W9-ANT-766

Maria Heindler

nsumer Behaviour

Maria Heindler

Male Consumer Behaviour

A Gender Perspective on Advertising Response

VDM Verlag Dr. Müller

Bibliographic information by the German National Library: The German National Library lists this publication at the German National Bibliography; detailed bibliographic information is available on the Internet at http://dnb.d-nb.de.

Copyright © 2007 VDM Verlag Dr. Müller e. K. and licensors
All rights reserved. Saarbrücken 2007
Contact: info@vdm-verlag.de
Cover image: www.photocase.de Aufseesianum
Publisher: VDM Verlag Dr. Müller e. K., Dudweiler Landstr. 125 a, 66123 Saarbrücken, Germany
Produced by: Lightning Source Inc., La Vergne, Tennessee/USA
          Lightning Source UK Ltd., Milton Keynes, UK

Bibliografische Information der Deutschen Nationalbibliothek: Die Deutsche Nationalbibliothek verzeichnet diese Publikation in der Deutschen Nationalbibliografie; detaillierte bibliografische Daten sind im Internet über http://dnb.d-nb.de abrufbar.

Copyright © 2007 VDM Verlag Dr. Müller e. K. und Lizenzgeber
Alle Rechte vorbehalten. Saarbrücken 2007
Kontakt: info@vdm-verlag.de
Coverbild: www.photocase.de Aufseesianum
Verlag: VDM Verlag Dr. Müller e. K., Dudweiler Landstr. 125 a, 66123 Saarbrücken, Deutschland
Herstellung: Lightning Source Inc., La Vergne, Tennessee/USA
          Lightning Source UK Ltd., Milton Keynes, UK

ISBN: 978-3-8364-2162-1

This book is dedicated to
Efrem and Brigitte.

Preface

Why Study Sex and Gender in Marketing?

Today's world is bustling with information and it is constantly getting faster, louder, and more complex. It is therefore getting more and more difficult for companies to reach consumers, which is only possible by standing out from the continuous flow of advertising information available. Marketing strategists have long responded to the increasing information overflow with concepts of market segmentation and target-specific product positioning. Companies hope that – through tailoring their messages to the preferences of their target group – those customers will pay more attention to their advertising because they are of greater relevance to them. There is a variety of variables which are used for segmenting consumer markets. Sex has been used very often for this purpose. Considering standard criteria for effective segmentation (e.g. Kotler, 2003) sex targets are particularly attractive to marketers for three main reasons (Darley & Smith, 1995, p. 41):

- Sex as a variable is easily identifiable and measurable.
- Sex segments are easily accessible, as most media provide information on the sex distribution of their audience.
- Sex segments are large enough to be profitable.

However, in recent decades differences between males and females, once very clearly observable, have begun to blur. Both researchers and to a lesser extent, marketers, started questioning the usefulness of the male-female distinction in marketing practice. Starting in the mid-1970s a new concept was introduced first in psychology and later also brought into consumer research: psychological sex. Research suggested that every person possesses a psychological gender identity. Psychological gender allows individuals to be either masculine or feminine or neither or both at the same time – independent of their biological sex. Thus it refers – contrary to sex, which defines the biological state of being – to a psychological and sociological self-definition.

Research interest in this new concept was considerable. From the 1970s on an increasing number of articles on sex and gender issues was published in almost all psychology journals (Deaux, 1985, p. 50). Specific sex and gender directed journals were established during this period (e.g. *Sex Roles* in 1975, *Psychology of Women Quarterly* in 1977, *Gender and Society* in 1987). The research findings cover a large array of scientific disciplines ranging from psychology and sociology to history or evolutionary theory, reflecting the broadness of the gender topic. As gender research established itself in the consumer behavior field, marketing practice also became increasingly aware about the possible impact of gender on consumer behavior. Marketers started responding to the challenge of designing new types of sex-targeted products and sex-specific advertisements which do not follow traditional role models.

To promote psychological sex as a new segmentation variable might be acting too eagerly, as biological sex is still a lot more common for segmenting markets. Also, psychological sex faces not only the problems usually associated with psychographic segmentation variables, such as measurement difficulties, but also studies of its impact on consumer behavior brought results which are far from unanimous and, therefore, its usefulness is still disputed among researchers.

However, though disputed the interest in psychological sex has not diminished. The topic is also more and more present in popular culture through public discussion on wage gaps, discrimination issues, transsexual laws, sex-change operations, and homosexual culture (reflected by articles in leading English-language newspapers). Especially the latter two topics seem to receive the particular interest of journalists. It is, however, important to realize that, contrary to the scientific treatment of the subject, gender identity in popular sources refers almost exclusively to disturbed gender identity. The scientific concept of gender infers no notion at all about mental disorders and does not view a state of femininity in a male as unpleasant or adversarial.

Probably one of today's most attention-getting marketing applications of the concept of psychological sex is metrosexuality.[1] Metrosexuals combine masculinity with traits associated with women (Zurawik, 2003). They are at the moment primarily targeted by cosmetic marketers introducing personal hygiene or make-up lines for the new feminine men. Although metrosexuals can be seen as having a more feminine-oriented psychological sex and thus a link can certainly be made between metrosexuality and psychological sex, the definition of the former is different from the scientific meaning of psychological sex. Femininity is

---

[1] The term *metrosexuality* was already invented in 1994 by the English journalist Mark Simpson, but it has not been for a few years that is received the amount of attention it has today.

There are two different definitions of what metrosexuality actually is which depend on the area where the term is used. In Great Britain metrosexuals pay a lot of attention to their appearance including using personal hygiene products formerly reserved for women and are thus a model of self-love and vanity, whereas in the United States metrosexual men look after their children, prepare meals for their families and more or less incorporate the feminine-attributed traits of caring and love-giving. The American definition therefore approaches far better than the English one what we mean by feminine and masculine qualities in the framework of psychological sex.

undoubtedly a key ingredient of metrosexuality, but the fact that women are per definition excluded from being metrosexual, leaves almost no possibility for integrating the two concepts. Academic researchers, however, have so far ignored metrosexuality.

Aims of this Book

This book is set in the field of information processing in an advertising context, specifically focusing on the differences between masculine and feminine subjects when processing and evaluating advertising information. Two research questions are addressed.

The first one examines the presentation of male images in advertising and male consumers' reactions to them. Jaffe and her colleagues (Jaffe, 1990, 1991, 1994; Jaffe & Berger, 1988; Jaffe, Berger, & Jamieson, 1992; Jaffe, Jamieson, & Berger, 1992; Jaffe & Berger, 1994) investigated the effectiveness of modern and traditional role portrayals in advertising by measuring and comparing reactions of females scoring high or low on masculinity and femininity scales. A similar research approach shall be used in this study, focusing on men's reaction to male role stimuli, namely how males differ in their perception of stereotypical and non-stereotypical male role portrayals in advertising, dependent on their scores on the dimensions of psychological femininity and masculinity.

The second part examines differences in information processing strategies between masculine and feminine subjects, again within an exclusively male sample. Studies show significant differences in the way males and females use message cues and deal with incongruent information (Meyers-Levy, 1988, 1989; Meyers-Levy & Sternthal; 1991; Meyers-Levy & Maheswaran, 1991). A study will be conducted to examine whether these differences are more a matter of biological or of psychological sex. If the latter is the case, processing strategies might be changing along with changing sex roles in society. Males who exhibit a greater degree of psychological femininity are hypothesized to employ female-attributed processing strategies.

Of course, these two research questions are not unrelated. Understanding information processing strategies is an essential part of understanding advertising. The objective of every advertisement is to enter the consumer's mind, to be noticed, processed and stored in memory. Clarifying what strategies people employ when processing advertisements, what message cues they use and how they form their judgments might provide helpful clues on how to design effective ads. The study will be designed in a way so that the interaction of the type of role portrayal and the processing strategy used can be assessed as well. In this book we will thus study three questions:

1. Do men react differently to varying *role portrayals* in advertising depending on their own gender?
2. Do men use different *information processing strategies* depending on their gender?
3. And, is there an *interaction* between the two?

This book will help advertisers in designing target-appropriate advertisements when employing sex- or gender-based segmentation. Of interest to both theory and practice is the yet unsolved question whether gender should play an important role in marketing and advertising. This study will shed further light on the usefulness of gender as an individual difference variable. From a theoretical viewpoint, a positive result will encourage future research in the area, opening up new perspectives on personal influence factors in consumer behavior.

Gender differences in advertising perception and information processing styles will also have considerable practical implications as they are questioning traditional sex-based segmentation strategies and stereotypical advertising approaches. To a certain extent practice has already responded to changing sex roles and adapted its advertising practice accordingly. Especially when it comes to women, companies build their advertising strategy on the existence of the strong, independent career women (see Hupfer, 2002, for some examples). This is true for a number of different industries, though the trend differs in strength. The new masculine image is, for example, widely used by insurance and banking companies. As mentioned, this development is observed more in female-directed marketing compared to male-directed marketing. Also it has been based on a rather intuitive assessment of what types of ads are appealing to the "new woman". With this research a theoretically and empirically grounded framework shall be provided for adapting also male-directed advertising practice.

Following this introduction I will first summarize gender research in the literature. The second half of this chapter will be dedicated to consumer research in this area. The next chapter will present evidence for changing male and female roles, focusing on past and current male roles and the meaning of masculinity. I will then investigate the use of sex roles and gender in advertising where gender-differences in advertising response will receive particular attention. Chapter four will examine past research on information processing differences between men and women, building on a short introduction on information processing theory in general. Consequently, I will describe the method used in conducting the empirical study and report and discuss the results at the end of this book, concluding with marketing implications both for research and marketing practice.

Table of Contents

List of Figures

List of Tables

> *"That a respondent is male or female is in itself of little psychological impact. What is of consequence are the patterns of attitudes or abilities or problems or interests that are presumed to go along with being male or female"*
> *(Sechrest, 1976, p. 6).*

1 Introducing Gender Research

Gender is not a self-explanatory construct. Neither is its use in everyday language identical with its meaning in social psychology. Therefore it is essential to find a useful and understandable definition for gender before starting in depth with its value for psychology and consumer behavior research. The purpose of this first theoretical chapter is thus to define what gender is and introduce selected fields of sex and gender research focusing on consumer behavior literature.

1.1 Defining Gender

The prevailing confusion in terminology has already been acknowledged by some researchers (e.g. Deaux, 1985, p. 51). Still, unanimous agreement on the use of terms and definition seems to be far away. Also, most authors do not dedicate much effort to a proper definition of the terms they employ. This lack of foundation can cause confusion when reading sex or gender related research papers and thus makes a short but thorough analysis of the most important terms inevitable. Although the concept of psychological sex seems to be intuitively understandable, due to the lack of precise definitions it continues as one of "the muddiest concepts in the psychologist's vocabulary" (Constantinople, 1973, p. 390).

Probably the most frequently and variably employed term in the literature is the word *gender*, though it can mean two different things: some authors use gender to refer to biological sex (e.g. Barak & Stern, 1986; Hurtz & Durkin, 1997; Ciabattari, 2001), while others relate the word to psychological sex (e.g. Deaux, 1985, Gould & Stern, 1989). The literature is rather consistent in its use of expressions for biological sex, though not without confusion, as authors use either the word *sex* or *gender*. Agreeing on a single term for psychological sex seems to cause more discussion where terms used vary greatly. The following expressions were found in the literature:

- *Sex role* (e.g. Areni, Kiecker, & Palan, 1998; Bem, 1974, 1977; Feather, 1978),
- *Sex-role self concept* (e.g. Golden, Allison, & Clee, 1979),

- *Gender identity* (e.g. Bereska, 2003; Fischer & Arnold, 1990, 1994),
- *Sex-role identity* (Kahle & Homer, 1985; Jaffe, 1990, 1991, 1994),
- *Sex-role orientation* (e.g. Gainer, 1993),
- *Gender role orientation* (e.g. Hoffman, 2001), or
- *Sex type* (e.g. Gould & Stern, 1989; Gould & Weil, 1991).

Although all these expressions essentially mean the same thing, slight differences between the terms still exist. This variety does of course not help to bring clarity into gender terminology. The ones most widely used are now analyzed in the following paragraphs.

Palan (2001) defines *gender identity* as the "degree to which an individual identifies with masculine or feminine personality traits" (p. 1). Kempf, Palan, and Laczniak (1997) specify it as "an individual's self-perceived endorsement of masculine *and feminine* personality traits which as such, may or may not be congruent with an individual's biological sex" (p. 444, italicized words added). Gender identity can be employed synonymously with psychological sex from a terminological point of view. But psychological sex should be conceptualized in a broader sense than done by these authors, namely not only by measuring personality traits. Therefore, from a conceptual point of view these definitions do not capture the manifold representations of psychological sex and are therefore not totally satisfying.

Sex-role identity is defined by Jaffe (1991) as "the degree to which one adheres to traditional female *and male* roles" (p. 57, italicized words added) and used in the same way as gender identity. The word degree in this definition already implies that there is no exclusive femininity or masculinity. This is one of the most important conceptual differences between biological and psychological sex, as an individual definitely has one biological sex – i.e. either male or female,[2] – but can possess two "psychological sexes", in the sense that he/she can incorporate masculine and feminine traits to the same extent. Jaffe uses sex role identity in the same sense as gender identity, but the latter term is to be preferred over the former. A *sex role* is "a role that is performed primarily by a person of a particular sex, [...] and societal factors tend to encourage this correlation" (Jaffe, 1990, p. 875).[3] As such sex roles are defined by society. The term is also often used to refer to commonly agreed-upon stereotypes of maleness and femaleness (e.g. Furnham & Bitar, 1993; Hurtz

---

[2] Some babies are born as intersexed. These infants have ambiguous genitalia, making sex assignment problematic. Diagnostic tests are then performed to determine the true biological sex of the child. Common practice also is to pronounce the child as male or female depending on its physical features – a distinction connected with cultural perceptions of maleness and femaleness (Kessler, 1990, in Palan, 2001).

[3] The term *gender roles* is sometimes used instead of sex roles. As aforementioned, sex roles refer to stereotypical roles of males and females and are thus connected to sex and not to gender as employed in this book. Therefore gender roles (and equally gender role attitudes etc.) will be replaced by sex roles or sex role attitudes, respectively.

& Durkin, 1997; Kolbe & Albanese, 1997). The expression does not accurately reflect the concept of psychological sex as an individual self-perception and personality variable. Nevertheless, sex role (sex role concept, sex role orientation, sex role identity) is very common in the literature as a synonym for psychological sex, as it has been introduced by Bem (1974) through the development of the Bem Sex Role Inventory (BSRI), the most widely used scale for measuring psychological sex.

Self concept (or *self schema*) is also employed in a number of studies (e.g. Bem, 1981; Crane & Markus, 1982). It refers to an individual's multifaceted self image – to one's whole personality. Therefore a sex-related self-schema can be only one part of a larger structure. Expressions, such as *gender schema* or *gender self concept* are therefore accurate for capturing the meaning of psychological gender, but *self concept* or *self schema* are not. However, gender schema is also used in information processing to describe a cognitive memory structure building on gender.[4] Using these terms might therefore cause confusion with information processing terminology and is thus not recommended.

In conclusion from this analysis of terminology, this book will employ the terms *sex* and *gender* for distinguishing psychological and biological sex according to psychological convention (Deaux, 1985, p. 51) and following a large number of influential researchers (e.g. Fischer & Arnold, 1994; Helmreich, Spence, & Holahan, 1979; Skitka & Maslach, 1990). Sex and gender will thereby be understood as two different words with separate meanings.

The term *sex* will be used to refer to an individual's biological sex. That is whether an individual is a man or a woman, genetically defined through the existence or absence of the Y chromosome in a person's genome. The expressions male and female, or maleness and femaleness, respectively, will analogically refer to biological sex.

Gender is the expression used for psychological sex. It is defined as the psychological identity of an individual and is both a social construct and a psychological self-perception. Analogous to the explanations above, the terms masculine and feminine, or masculinity and femininity, respectively, will be used as terms relating to gender in contrast to male/female when talking about sex. A chapter on how gender is finally operationalized for study purposes will further enhance understanding of the concept.[5]

---

[4] See Chapter 4 "Gender and Information Processing".
[5] See section 1.2.5 "Conclusion: Conceptualizing Gender".

The definition of the words above is also common in everyday English language, as reflected in newspaper articles of daily English speaking newspapers (e.g. Ahlstrom, 1999). However, cultural influences seem to play a role. British use the word sex more often than Americans, e.g. the British "sex-change operation" is, when crossing the Atlantic, converted into "gender conversion surgery". It might be, though, that gender is perceived as the more sensitive and less rude word. However, with the intention of not offending anyone, this book will use the word sex in the sense specified above.

A last point that deserves some emphasis is that gender does not refer in any way to the sexual orientation of the individual. Thus, high or low femininity in a man's personality is not correlated with this man being less or more likely to exhibit homo- or heterosexual preferences, but not dependent or predictive for it (e.g. Constantinople, 1973, p. 390).

1.2 Psychologists on Gender

All societies across all cultures distinguish between male and female. The relevance of gender in the organization of human society is as old as society itself. Gender roles and associated identities and role-, or rather sex-specific tasks – what it means to be "a man" or "a woman" – have been prevalent in all forms of human cohabitates since the beginning of time (e.g. the division of labor into hunting (men) and gathering (women) in the very early forms of human existence). There seems to be indeed "no other dichotomy in human experience with as many entities assimilated to it as the distinction between male and female" (Bem, 1981, p. 354). However, the start of academic research on the subject is, naturally, a more recent event. The earliest roots of sex and gender research can be dated back to 1879, the year of the beginning of formal psychology (Hyde, 1990, p. 56), as both gender and sex have been an important part of the individual's personality. Thus both research fields could not emerge until formal scientific interest into individual personalities was prevalent enough. Scientific analysis of gender as a psycho-social variable started later during the early 1930s of the last century (see Constantinople, 1973, for an analysis of early research), where the first scales for its measurement were constructed (e.g. Terman & Miles, 1936). As indicated by Bem (1981, p. 362), interest in gender requires a certain political background. In a more general interpretation this means that gender issues have rarely been brought into research before society has achieved a certain readiness and sensibility for this topic, which presumably started with the women and feminist liberation movement. Although first movements of this kind already existed in the early beginnings of the 20th century (e.g. the Suffragette movement in the United States of America) it can be said that the late 1960s and 1970s were probably the most fruitful and progressive decades of women liberation movements. Modern gender research as conducted and interpreted today did not start before 1973, when Constantinople published an article which proved to be "a watershed for research in this area" (Deaux, 1985; p.58).[6] Since then researchers in areas as diverse as sociology, anthropology, history, biology, or evolutionary theory have embraced the concept of gender.

This chapter shall provide a short introduction into the extensive field of gender related research in psychology. Because of the marketing focus of this book psychological literature will only be used for providing the necessary groundings, including sex differences, the gender revolution in the 70s, gender theory, and

---

[6] See section 1.2.3 "Rethinking Sex and Gender".

gender measurement instruments, ending with a detailed conceptualization of gender.

1.2.1 Differences Between Males and Females

The longest and most extensive research history in the field of sex and gender can be found on sex differences between men and women (see Maccoby & Jacklin, 1974, for an early review of the topic). While gender research tries to ascribe observed differences to personality, i.e. psychological identity as masculine or feminine, this area focuses exclusively on the male-female dichotomy. Deaux (1985, p. 54) identifies three main fields of research on sex differences: cognitive skills, personality traits and dispositions, and social behaviors.

Maccoby and Jacklin (1974) found convincing evidence for sex differences only in two areas:

- cognitive skills (verbal ability, mathematical ability, visual-spatial ability) and
- aggression.

Boys were found to be superior to girls on mathematical tasks as well as in certain tasks aimed at testing visual-spatial ability, such as tests of mental rotation. Alternatively, girls seem to perform better on test of verbal skills.

Regarding personality traits and dispositions, achievement and motivation research reported women to be more concerned with work, while men seemed to be more concerned with mastery and scored higher on competitiveness. Moral development and behavior research indicates that men and women have different principles of moral development. Whereas men emphasize separation and individualization, women are concerned with attachment and caring. Of course, masculinity and femininity research would also be an issue in this context, but is omitted for now, as it will be analyzed extensively later in this chapter.

Maccoby and Jacklin (1974) identified aggressive behavior as a social behavior variable showing particularly strong sex differences. Women seem not only to be less aggressive than men, but are also more easily influenced and more likely to conform in group pressure situations. Additionally, they are better at both encoding and decoding nonverbal cues and recognizing faces. Females were found to possess more expressive faces, are approached more closely by others, and emit fewer speech errors. To summarize, sex differences where found in three fields (cf. Deaux, 1985):

- Cognitive skills (e.g. verbal, mathematical, visual-spatial ability,…)
- Traits and dispositions (e.g. achievement, motivation, competitiveness, individuation, attachment,…)
- Social behavior (e.g. aggressiveness,…)

Although the studies reported were conducted around thirty years ago they still serve as popular references for this field as not much change in sex differences has been observed in the years following their publication (e.g. Maccoby, 1998; see Mealey, 2000, p. 21, for a summary of recent references on sex differences). Also, research interest was leading away from the examination of sex differences "in the sense of comparisons between males as a group and females as a group" (Maccoby, 1998, p. vii). Newer research on sex differences focused on topics such as the development of sex differences (Mealey, 2000) or interaction of the sexes (Maccoby, 1998) to name only two examples.[7]

One reason for the decline in research interest could have been that the meaningfulness of the results obtained was heavily disputed. Deaux (1985) calls research on personality differences "atheoretical at best and opportunistic at worst" (p. 56-57) as their topics include a random assortment of issues and the research flow was rather provoked "by the ease of administering personality questionnaire and the equal convenience of sex as a variable" (Deaux, 1985, p. 56) than by any other factor. Hyde (1981) conducted a meta-analysis with the studies used by Maccoby and Jacklin (1974) and found sex differences to be very small. A comparison of studies found that sex differences usually account for one to five percent of variance in different variables (Deaux, 1984, p. 108). A more detailed analysis by Hyde and Plant (1995, p. 160) reported great variability in the magnitude of gender differences across different behaviors. However, they found that 60 % of observed sex differences fall into the below-moderate category (effect size $d \leq 0,35$, see Figure 1 for mean sex differences on a range of psychological variables).

---

[7] This area of research is far too large to be covered adequately in the frame of this book. The excellent books by Maccoby (1998) and Mealey (2000) are recommended to readers who wish to learn more about male and female differences, their development, and evolutionary strategies.

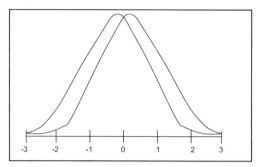

Figure 1: Mean sex differences (standardized units) on a range of psychological attributes.
(Either sex may have the higher score.) (Source: based on Maccoby, 1998, p. 80)

Also, same-sex individuals are far from being homogenous (Hyde, 1990, p. 62). Carlson (1971, p. 275-276) reports ethnic and cultural diversity in differences, questioning the ability to generalize the results. Another question which still remains unanswered is what actually causes the reported sex differences.

1.2.2 Where do Sex Differences Come From?

At different points in this book references will be made to the origin of sex differences in general and differences in information processing specifically. Naturally, postulating that sex differences exist leads to the question of where these differences originate. The answer to this question is not easy and – despite heavy discussions – still not solved.

1.2.2.1 Socialization vs. Biology

Two main perspectives are competing in this field: biological predispositions on the one hand and social development on the other (Darley & Smith, 1995, p. 42).

1. The *biological perspective* assumes that human behavior and personality is shaped by their biological configuration, of which sex is an important part.
2. The *sociological perspective* postulates that human beings are born tabula rasa and all behaviors and personality traits are in consequence acquired through socialization processes.

The pros and cons of these two perspectives are heavily debated. Probably the strongest indicator for social influence is the fact that sex differences are not constant over time. Rosenthal and Rubin (1982) found that differences in cognitive skills were diminishing over a 20-year period. Hyde (1990, p. 70) reported diminishing differences in aggression between males and females.

Some differences emerge only later in development, such as males' predominance on numerical tests, which does not appear until well into elementary school (Hyde, 1990, p. 64). Whereas Tieger (1980) suggests that reliable differences are observed in humans only after five years of age, Maccoby and Jacklin (1974) found evidence for the existence of differences prior to the age of six. Even if evidence on the development of sex differences were more consistent, it would still not solve the question at hand. It might be that sex differences are rooted in biology but only take some time or require some biological state, such as the changes occurring during puberty, to fully develop (Maccoby & Jacklin, 1974). On the other hand it is as well possible that through subtle influences society determines which sex develops what kind of abilities. However, once sex differences are established they remain present throughout the life span (Hyde, 1990, p. 64). Pajares and Valiante (2001) found that gender differences in mathematical ability (male superiority) and writing (female superiority) seemed to decrease or disappear when gender-orientation was controlled. In her recent book Maccoby (1998) studies the development of sex differences from childhood to adulthood and also gives a comprehensive account of different explanations from biological to social theories, concluding that "nature and nurture are jointly involved in everything human beings do" (Maccoby, 1998, p. 89).

It can be speculated that there is more reason to assume that differences in cognitive abilities are at least partly based on biological facts, such as differences in brain organization, than are personality traits and social behavior which can be assumed to be largely socially shaped. If now even cognitive sex differences cannot be traced back to biological differences for sure, it is even more unlikely that personality traits and social behavior are predetermined instead of externally shaped. Whatever conclusion may be drawn – even after a more thorough analysis of research than done here –, the dispute on "nature versus nurture" (Deaux, 1985, p. 64) will probably never be solved. Social influence as a main factor in shaping especially an individuals personality and behavior is quite likely. In the meantime both explanations continue to coexist and complement each other. Furthermore, the multifactorial nature of gender discussed below implies that gender is determined by a number of different factors, some of them of social, others of biological origin.

There is, however, not enough evidence to reject either of the two explanations. It seems intuitive that neither of those extreme perspectives can give a satisfactory answer to the question posed. Even supporters of one or the other do not claim that their view gives the ultimate answer: "Few of those who argue for biological influence would insist upon biological determinism; the malleability and even reversibility of human behavior is recognized by most" (Deaux, 1985, p. 64). Cross-cultural variety is enough to make it obvious that biology can only tell part of the story and environmental contributions to individual development and behavior cannot be ignored (Mealey, 2000, p. 61). On the other hand, explanations by social forces may be too narrow – not wrong but too limited" (Maccoby, 1998, p.9).

These two perspectives have remained largely unintegrated in the literature (Mealey, 2000, p. 189) but there is an area of research trying to give a comprehensive explanation on why sex differences have emerged: evolutionary psychology.

1.2.2.2   Evolution and Evolutionary Psychology

A main component of the biological perspective is *evolution theory*. Evolution theory postulates that mankind acquires behavioral mechanisms through adaptation in a process of natural selection in order to achieve fitness maximization (i.e., mainly reproductive success). Thus, it is not assumed that people are completely shaped by society but that they possess traits and behavioral mechanisms which have developed over a long period of time. Evolution theory is not denying that human beings are changing, but the change – through adaptation – is so slow that when monitoring only a few it might seem that there are indeed fixed innate qualities which vary with biological variables, such as sex.

In the tradition of gender research and social science in general (cf. Maccoby, 1998, p. 3) this book focuses on the ability of human behavior and personality to be socially influenced; a truly biology-based argument might be too far off the topic. However, it might still be necessary for some aspects. Especially interesting in the current context is an area of research applying evolution theory to psychological processes: *evolutionary psychology*. Evolutionary psychology has become increasingly popular during recent years (e.g. Saad & Gill, 2000, p. 1012) and its relevance for marketing has been examined more than once (e.g. Lynn, Kampschroeder, & Pereira, 1999; Colarelli & Dettmann, 2003; Hantula, 2003). It focuses on evolved psychological mechanisms in people's minds and thus seeks to unify evolutionary biology and cognitive psychology. Whereas these two extreme perspectives are often contrasting each other, evolutionary psychology and traditional psychology/sociology seek to coexist and complement each other. The main difference between the two may be summarized as such:

"In contrast to the traditional psychological paradigm, the emphasis in evolutionary psychology is on the ultimate rather than proximate explanations. That is, evolutionary psychology also tries to answer the question as to why a particular behavior, cognition, or emotion exists, rather than only answering how it operates and what it results in. [...] The human mind is a result of an evolutionary process that operates on the principle of natural selection." (Saad & Gill, 2000, p. 1006)

The difference is further illustrated with a concrete example for the study at hand: while psychology tries to assess the magnitude of gender differences and argues whether they are or are not diminishing due to changing sex roles, evolutionary psychology would ask where these differences originally come from and search for causes in the long period of human existence. As gender research mostly focuses on social and psychological – "proximate" – causes an evolutionary perspective can be a valuable complement to the reported knowledge. However, the fact that evolutionary psychology tries to explain sex differences with evolution theory does not invalidate psychological research and sociological theories about the origin of such differences.

Evolutionary psychology simply gives a broader and deeper framework for explaining sex differences than sociological and psychological theories. Even evolutionary psychologists argue that socialization plays a role in maintaining sex differences (Saad & Gill, 2000, p. 1015). As evolution is a slow process (Hantula, 2003, p. 758), there must be some force working besides evolution to ensure immediate and small scale adaptation of human beings to their (social) surroundings (see Figure 2). Thus evolution forces have been shaping human behavior on the long run since the beginning of mankind, while the social environment provided short-term orientation.

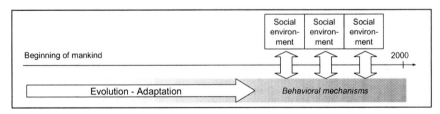

Figure 2: Connection between evolutionary psychology and sociology/psychology

Evolutionary psychology argues that some innate behaviors continue despite changing roles (Saad & Gill, 2000, p. 1017). But it also concedes that innate characteristics "may not be present at birth" and are not "unlearned or inevitable" (Lynn et al., 1999, p. 226). Psychological mechanisms may have been shaped by natural selection but they are also subject to further changes – through evolutionary processes in the long run, but possibly through social forces also in the short run. Saad (2004) states that "our innate predispositions [...] interact with the environment" as "humans are equipped with extraordinary behavioral plasticity and as such are hardly constrained by preordained biological determinism" (Saad, 2004, p. 597).

There are actually two different evolutionary perspectives which can be found in the social sciences (Colarelli & Dettmann, 2003, p. 839-842):

- evolutionary psychology and
- cultural evolution.

These two illustrate even better the different concepts of adaptation which distinguish themselves by their time horizon, their ability to generalize over populations, and their responsiveness to change. While evolutionary psychology examines mechanisms of the human mind developed over a long period of time which are common for (almost) all human beings, cultural evolution is "a process whereby social systems and practices develop from variations and by a process of trial and error" (Colarelli & Dettmann, 2003, p. 841). Behaviors and values are culturally selected and retained by social systems and are thus more specific and more open to change. However, cultural evolution processes still rely on long-developed behaviors and mechanisms in people. Socialization, then, is responsible for the short-term immediate adaptation to the environment, building on both evolutionary and culturally-evolved foundations (see Figure 3).

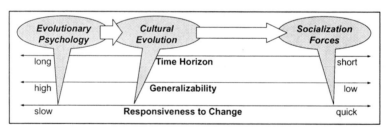

Figure 3: Evolutionary psychology, cultural evolution, and socialization forces

However, how deep socialization influences the psychological mechanisms at the bottom is a question which still needs to be answered. An example will be given: One basic difference in males and females – according to evolutionary psychology – lies in different mating strategies of the sexes (see Mealey, 2000, for an ample analysis). Females are generally more selective than males in the choice of their partner, also because the parenting cost for them is usually higher than that for males once they bear a child. Changing sex roles, with fathers investing increasingly more resources in fathering and child raising could thus also influence mating strategies. Although this might not change the long-evolved instinctive differences in mating strategies and preferences between men and women, a certain social environment might influence them at least in the short run.

1.2.3 Rethinking Sex and Gender

Before 1973, healthy individuals were those who conformed to sex-appropriate behavior and manifested only traits considered to be socially adequate for their sex. Masculine traits were attributed to men and feminine ones to women, and it was neither thought of nor judged desirable that men exhibited feminine or women masculine traits. This model of mental health is called the *congruence model of mental health* (Whitley, 1984), because it postulated congruence of psychological and biological state as a prerequisite for mental well-being. Also, for a long time masculinity and femininity were seen as two interdependent dimensions on a bipolar scale. This means that an individual who is high in masculinity can not be high in femininity and in turn, a feminine person cannot be masculine.

In 1973, Constantinople published an article, questioning three basic assumptions underlying previous gender research:

- Gender is a bipolar dimension ranging from extreme masculinity to extreme femininity (bipolarity assumption).
- Gender is unidimensional and can be adequately measured by a single score (uni-dimensionality assumption).
- Gender is best defined in terms of sex differences in item responses.

The last point is criticized by Constantinople because of its dependence on time and cultural circumstances and therefore its tendency to change. However, the use of other criteria for gender measurement is far more difficult and complex, therefore this point has been largely ignored by most researchers. Constantinople (1973) reviewed a large number of tests of masculinity and femininity and drew the following conclusions:

- There is not enough evidence for a negative correlation between masculinity and femininity measures in order to conclude that they form a single bipolar dimension. Further research on the relevance of an orthogonal model is needed (see Figure 4 for a comparison of the two models).
- Available data point to a multidimensional construct, thus suggesting that gender is better defined as a set of submeasures than by a single score.

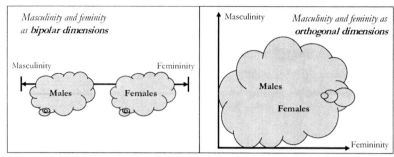

Figure 4: Comparing the bipolar and orthogonal gender model

As can be seen in Figure 4, the masculinity-femininity distinction was closely linked to maleness and femaleness before 1973. One of the most important merits of the new approach was to disentangle this relationship. The separation of the two dimensions masculinity and femininity has been favored in research and incorporated in gender measures developed from the 1970s onwards. Out of the multi-dimensionality assumption, multifactorial gender theory has been developed (Spence, 1993).

Although the turning point in gender research can be tied to the article of Constantinople, when she first summarized the problematic assumptions underlying the definitions of gender and provoked a large amount of follow-up research, it was not a sudden turnaround in opinions, but rather a gradually coming change. Two years before, in 1971, Carlson already criticized that "strictly dimensional approaches fail to reflect adequately the nature of psychosexuality" (p. 267) and suggested the "presence of both male and female qualities within the individual" (p. 271). Even earlier, Bakan postulated in 1966 the necessity of both male and female qualities within an individual for psychological health. This new approach is called the *androgyny model of mental health*; now possessing simultaneously both masculine and feminine personality characteristics is seen as a prerequisite for mental health (e.g. Bem, 1974, p. 162). A new group of individuals emerges, the androgynous, which is both masculine and feminine at the same time, the word being a composite of the two Greek words *andro* (= male) and *gyne* (= female). Androgyny is viewed as a desirable state, as it is not only associated with mental health, but also with emotional maturity (Fischer & Arnold, 1994, p. 166).

Two other pairs of expressions are frequently used as well in the context of masculinity and femininity, sometimes even synonymously: Parsons and Bales introduced the distinction between instrumentality and expressiveness in 1955. Eleven years later Bakan (1966) came up with a very similar model, the dimensions in which he called the dimensions agency and communion. These two dimensions can be defined as follows: Instrumental or agentic individuals are "concerned with the attainment of goals external to the interaction process" (Gill, Stockard, Johnson, & Williams, 1987, p. 379) and are characterized by traits such as independence, assertiveness, reason, rationality, competitiveness, and focus on individual goals (Palan, 2001, p. 3) – or generally spoken, traits classified as masculine.[8] An expressive or communal orientation "gives primacy to facilitating the interaction process itself" (Gill et al., 1987, p. 379-380). Personality traits associated with expressiveness are understanding, caring, nurturance, responsibility, considerateness, sensitivity, intuition, passion, and focus on communal goals (Palan, 2001, p. 3) – or traits generally classified as feminine. These two dimensions are also often referred to as self- and other-orientation.

Usually men are considered to be agentic and women communal. However, researchers concluded that men are usually only seen as more instrumental than women, rather than as instrumental instead of expressive (Deaux, 1984, p.112). It is problematic to set their meaning equal to the dimensions of masculinity and femininity, although it is often done. Instrumentality and expressiveness or agency and communion, respectively, are usually used to characterize personality traits and their connection to sex is generally questionable.

Not only has Constantinople (1973) questioned the bipolarity of masculinity and femininity, but also the uni-dimensionality of the gender construct. In following research (e.g. Bem, 1974) masculinity and femininity were operationalized as two independent, orthogonal dimensions, but it was often still assumed that measuring masculine and feminine traits constitutes an adequate and sufficient measure of an individual's gender, thus neglecting possibly inherent multi-dimensionality. It was not long until this implicit assumption was called into question. Spence and Helmreich (1981) or Deaux (1985) were not the only ones to suggest that "gender phenomena form neither a single bipolar factor nor two separate factors" (Aube & Koestner, 1992, p. 485) but are made up from a large variety of thoughts, feelings, and behaviors instead. Koestner and Aube (1995) suggested that "trait approaches fail to account for the fact that much of human behavior is conditional, varying across situational contexts and developmental stages" (p. 700). But also multidimensional models were criticized in that they fail to explain how individuals can make up a single gender identity out of the various dimensions associated with it.

---

[8] Often instrumental personality traits are set equal to masculinity (and expressive personality traits to femininity). However, from a theoretical perspective this equation was heavily criticized (see sections 1.2.4 "Measuring Gender" and 1.2.5 "Conclusion: Conceptualizing Gender").

This debate led to the development of the multidimensional gender identity theory (Spence, 1993).[9] What dimensions actually constitute gender is disputed among researchers. The following table (Table 1) displays different concepts used in the examined gender literature ranging from rather simple to more complex ones and thus serving as an illustration of the multidimensional gender model. However, this list is not at all meant to be exhaustive. Columns highlighted with grey color indicate the most common dimensions present in nearly every gender model.

Model	Sex	Global Identity	Personality Traits	Interests, behaviors, attitudes	Sexual orientation	Sex roles	Symbolic contents of sex typing	Social relation-ships	Physical appearance	Occu-pations
Deaux & Lewis, 1983			X	X	X				X	X
Huston, 1983	X		X	X			X	X		
Stern, 1988	X		X	X						
Spence, 1993		X	X	X	X					
Fischer & Arnold, 1994	X		X	X						

Table 1: Illustrating multifactorial gender models

The probably most prominent and influential model was proposed by Spence (1993). This four-component gender model will serve as a starting point for operationalizing gender for the purpose of this study. Following Spence (1993), gender consists of:

- gender identity, i.e. one's global sense of maleness or femaleness,
- instrumental and expressive personality traits,
- gender related interests, role behaviors, and attitudes, and

[9] Multidimensional Gender Identity Theory is usually seen as the counterpart of Gender Schema Theory (e.g. Palan, 2001). Though, there seems to be no theoretical reason for this. As explained, multidimensional theory was developed as a response to criticisms that gender is not unifactorial in nature. Therefore it makes sense to distinguish between unidimensional and multifactorial approaches. Gender Schema Theory, in contrast, was developed by Bem in 1977 and proposes a framework of how individuals process information on the basis of gender. An alternative to Gender Schema Theory was provided by Marcus, Crane, Bernstein, and Siladi (1982) who explained gendered information processing on the basis of their Self Schema Theory (see section 4.2.1 "A Theoretical Framework"). It makes sense to compare these two approaches in an information processing context but not to contrast Multifactorial Gender Identity Theory and Gender Schema Theory.

- sexual orientation.

Whatever dimensions are used by researchers to construct a multidimensional measure of gender, research has shown that these dimensions are usually not or only slightly interrelated (e.g. Koestner & Aube, 1995, p. 693; Spence, 1993, p. 633). Thus, for example, a person possessing expressive personality traits does not necessarily need to endorse traditional role attitudes or enjoy traditionally feminine activities. Multi-dimensionality also allows for the fact that people experience themselves as perfectly masculine or feminine on a global scale and still exhibit a large number of feminine or masculine traits, interests, and attitudes.

Multi-factoriality abandons the simple, convenient way of defining gender by means of masculine and feminine personality traits and therefore adds its share to the prevailing confusion on what gender is. It also renders gender measurement significantly more complicated, but it has been shown to be a far better approximation for covering the complexity of gender than unidimensional explanations (e.g. Koestner & Aube, 1995, p. 693). Thus, its application in research seems not only warranted but also necessary if meaningful results are to be obtained (Palan, 2001, p. 17).

1.2.4 Measuring Gender

Before Constantinople and Bem re-conceptualized gender in the early 70s, a number of scales already existed to measure gender related traits and similar concepts. However, from a current point of view these scales have two major limitations: Firstly they used a bipolar gender model, and secondly they implicitly assumed that it is desirable for women to only be feminine, just as it is for men to be only masculine. In research these assumptions were no longer supported (e.g. Carlson, 1971; Bem, 1974). Additionally the scales have not been used much since the new inventories were developed. Older inventories such as the California Psychological Inventory Femininity Scale (CPI Fe-scale; Gough, 1952) differ completely from later measures in their purpose because they were mostly designed to detect deviant sex-role orientations or homosexual preferences which were considered psychological dysfunctions and psychopathies. The assessment of their validity has accordingly been focused on their capacity to distinguish between males and females or between homosexuals and heterosexuals. For all these reasons a closer examination of pre-1970 measures is of little importance in the context of this work (see Constantinople, 1973, for a review of older measures and Beere, 1990, for an ample collection of various scales related to gender). The new scales developed from 1973 onwards (e.g. Bem, 1974; Spence, Helmreich, & Stapp, 1974) were called *androgyny scales* because they allowed individuals to be masculine and feminine (i.e. androgynous) at the same time.

When measuring gender identity two things have to be kept in mind:

- First, gender identity is usually measured on the basis of items, i.e. traits, which reflect society's definition of masculinity and femininity. Measures are always dependent on the time and culture in which they were developed and should be checked for their validity and applicability in the given research situation before developing questionnaires if possible.

- Second, an individual's personal definition of his or her gender might not be consistent with the definition implied by measurement instruments (Constantinople, 1973, p. 391).

Thus a man might exhibit traits classified as feminine but still experience himself as a perfectly masculine person. This difference does not impact measurement validity itself if the gender construct has been properly defined previously and a validated test inventory is used. Differences between subjects with different personality traits or role orientations and their implications can still be assessed. An additional test item asking subjects for their overall subjective self-assessment on the dimensions of masculinity and femininity might, however, provide interesting insights and also allow some ex-post analysis of the ability of the instrument to capture masculinity and femininity of personality traits under given cultural and temporal constraints. If a multidimensional gender model is used, global self-concept should be assessed anyway, forming one of the four dimensions of gender (Spence, 1993).

The four most important inventories for measuring gender will consequently be introduced. The CPI Fe-scale belongs to the pre-1973 group. The other three are androgyny measures (see Figure 5).

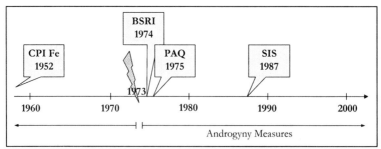

Figure 5: Selected scales for measuring gender

The California Psychological Inventory Femininity-scale (CPI Fe-scale) was chosen because it was the most commonly employed measure before the androgyny scales were developed and also because it was already used in consumer research. The Bem Sex Role Inventory (BSRI) and the Personal Attributes Questionnaire (PAQ) were chosen because they are far more widely used in both psychology and consumer behavior research than any other measure. The Sexual Identity Scale (SIS) finally provides a totally different approach to measuring gender.

1.2.4.1 *The California Psychological Inventory Femininity Scale (CPI-Fe scale)*

The CPI-Fe scale (Gough, 1952; 1966) shall be briefly mentioned here as the only instrument developed before 1973 because it is the only of the early scales which gained some importance in research. It was also used on four early marketing studies (Aiken, 1963; Fry, 1971; Morris & Cundiff, 1971; Vitz & Johnston, 1965) and as well in two later studies together with the PAQ (Gentry & Doering, 1977; Gentry, Doering, & O'Brien, 1978). The CPI-Fe scale is part of the larger California Psychological Inventory (CPI), a set of 18 scales designed to evaluate interpersonal behavior and social interaction within individuals. Assuming that masculinity is strongly linked with being male, the purpose of the scale was to differentiate males from females and distinguish "sexual deviates from normals" (Gough, 1952, p. 427). Gough (1966, p. 136) also explicitly refers to the bipolar gender model as a basis. During its construction 58 items were selected out of a starting pool of 500 by comparing responses of male and female student subjects. Later they were further reduced to 38 in the course of a cross-cultural extension and validation of its differentiating abilities (Gough, 1966).

1.2.4.2 *The Bem Sex Role Inventory*

The BSRI (Bem, 1974) was the first gender measure to contain separate scales for masculinity and femininity. The inventory was constructed to identify personality traits that are more desirable for men than for women – and vice versa. The original BSRI consisted of three groups of attributes: masculine, feminine, and neutral ones, which were then rated by respondents on a seven-point scale ranging from "never or almost never true" to "always or almost always true".[10] Accordingly, three scores were calculated: a masculinity score (m-score), a femininity score (f-score) and an androgyny score, computed as the difference between m-score and f-

---

[10] For the original inventory see the Appendix.

score. Bem (1974, p. 159) reported high internal consistency ($\alpha \approx 0,8$) and a high test-retest reliability ($r \approx 0,9$). According to Bem (1974, p. 160-161), respondents were divided into three groups:

- *androgynous* (low m- and f-score or high m- and f-score; see Figure 8 later in this chapter),
- *feminine* (high f-score, low m-score), and
- *masculine* (high m-score, low f-score).

The term *sex typed* refers to a person who behaves according to their biological sex, i.e. a masculine man or a feminine woman. Contrarily, *not sex typed* includes androgynous, undifferentiated and cross-sex typed subjects with *cross-sex typed* denominating a feminine man or a masculine woman. Figure 6 explains sex-typing graphically.

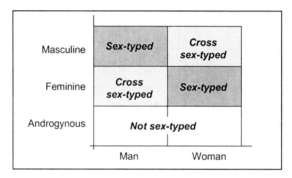

Figure 6: Sex-typed, not sex-typed and cross sex-typed

The BSRI is the most commonly used measure in consumer research (Palan, Areni, & Kiecker, 1999, p. 366) and probably also the most thoroughly examined instrument for measuring gender. However, follow-up research is not at all uniform in its judgment of validity and reliability of the BSRI. An early and probably also the most extensive critique has been written by Pedhazur and Tetenbaum (1979). They claim, however, that the points criticized apply to a variety of other masculinity-femininity-scales as well. It can thus be used for further specifying the demands for a proper measurement of gender. In that, the following paragraph is important not only for evaluating the BSRI. Pedhazur and Tetenbaum's (1979) most important points are summarized below:

- The strictly empirical approach might lead to a substantial lack in construct validity (p. 998).

- Social desirability is no adequate criterion to decide on the inclusion of attributes in a questionnaire. Not only is a definition of the term *desirability* itself lacking, but it might have also led to the inclusion of items which are in fact less undesirable for one sex, but still not really desirable for any of the both sexes. Pedhazur and Tetenbaum (1979, p. 999) found that mean desirability ratings for feminine items are generally lower than those for masculine items, possibly diluting results obtained with the BSRI.

- The inclusion of the items masculine and feminine themselves does dilute the scale, as discrimination between males and females is almost exclusively due to their self-ratings on these two items. The percentage of correct classifications into the three gender groups with the values of these two items only is just slightly lower than when using the whole sixty-item inventory (p. 1004).

- The factor structure underlying the three-dimensional construct by Bem (1974) was not replicated in their study. Furthermore, the feminine items lack evidence to allow their treatment as a single summated rating scale (p. 1004-1007, 1013).

As a result Pedhazur and Tetenbaum (1979) have suggested excluding the items masculine and feminine from the scale, as well as the few traits that have been shown to be particularly low in desirability. But there have been more examinations conducted on the BSRI.

Wong, McCreary, and Duffy (1990, p. 255) found the BSRI to be reliable, but lacking convergent and discriminant validity, essentially questioning the orthogonality of masculinity and femininity as measured by the BSRI. Ramanaiah and Martin (1984) reported similar low convergent validity, contrary to Lubinski, Tellegen, and Butcher (1983). Criticims come as well from Feather (1978), Gaudreau (1977), and Whetton and Swindells (1977). In their replications of Bem's studies they generated a multiple-factor solution (e.g. four in Gaudreau, five in Whetton & Swindells, and even 18 in Feather). Feather (1978, p. 251) concludes that the two-dimensional orthogonal structure of masculinity and femininity might represent an oversimplification of the actual complex network of personality characteristics measured by the BSRI. Gaudreau (1977), on the other hand, who reports a four factor structure representing masculinity, femininity, actual sex, and a neutral maturity factor, supports Bem's contention of treating masculinity and femininity as orthogonal dimensions rather than as bipolar. Orlofsky (1981, p. 929) warned that, although m- and f-scales were found to be independent of each other, individual items might still be positively or negatively correlated. The way in which the BSRI was constructed meant it did not distinguish between aspects of masculinity/femininity that were stereotypically desirable for both sexes, and those that were desirable for only one sex.

Other researchers report results encouraging the use of the BSRI as a masculinity-femininity inventory: A factor analysis of the BSRI by Ballard-Reisch and Elton (1992, p. 296) yielded the expected two-factor orthogonal solution as did the analysis by Lubinski et al. (1983, p. 432) and Palan et al. (1999, p. 369). Conducted almost twenty years after the construction of the BSRI, Ballard-Reisch and Elton (1992, p. 300-301) concluded that the original factor structure is still reliable and highly consistent (α = 0,89 for femininity and 0,87 for masculinity). Consistently, Holt and Ellis (1998, p. 936) suggested in their rather recent study that the BSRI may still be a valid measure of gender role perceptions. Nevertheless, they examine changes in the desirability of traits between 1974 and 1998 and conclude that gender role stereotyping has weakened to some extent over the last 24 years.

As the study will take place in Austria and the BSRI is an instrument developed and tested in the United States the question of the cross-cultural validation of the BSRI remains as well as the problem of possibly decreasing validity through translation effects. Studies examining the cross-cultural validity of the inventory yielded different results. While, for example, the BSRI was found to be a valid measure among Africans (Wilson, McMaster, Greenspan, & Mboyi, 1990), this was not the case for South Indians and Malaysian populations (Ward & Sethi, 1986). As results as contrary as these do not allow for a generalization of the validity of the BSRI across countries, it was deemed sensible to use a validated German version of the inventory. Such a validation study was performed by Schneider-Dueker in 1978. The resulting inventory has already been used in research in German-speaking countries (e.g. Krahe, 1989). A refined inventory using results from studies employing the inventory was presented ten years later (Schneider-Dueker & Kohler, 1988). The authors reports sufficient reliability (α ranging from 0,74 to 0,85) and validity. The individual items are displayed in the Method chapter.

In conclusion, there is no convincing reason not to include the BSRI in a list of possibly useful measurement instruments although some weaknesses have to be acknowledged.

1.2.4.3 The Personal Attributes Questionnaire

In constructing the PAQ Spence et al. (1974) asked students to rate either the typical or the ideal male or female on a series of bipolar characteristics. The original PAQ is made up by 55 items divided into three subscales (see Figure 7):[11]

- Male-valued items (23; equally desirable for both sexes, but believed to occur to a greater degree in males; both ideal male and female, typical male)
- Female-valued items (18; equally desirable for both sexes, but believed to occur to a greater degree in females; both ideal male and female, typical female)
- Sex-specific items (13; judged desirable for either males or females; ideal for either female or male).

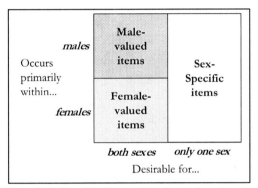

Figure 7: Scales of the Personal Attributes Questionnaire

The male- and female-valued items reflect the agency-communion distinction by Bakan (1966) or the instrumental-expressiveness distinction, respectively (Parson & Bales, 1955). Spence et al. (1975) built on the conceptualization of masculinity and femininity as a dualism. They also (1975) criticized the original three-group classification by Bem (1974) and extended it by differentiating between individuals scoring high (androgynous) and those scoring low on both dimensions of the BSRI, labeled *undifferentiated*. They demonstrated the sense of this differentiation by showing that undifferentiated and androgynous individuals differ regarding personality characteristics, such as self-esteem. Though Bem adopted this new schema, she still doubted that "the two groups differ fundamentally in their basic assumptions about gender." She emphasizes that "androgynous and undifferentiated subjects are still alike in not being sex typed" (Bem, 1977, p. 204). Figure 8 compares the two classification schemes.

---

[11] The original inventory is displayed in the Appendix.

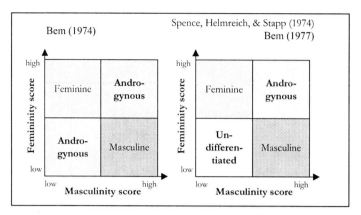

Figure 8: Comparison of the two classification schemes

As no studies have been found examining the PAQ separately (as it has been the case for the BSRI criticisms reported above) but always together with other measures (usually the BSRI) further data on the advantages and limitations of the PAQ will be reported below when explicitly comparing the two measures.

1.2.4.4 The Sexual Identity Scale

The SIS (not to be confused with the SIS – Social Intimacy Scale by Miller & Lefcourt, 1982) was developed by Stern, Barak, and Gould (1987) in an attempt not to measure researcher-defined personality characteristics, but rather to encompass individual subjective self-evaluation of their masculinity and femininity. It consists of four 5-point scales (ranging from "very feminine" to "very masculine") – thus using a single, continuous bipolar conceptualization of the masculinity-femininity characteristic – representing four gender dimensions:

- how/what individuals feel (personality/emotional dimension),
- how individuals look (physical/biological dimension),
- what individuals do (societal/occupational dimension), and
- what individuals are interested in (cognitive/intellectual dimension).

It was reported to possess both face and discriminant validity in terms of its relationship to biological sex and two multitrait indices for masculinity and femininity by its authors. The authors also found that the SIS provides additional information apart from biological sex, but heavily correlated with biological sex, though this relationship is stronger for the *look* and *feel* than for the *do* and *interest* dimensions.

Thus, it avoids operationalizing gender in form of personality traits as criticized by Constantinople (1973, p. 405). Additionally, Stern et al. (1987) suggested that the SIS might be "particularly useful in an era when rapidly evolving definitions of masculinity and femininity render previous sex role categorizations obsolete" (p. 514) because it relies on self-definitions instead of potentially out-of-date researcher-defined traits. But this is also one of the weaknesses in using the SIS as a gender identity measure: Changing gender identities can be attributed to two different phenomena: on the one hand an individual's embracement of masculine and feminine qualities can change over time, while on the other hand the definition of masculine and feminine qualities itself can shift. Thus, an individual can rate himself or herself equally masculine on a self-assessment measure compared to ten years ago, but still exhibit different personality traits. These two effects are undistinguishable with a self-assessment measure such as the SIS. Another disturbing factor may be found in the very open nature of the four statements and their wording. Individuals, especially males, may encounter troubles classifying themselves openly as "feminine". Such reservations may not be equally strong when the task is to state the degree of prevalence of personality traits traditionally associated with femininity or showing modern sex role attitudes. In an area of such sensitivity as gender and the male-female distinction open questioning is deemed a little problematic. The SIS is moreover lacking further validation studies which are available in large numbers for both the BSRI and the PAQ. Only one study was found using the SIS again in consumer research (Gould and Stern, 1989).

1.2.4.5 Comparing Available Measures

Palan et al. (1999) point out the importance of proper instruments for measuring gender: "The promise of gender identity to be a significant explanatory variable in marketing research has not yet been fulfilled, perhaps because of how it is operationalized" (p. 364). Thus, choosing a valid and reliable measure seems to be one of the most critical decisions when conducting gender research as it can substantially impact results.

Both the BSRI and the PAQ are refined inventories and widely used in research. This is not the case for the SIS. Though this self-assessment measure was with good reason suggested by Stern et al. (1987) it is still mostly lacking further examination (for one exception see Palan et al., 1999) and holds other potential difficulties. It might be useful for complementing, but not for substituting other measures of gender identity.

The decision between BSRI and PAQ does not seem to be too critical because studies found a substantial overlap between these two measure (Lubinski et al., 1983, p. 433; Spence, 1993, p. 626). Kelly, Furman, and Young (1978, p. 1575) compared the BSRI and the PAQ and found rather high correlations between the corresponding masculinity and femininity scales (0.85 and 0.75). They suggest that the two inventories can be used interchangeably. Palan et al. (1999) compared the three measures and conducted confirmatory factor analyses for all three inventories. While the BSRI items yielded a two-factor solution representing masculine and feminine traits ($\alpha = 0.88$ and 0.94, respectively), the PAQ analysis resulted in six factors (expressiveness, instrumentality, vulnerability, emotionality, composure, and autonomy) which does not facilitate interpretation of PAQ results with respect to instrumentality and expressiveness. The SIS resulted, as expected, in a one-factor solution. Internal consistency of the factors varied from very low to good. They also investigated the relationship of biological sex and the gender identity instrument: for both the BSRI and the PAQ sex accounted only for a low amount of variation in the results (18 % and 16 %), thus suggesting that these instruments do indeed measure something other than biological sex whereas 87 % of variation in scores in the SIS is explained by sex.

These findings further disqualify the SIS as an instrument for measuring gender. The number of different factor solutions for the inventories is large as it has already been shown above for the BSRI. Both the PAQ and the BSRI have been heavily criticized for their lack of theoretical foundation (e.g. Pedhazur & Tetenbaum, 1979) and reliance on college students' stereotypical ideas in their construction (e.g. Gill et al., 1987, p. 376) which may "limit their ability to transcend cultural changes over the [...] years" (Palan et al., 1999, p. 364). These authors question the assumptions made by Bem.

Bem (1974) and Spence, Helmreich, and Stapp (1975) that the masculinity and femininity scales measure instrumentality and expressiveness. Kelly et al. (1978, p. 1576) also point out that both inventories do not measure masculinity and femininity – thus gender per se – but rather instrumental and expressive personality traits as it has already been acknowledged by Spence at al. (1975, p. 38) but not by Bem (1974). Similar concerns are expressed by other researchers as well (e.g., Ballard-Reisch & Elton, 1992, p. 302). Thus, although care should be exercised when claiming that the two inventories measure masculinity and femininity, they do indeed seem to adequately capture masculine and feminine personality traits in a multidimensional gender model.

Expressiveness in the two inventories encompasses emotionality, passivity, and dependence, qualities in personality theory associated with expressiveness. In another conceptualization, Gill et al. (1987, p. 391-396) find support for their three-dimensional model (expressiveness, instrumentality, independence/autonomy). The only difference found between men and women was that women reported significantly higher levels of expressive personality traits. They argue that the inclusion of items reflecting emotionality and dependence in an expressiveness scale supposed to measure femininity might disqualify this scale as a useful measurement tool because then "the term feminine seems to connote deference to males, emotionality, and lack of assertiveness, rather than the more positive qualities that facilitate interpersonal interaction" (Gill et al, 1987, p. 396). "Masculinity is glorified and femininity devalued" (Kacen, 2003, p. 347).

Kelly et al. (1978, p. 1575) not only compared the two scales, but classified their respondents with each measure into masculine, feminine, androgynous and undifferentiated individuals. The percentage of agreement was surprisingly low. In fact, the majority of subjects were classified discrepantly with one inventory compared to the other inventory. If an individual can be androgynous when assessed with the PAQ, but masculine when measured with the BSRI, the classification scheme does not seem to cover real personality values at all and seems to be of very little worth. Kelly et al. (1979, p. 1576) are not the only authors who recommend refraining from categorization and relying on the original masculinity and femininity scores instead. A couple of other arguments also advocate for the use of original scale score instead of the rather arbitrary gender group pertinence:

- There was little empirical basis found for the classification (Kelly et al., 1978, p. 1575).
- The median-split method is inappropriate, as it is arbitrary rather then systematic (Kelly et al., 1978; Pedhazur & Tetenbaum, 1979, p. 1575).
- Through downscaling interval into nominal-scaled data by grouping, information is lost and the set of methods for data analysis is severely limited. Thus classification procedures are not warranted from a methodological and practical point of view either.

As a final note, it shall be emphasized that neither the masculinity schema nor the femininity schema does refer exclusively to men or women respectively. One might still argue that men are more likely to fall into the high masculinity/low femininity – masculine – schema and that the same – in reverse – is true for women. This might indeed still be the case with most individuals. But the important notion is that masculinity or femininity is not necessarily the consequence of being a man or a woman but separately determined by social and psychological influence factors.

1.2.4.6 Measuring Sex Role Attitudes

As suggested in Multidimensional Gender Identity Theory (Spence, 1993) interest, attitudes, and behaviors constitute separate dimensions of gender. However extensive and controversial the discussion on personality measures might be, research on attitude measures is far more restricted and less debated. A measure widely used in research for assessing sex role attitudes is the Attitudes Towards Women Scale (AWS; Spence, Helmreich, & Stapp, 1972). The AWS consists of 55 statements about the rights and roles of women in areas such as vocational, educational, and intellectual activities, dating and sexual behavior, and marital relationships. Respondents are asked to indicate their degree of agreement on a four-point Likert scale. In 1973 the authors developed a shortened form of the AWS (Spence, Helmreich, & Stapp, 1973). Spence et al. (1973, p. 220) showed that the long and short version are almost perfectly correlated. The short scale still reflects the degree to which an individual holds traditional or liberal views and thus permits comparison of different groups on this dimension as well as prediction of behavior on the basis of the individual attitude score but is still easier to administer than the lengthier version. Factor analysis of the scale yielded a one-factor solution.

Another scale better fitting the study at hand is the Male Role Norm Scale (MRNS) by Thompson and Pleck (1988) which has already been used in subsequent research (e.g. McCreary, Newcomb, & Sadava, 1998). As male role attitudes were found to be independent of attitudes towards women (Pleck, Sonenstein, & Ku, 1994) the decision which part to assess had to be made carefully. The MRNS consists of three dimensions: the Status Norm Scale (11 statements), the Toughness Norm Scale (8 statements), and the Anti-femininity Norm Scale (7 statements).

The three dimensions reflect men's need to achieve status and others' respect (status norm), the expectation that men should be mentally, emotionally, and physically tough and self-reliant (toughness scale), and the belief that men should avoid stereotypically feminine activities and occupations (anti-femininity norm). These dimensions reflect to a certain extent personality traits classified as masculine in trait inventories. Respondents answer on a seven-point Likert scale anchored with "very strongly agree"). This scale reports high values for reliability (α ranging between 0,74 and 0,81). However, when questioned men do not always embrace the attitudes stereotypically prescribed for their sex. The toughness norm was supported only slightly, and the anti-femininity norm was slightly rejected. It can be concluded that today's men's attitudes differ to a certain extent from traditional attitudes. Nevertheless individual differences are surely observable within samples.

Unfortunately neither a validation study in a German or at least European context nor some German measure developed for a similar purpose could be identified. The study therefore has to rely on a carefully conducted and multiply revised translation by the researchers and assume that the stereotypes of male role attitudes is at least to some extent transferable from American to European culture. The items of the Male Role Norm Scale are displayed in the Method chapter.

1.2.5 Conclusion: Conceptualizing gender

Gender – like any personality variable – is not readily observable within individuals. It is therefore necessary to find underlying indicators which constitute gender and can therefore be used in determining psychological masculinity and femininity. This study will use Spence's (1993) model, which is a multidimensional gender construct, as a starting point for developing a measurable concept of gender:

- gender identity,
- instrumental and expressive personality traits,
- gender related interests, role behaviors, and attitudes, and
- sexual orientation.

Dimensions one to three (gender identity, personality traits, and sex role attitudes) will be measured by appropriate scales developed for that purpose. The scales will be carefully selected, analyzing supporting and criticizing evidence from previous research.

Global gender identity will be measured by a global scale score. Despite criticisms a German version of the BSRI (Schneider-Dueker & Kohler, 1988) will be employed for measuring instrumental and expressive personality traits. Attitudes will be assessed with help of the Male Role Norm Scale by Thompson and Pleck (1988). Dimension four, sexual orientation, will be omitted from the framework for two reasons. First, including a question on sexual orientation in a questionnaire might cause considerable resentment from respondents and will quite probably be only rarely answered anyway. Secondly, the percentage of men showing homosexual preferences in Austrian population is not high enough that a relevant number of respondents can be expected to fall into this group (around 5 %).[12] Instead, the variable sex will be included, because it is frequently cited by researchers as part of the gender model (e.g. Fischer & Arnold, 1994, p. 167).[13] Figure 9 shows this fourfold gender model:

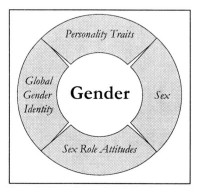

Figure 9: Four-dimensional Gender Model

Hopefully that the preceding pages have given a comprehensive introduction into the basic assumptions of gender research and also the problems associated with this field. A conclusion has been reached on how to define gender, how to differentiate it from sex and how to conceptualize and measure it for the study at hand. Building on these theoretical groundings the focus in the next section will be narrower as gender research in consumer behavior is examined in particular.

---

[12] Source: Männergesundheitsbericht Wien 1999, (http://www.wien.gv.at/who/manngb/99/).
[13] For a detailed reasoning of gender operationalization and scale selection see the Method chapter.

1.3 Consumer Behaviorists on Gender

A collection of studies will illustrate the history of gender research in marketing and consumer behavior, a topic which used to polarize and fuel debates amongst researchers.

Some authors draw a very fundamental marketing distinction between men and women regarding their economic roles: men are regarded as the producing sex whereas women are the passive sex who takes over primarily consuming roles (e.g. Kacen, 2000, p. 345). While this thesis is undoubtedly untenable in its extremity, more subtle role differences are recognized by a larger number of researchers: There seems to be a perfect relationship between female-stereotyped personality traits and female consumerism. The ideal female consumer is irrational, passive, conforming, and easily influenced (Marchand, 1985). These are traits which are also contained in femininity scales. By now marketing has become accustomed to changing roles by transforming everyone into a consumer. The male consumer role is most clearly evidenced by exclusively male-directed campaigns for products where, some decade ago, men when buying them would have undergone substantial social trouble. The impact of this change and the difficulties associated with it has been acknowledged by most researchers (e.g. Tucker, 1976, p. 351).

Topics of gender research in consumer behavior are manifold. Burns (1977) and Qualls (1987) for example investigated the impact of husband and wife's gender on household decision making. Burns (1977, p. 521) found masculinity in females to be significantly related to a shift away from husband influence to wife influence. Qualls (1987) confirmed the influence of gender on family member influence, mode of conflict resolution, and decision responsibility. Komer and Kahle (1985, p. 244) examined lunch preferences based on sex and gender and concluded that sex is a better predictor for eating habits and food preferences than gender. However, this is quite possibly due to factual physical differences between men and women (e.g. "men eat more than women"; Kahle & Homer, p. 244) whereas gender differences might be more prevalent in situations where physical predispositions do not play an important role. Gould and Stern (1989, p. 143) studied fashion-consciousness and found sex to be a better predictor of fashion attitudes than gender but suggested that gender might nevertheless be useful when examining within-sex rather than between-sex differences. Before going into more detail Table 2 lists the studies and summarizes the findings of gender studies in consumer behavior.

Study	Sample	Method	Results
Aiken, 1963	300 F	Descriptive Research, Structured questionnaire	Significant positive correlation between femininity traits and decoration, interest, and conformity dress "clusters."
Vitz & Johnston, 1965	97 F 97 M	Descriptive Research, Structured questionnaire	Among smokers, significant positive correlation between masculine cigarette brand image and (1) masculine personality traits; and (2) being male.
Fry, 1971	216 M & F Non-students	Descriptive Research, Longitudinal Study, structured questionnaire	Feminine males and females prefer cigarette brands with feminine images, although stronger effect when also have high self-confidence.
Morris & Cundiff, 1971	223 M	Descriptive Research, Structured questionnaire	High feminine/high anxiety males have more unfavorable attitudes toward feminine hair spray product than do low-or-medium feminine males.
Burns, 1977	81 F Non-students	Descriptive Research, Structured questionnaire	Masculinity is significant determining factor in wives' decision making power.
Gentry & Doering, 1977	100 M 100 F	Descriptive Research, Structured multiple questionnaires	Gender identity is strong predictor of attitudes toward leisure activities, but poor predictor of attitudes about products, brands, and media. Biological sex is better predictor than gender identity for both attitudes and usage differences in all categories.
Gentry, Doering & O'Brien, 1978	100 M 100 F	Descriptive Research, Structured multiple questionnaires	Biological sex accounts for more variability than gender identity with respect to perceptions and use of products and leisure activities.
Gentry & Doering, 1979	100 M 100 F	Descriptive Research, Structured questionnaire	Biological sex is more strongly related to attitudes and usage of leisure activities than is gender identity.
Golden, Allison, & Clee, 1979	307 M & F	Descriptive Research, Structured multiple questionnaires	Biological sex is significantly related to product sex-typing, while gender identity is not.
Allison, Golden, Mullet, & Coogan, 1980	307 M & F	Descriptive Research, Structured questionnaire	Biological sex is a better predictor of differences in product sex-typing than is gender identity.
Martin & Roberts, 1983	125 M & F	Laboratory experiment	Gender identity is significantly related to performance expectations of women entrepreneurs; sex-role attitudes significantly related to expectations of proven individuals regardless of their sex.
Kahle & Homer, 1985	84 M 55 F	Descriptive Research, Structured questionnaire	Biological sex is better predictor of food preferences than is gender identity.

Table 2: Gender studies in consumer behavior

Stern, 1987	---	Conceptional paper	Gender characteristics may affect services consumers in different ways. Gender research has special implications for services consumers.
Qualls, 1987	89 M 89 F	Descriptive Research, Structured questionnaire	BSRI, as a measure of sex-role orientation, is positively related to household influence.
Stern, 1988	---	Conceptional paper	Marketing studies have generally found that (1) sex is more influential than gender and (2) masculinity is more influential than femininity. Socio-economic changes suggest future directions for gender research.
Gould & Stern, 1989	65 M 70 F	Descriptive Research, Structured questionnaire	Biological sex is better predictor of fashion attitudes than gender identity, but gender identity research may be more important when examining within-sex vs. between-sex differences.
Fischer & Arnold, 1990	299 M & F Non-students	Descriptive Research, Structured questionnaire	Feminine gender identity positively related to involvement in Christmas gift shopping for both men and women; gender role attitudes moderate involvement.
Gould & Weil, 1991	59 M 68 F	Experiment	Biological sex is better predictor than gender identity of self-descriptions, feelings, attitudes, and gift choice. Gender identity useful in explaining within-group differences in specific contexts.
Worth, Smith, & Mackie, 1992	40 M 72 F	Experiment	Preference for gendered images of beer and jeans consistent with gender identity self-ratings.
Gainer, 1993	147 M 210 F	Descriptive Research, Structured mail questionnaire	Both biological sex and feminine gender identity positively affect attendance at the arts indirectly through involvement; further, feminine gender identity directly affects involvement, while biological sex indirectly affects involvement as a result of childhood experience in the arts.
Stern, Gould, & Tewari, 1993	70 M 79 F	Descriptive Research, Structured questionnaire	Both consumer variables (sex and gender) and service variables influence a service's sex-typed image.
Areni, Kiecker, & Palan, 1998	64 M 51 F	Qualitative Research, analysis of written narratives	Feminine and masculine scales of BSRI and PAQ are not internally consistent. SIS highly correlated to biological sex.
Kacen, 2000	---	Conceptional paper	Gender identity is foremost among the concept that need to be updated in the new millennium. The historical (modern) significance of gender identity to marketing is reviewed, the postmodern consumer condition explored, and a paradisal vision of gender identity in the consumer society to come is prophesized.

Table 2: Gender studies in consumer behavior (cont.)

Palan, 2001	---	Conceptional paper	Significant gender identity findings in consumer research have been rare because of operationalization problems, inappropriate interpretation and application of gender identity to consumer variables, or blurring gender categories.
Palan, Areni, & Kiecker, 2001	64 M 51 F	Descriptive and qualitative Research, Structured questionnaire and free narrative	Masculine males more likely than feminine males to recall gift giving experiences; feminine individuals (both males and females) were person-focused while masculine individuals (both males and females) were object-focused.

Table 2: Gender studies in consumer behavior (cont.)

To give a systematic overview, studies published before 1973 using the old conceptualization of masculinity and femininity as bipolar adjectives will be presented first. Then I will analyze two research themes in greater detail: firstly, gender and products and secondly, gender and gift-giving. Research on advertising response and information processing, the by far largest fields of research in the area, is the topic of the next chapter.

1.3.1 Before 1973: The Age of Bipolarity

Only four consumer studies were published before the new concept of gender started to emerge in the early 1970s. Out of lack of alternative inventories all four studies use the CPI Fe-scale for measuring masculinity and femininity. Additionally, the study by Vitz and Johnston (1965) employed the Minnesota Multiphasic Personality Inventory (MMPI), another pre-1973 inventory.

The first consumer study concerned with masculinity and femininity was published by Aiken in 1963. Although it is essentially a psychology paper, it was included in the literature review on gender identity in consumer research by Palan (2001) because of the relevance of its results to marketing. Aiken examined dress behavior and preferences to selected personality variables, among those the CPI measure for femininity. Variables did include masculine and feminine personality characteristics, although Aiken did not make this distinction. As his respondents were only women, his results indicated substantial differences in personality traits within the female segment. Thus they already pointed towards a possibility of female masculinity, although this was not concluded by Aiken (1963, p. 125) himself.

Aiken was followed two years later by Vitz and Johnston (1965). They examined the relationship between the masculinity of smokers and cigarette brand image and found a significant positive correlation between the perceived masculinity of the brand, masculine personality traits and being male. They allowed for the fact that females may have masculine personality characteristics, although they assumed that "men are more masculine than women" (p. 158). (Their results should be evaluated while taking into account that cigarettes are a rather image-intensive product category and thus the results might not be generalizable to other product categories which are less image-sensitive.) Using the same product category but with a different focus Fry's (1971) intention was to determine the effect of personality on cigarette brand choice. Respondents were administered scales for ten different personality traits, among those the CPI-Fe scale for femininity. Other variables measured represented traits frequently associated with masculinity, such as aggression, autonomy, and dominance, although this was not explicitly acknowledged by Fry. Compared to other personality measures femininity seemed to have a larger impact on cigarette brand choice especially for males. Thus the explanatory value of biological sex was a far stronger predictor. However, Fry nevertheless concluded that "personality variables [...] appear to have considerable potential for improving understanding of the psychological basis of brand choice" (p. 303). He admitted, though, that only part of the variation in brand choice could be explained by personality.

Cigarette brands were split into masculine and feminine brands in the two previous studies, on the other hand men's attitudes towards products with a defined feminine appeal were investigated by Morris and Cundiff (1971). In addition to assessing femininity they also measured manifest anxiety within the individual. They reported that there is no relationship between femininity and product attitudes or between anxiety and product attitudes. They found a strong connection between femininity, anxiety, and product attitudes. High anxiety combined with high femininity resulted in the most unfavorable attitudes. Low anxiety and high femininity individuals seemed to possess by far the most favorable attitudes towards feminine products. Anxiety to openly display socially undesirable attitudes, such as liking of a defined feminine product by a male person, thus seemed to impede feminine men from stating their otherwise positive attitudes openly. Interestingly, low femininity and high anxiety also lead a to comparably positive attitudes, perhaps because extreme positions – in which one direction indicates extreme femininity where the opposite direction represents extreme masculinity – are felt to be socially less accepted.

Apart from Aiken's (1963) study all these early precursors are part of one large field of gender research, namely the relationship of gender and product image. Vitz and Johnston (1965) as well as Fry (1971) investigated some aspects of the relationship between gender image and product image. While they focused on the actual use of products, Morris and Cundiff (1971) examined attitudes which are linked to usage in that sense that favorable attitudes generally precede a buying decision or are at least influencing repurchase of a product. As this field of research now has already been introduced the next section will continue to analyze research from 1973 onwards all of which examine relationships between product and gender.

1.3.2 Who Likes What? – Gender and Products

The congruence of product image and gender image constitutes a basic link between gender research and marketing (Stern, 1988, p. 87). More precisely, gender is an important part of an individual's self-concept or self-image, i.e. "the totality of an individual's thoughts and feelings having reference to himself as an object" (Rosenberg, 1979, p. 7; cited after Sirgy, 1982, p. 287). Self-concept is thought to have a relationship to product image, so that a positive congruence of the two (a positive product-image perception and a positive self-image belief) will motivate this individual to a purchase (Sirgy, 1982, p. 289). Additionally, substantiating the interest in sex-typed product images is the idea that consumers purchase products not so much for their functional value as for the match between their own personality and the image of the product (proposed as early as in 1959 by Levy). Products not only satisfy consumption needs but are also used to express attitudes and status.

The first authors to follow Fry (1971) were Gentry and Doering in 1977. They collected data from 200 college students about their product perceptions in terms of masculinity and femininity, product attitudes, and the degree to which brands were used, for a large number of brands in different product categories, as well as for leisure activities and magazine readership. In general, they found that biological sex is a better predictor than gender for both attitudes and usage in all categories, although for several specific products or activities, such as cigarettes or hair spray, this hypothesis did not hold. Sex seemed to have a greater impact on the use or non-use of a product category than on the choice of a specific brand. When using the CPI-Fe scale as a measure of masculinity and femininity, stronger relationships between gender and the dependent variables were found than when using the newly-developed PAQ. Gentry and Doering (1977, p. 427) concluded that, although gender did not seem to play a crucial role in determining consumer behavior, it might well do so in the future because of changing sex roles. In a 1978 paper, Gentry et al. investigated the sex-stereotyping of products and found surprisingly little differences between masculine and feminine product perceptions. In fact, only one product (Cologne) was viewed as distinctly masculine by males. Even products like hair spray, razor blades, beer, or shampoo received approximately equal masculinity and femininity ratings. The authors interpreted the results as support for an increasing convergence of male and female sex roles. The examination of data on attitudes towards and usage of leisure activities (Gentry & Doering, 1979) confirmed previous findings: sex was a strong predictor of activity preference with usage and attitude patterns reflecting prevalent stereotypes. But the researchers also found androgynous individuals to be more likely to participate and have positive attitudes towards activities not traditionally associated with their sex, thus encouraging further research in this area.

Another pair of researchers investigating sex-typed product images was Linda L. Golden and Neil Allison. Contrary to Gentry et al. (1978) they concluded that products have very definite masculine or feminine images (Golden et al., 1979, p. 604) and that these two dimensions are perceived as orthogonal rather than bipolar (Allison, Golden, Mullet, & Coogan, 1980, p. 609). These images seem to be developed based on which sex most often uses the product. The strength of perceived masculinity and femininity is influenced by gender and sex, where sex seems to be the stronger influencing factor. Males tend to perceive products as more masculine whereas females usually consider these same products to be more feminine (Allison et al., 1980, p. 608).

In two experiments Worth, Smith, and Mackie (1992) presented stimulus material to respondents that described products in either masculine or feminine terms. Subjects liked the product whose description most closely met their individual gender best, regardless of their actual sex. Additional insight into the relation between product image and gender identity was delivered by Gainer (1993) who investigated the role of involvement as a mediator between feminine gender and arts attendance. The results suggest that neither sex, nor gender has a direct affect on purchase, but rather impacts involvement which in turn influences purchase frequency.

As the term *product* usually includes both physical goods and intangible services some results on gender and services shall also be included in this section. An interesting aspect of services in a gender context is that services are the only economic sector that involves women as producers as well as consumers (Stern, 1987, p. 515; cf. Kacen, 2000, p. 345). Parallel, studies from researchers such as

Golden et al. (1979), Stern and her colleagues (1993) investigated the sex-typing of services. Images can be assigned to services as to products, either on the basis of the individual's own sex or gender or by the sex of the stereotypical user or provider of the service. They found that service images are clearly sex-typed (masculine, feminine or neutral) and that generally neither sex nor gender do influence service sex-typing. Images seem to be more strongly influenced by which sex is perceived to be the typical consumer of the service, just as the perception of a typical male provider was associated with higher masculinity of the service. Martin and Roberts (1983) investigated performance expectations of male and female entrepreneurs in the service industry. Contemporary or traditional sex role attitudes did not affect the level of expectations towards male and female entrepreneurs. Masculine individuals, however, held lower performance expectations of unproven (without previous accomplishments) when compared to proven (with previous accomplishments) businessmen or women with a particular tendency to devalue unproven females.

Several conclusions can be drawn from research on the gender and product relation. First, most authors agree that a certain amount of sex-stereotyping occurs for products (e.g. Gainer, 1993, p. 265) although image perceptions might be blurring due to changing sex roles (Gentry et al., 1978). The reasons for the development of sex-typed images are less clear. They might lie in who most often uses the product (Golden et al., 1979) but could also be due to characteristic product features which are associated with either one or the other sex (Gainer, 1993, p. 265). This question was investigated for services by Stern et al. (1993, p. 92) pointing to a typical user influence rather than to influence of the respondent's own sex or gender. The gender concept seems nevertheless to hold great promises for the service industries (Stern, 1987, p. 518). Gender – or more precisely – gender-product image congruency seems to play a role for attitudes towards products. This hypothesis will be further investigated when examining consumer responses to gendered ads where congruence between advertisement portrayal and gender is suggested to be important for consumers' attitudes towards the ad and resulting purchase probability. Finally, when interpreting data from such studies it should be taken into account that there might be variables interfering in the relationship, as shown for involvement by Gainer (1993).

1.3.3   To Give or To Receive – Gender and Gift Giving

A surprisingly large amount of research focuses on a rather unusual field: the giving and receiving of gifts. The relationship between gift-giving and gender seems to exert fascination on researchers as five out of 31 studies (16 %) contained in the literature review by Palan (2001) examined some aspect of gift-giving. In this context gender seems to be of particular relevance as most of the studies found gender to be a better predictor of gift-shopping behavior than sex. Fischer and Arnold (1990, p. 342) report that feminine gender identity significantly impacts involvement with Christmas gift shopping. Feminine individuals start shopping earlier and spend more time shopping per individual, indicating a more communal orientation. Using a multidimensional gender framework Fisher and Arnold also assessed sex role attitudes and found a significant relationship between egalitarian sex role attitudes and the number of people to whom gifts were presented as well as time spent for shopping. However, gift-giving still seems to be strongly associated with women's tasks and women are still more involved than men. Gould and Weil (1991) provided further insight by taking sex of gift recipients (same-sex versus opposite-sex) and thus the situational dependency of self-perceptions into account. Men's self-perceptions as masculine or feminine varied significantly more than women's. When giving to opposite-sex recipients males tended to become more feminine whereas they judged themselves as more masculine when giving to same-sex recipients. This variability could not be clearly observed in females. Areni et al. (1998) extended the topic to the dimension of gift-receiving. They found that men surprisingly recall more gift-giving experiences while women recall more gift-receiving situations. This is contrary to the stereotypic notion of female other-orientation and male self-focus. In this study, however, no attempt was made to assess the impact of gender on the receiving of gifts. In another paper Palan, Areni, and Kiecker (2001) extended the findings of the previous study taking gender into account. According to this, masculine men were more likely to recall gift-giving experiences than feminine men which is again incongruent with traditional male role expectations. Another finding which fits better into expectations of male and female behavior is that feminine men were found to be very person-oriented in their gift-giving.

Probably the most interesting conclusion that can be drawn from this unusual field of research is that gender identity does indeed seem to influence people's attitudes and behaviors. Though this might not be the case with any attitude or behavioral situation, such findings encourage further research on the gender topic and add value to the concept itself.

1.3.4 Conclusions from the Past – Implications for this Research

The first conclusion to be drawn from the variety of research results reported above is simply that no unanimous conclusion can be drawn at all. Undeniably there are a large number of studies negating the importance of gender as an individual differences variable in marketing, which have led to calls to abandon gender-role research in marketing (e.g., Roberts, 1984). However, Stern (1988, p. 96) was not the only one to conclude that it may be premature to completely cancel marketing related gender research altogether, arguing that the consequences of the changes brought about by the feminist movement during the 70s might need some time to be fully effective in society. This view is supported by Widgery and McGaugh (1993, p. 37), who believe that changes will not occur until at least one generation later, because only children being brought up in a new societal environment can eventually exhibit different traits and attitudes. This is one reason why most researchers use students samples (e.g. Gentry & Doering, 1977), which will also be the case in this study.

Findings of past research can be summarized on two points (Stern, 1988, p. 92-93):

1. High masculinity explains more than typological combinations (masculine, feminine, androgynous, undifferentiated) in terms of family decision making, reactions to women's roles in advertisements, and a variety of consumer behavior variables (Barak & Stern, 1986, Burns, 1977; Coughlin & O'Connor, 1985).

2. Biological sex is an explanatory variable at least as good as sex-role self-concept (gender), for product use, brand choice, media use, product perception, product sex-typing, attitudes towards women business owners, and advertising recall, although results are not unanimous (Allison et al, 1980; Gentry & Doering, 1977; Gentry et al., 1978, Gentry & Haley, 1984; Golden et al, 1979, Kahle & Homer, 1985; Martin & Roberts, 1983).

Palan (2001, p. 15-19) concludes in her review of gender identity in consumer behavior that gender can explain meaningful differences in consumer behavior if studies are carefully conceptualized and thus encourages further research in this area. She also provides some recommendations on how gender identity studies should be conducted which are also followed in the present study:

- A multidimensional gender approach should be used. Of the studies included in Palan (2001) using multifactorial gender identity as a basis, all studies yielded significant results with respect to gender. At the very least, personality traits and global gender self-concept (as defined by Spence, 1993) should be assessed.
- Regardless of the theoretical basis used, studies employing the BSRI yielded more often significant results than did studies using the PAQ.
- There should be some logical reasoning behind including gender as a variable in the survey. Gender should be logically argued to have some potential explanatory power (to "be relevant") for the variables in question. Both studies on advertising response (e.g. Coughlin & O'Connor, 1985; Jaffe & Berger, 1988; Jaffe, 1991) and information processing (e.g. Schmitt, LeClerc, & Dubé-Rioux, 1988) fulfill this criterion (Palan, 2001, p. 7-9) and therefore justifying the examination of gender differences in these two fields.

Gender identity seems to

1. possess explanatory value regarding women's responses to advertising and
2. may also influence information processing.

The examining of three decades of gender related research encourages the objective undertaken in this book as continuing social change might further enhance the value of gender in understanding consumer behavior. The value itself has already been demonstrated in some consumer research areas (e.g. gift-shopping behavior). The next chapter will examine in greater detail the origins and consequences of this change and ask whether change can be observed at all.

One is not born, but rather becomes a women.
(Simone de Beauvoir)

2 Masculinity in a Changing World

This book is based on the assumption that males and females do not only exhibit their stereotypically attributed range of personality traits and behaviors but have changed considerably on these dimensions within the recent decades. Though there is probably no one to argue that some change of this kind has *not* taken place, the assumption that is has is often taken as a fact without further efforts for verification. Therefore, with the help of previous research we need to assess whether there is enough evidence for actual shifts in society to be able to conclude that males and females might indeed exhibit traits and behavioral patterns different from those some decades ago. This conclusion is of course only valid if these patterns are at least to some extent dependent on social influence and not completely predetermined by biological sex. Because of the extensiveness of this question – whether "nature or nurture" actually shapes human personality – will only be addressed briefly. Furthermore, as males are subject to study here part two of this chapter will deepen understanding of the male role by examining past (rare) research on masculinity.

2.1 Changing Sex Roles – Evidence for Shifts in Society

This section is titled Changing Sex Roles although it is not only about sex roles. The evidence for change includes personality traits, sex role ideologies and attitudes, and power relations. However, for easier readability the term sex roles is considered a good descriptive umbrella term. Nevertheless, it is important that research on "soft fact" changes, such as personality traits, is supported by some "hard facts" to show whether and where sex role change has visible implications on social structure. One fact frequently made responsible for the change in sex roles is the increasing work force participation of women (e.g. Jaffe & Berger, 1994, p. 32; Coltrane, 1994; Zuo, 1997, p. 813). Some European and, in particular, Austrian evidence for this claim and other potential demographic manifestations of sex role change are consequently reported in the next section.

2.1.1 Demographic Evidence

Because the literature claims that work force participation of women is the driving factor of sex role change, this issue will be investigated first. In Austria female work force participation (the percentage of women who were involved in the job market) was 44 % in 1971, rising steadily to 58 % in 1999. In the same period the male work force participation declined slightly from 71 % to 68 % (see Figure 10). Compared to the European average, Austria takes a rather favorable position. In the year 2000 only 51 % of European women were part of the workforce. However, efforts are being undertaken by both EU and national administrations to increase this figure. On the long run the EU hopes to push women work force participation above 60 % by 2010.[14]

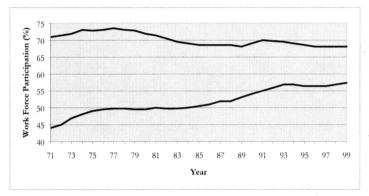

Figure 10: Work force participation rates of men (upper line) and women (lower line) in Austria from 1971 to 1999, adapted from Prenner & Scheibenhofer (2001)

The difference in work force participation rates between the sexes is therefore diminishing, though this is almost exclusively due to rising women's rates rather than to men's decreasing rates. The difference, in 1971 amounting to 27 %, has decreased to only 10 % within the last three decades.[15] Although work force participation rates do not take into account the amount of part-time work and the quality of the job, it is nevertheless clear that women continue leaving their traditional home working place.

---

[14] Source: European Council (cf. Beckmann, 2003).
[15] An interesting concept in this context is the *Full Time Equivalent*. This modified participation rate takes diluting effects of part time work into account and is calculated by dividing total work volume (hours) by the average number of working hours for a full time job. If participation rates are therefore purified and recalculated, then the rates for women are approximately 10 % lower than those reported above. Men show about the same regular participation rates and full time equivalents (Source: Eurostat 2002; cf. Beckmann, 2003).

The average level of education of women in Austria is also increasing. Today more women complete higher education (A-levels, University diploma) than before. When comparing education levels of men and women, the proportion of men is higher at universities, A-level schools and apprenticeships, whereas women more numerous in the group finishing their education after reaching the compulsory education level. Women who have completed higher education are generally more active in the work force (Prenner & Scheibenhofer, 2001).

Now there is obviously an abundance of research and data on female work force participation. Male data seems to be simply less interesting because it has not changed much within the last 30 years. However, although male work force participation might not have decreased, there might be some other areas where evidence of changing sex roles can be obtained. Two of them are investigated here: male household work participation and the taking of child rearing responsibilities. The first one is chosen because it is the best manifestation of changing sex roles and crossing gender boundaries since men take over tasks stereotyped as feminine[16] and the household is the stereotypical female work environment. The second indicator was selected because child rearing refers especially to the nurturing, caring role associated with femininity.

The distribution of household responsibilities is still heavily skewed towards the female side. On average women dedicate four hours daily to household work while men spend only one. In relationships where both partners are working fulltime, men spend approximately two hours a day with household work, women about five (see Figure 11).[17]

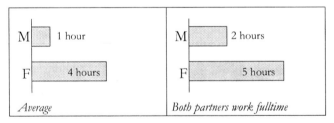

Figure 11: Household workload distribution between men and women

This is possibly due to the fact that men whose spouses are also working generally exhibit more egalitarian sex role attitudes (Ciabattari, 2001, p. 579-580) and therefore might be more willing to share tasks. Also simple time constraints

---

[16] A study by Bem and Lenney (1976) found that sex-typed individuals show an especially strong dislike against performing tasks stereotypically linked to the other sex. Cross-sex typed and not-sex typed individuals exhibit weaker resentments.
[17] Source: Statistik Austria, 2002 (cf. Weinzinger & Wagner, 2004).

from both partners working might lead to a greater readiness to share responsibilities overall. However, husband participation in the household work has generally increased, as has joint household decision making (e.g. Helmreich, Spence, & Gibson, 1982; Mason, Czajka, & Arber, 1976). Thus, men high in expressiveness tend to do more household work, as well as they show greater interest in household products. This establishes gender as one variable potentially explaining such differences within sexes (Nyquist, Slivken, Spence, & Helmreich, 1985, p. 27), but the assignment of specific tasks to either the male or the female partner is still dependent on sex. While women are still largely responsible for domestic tasks, such as cooking, cleaning, laundry, and food shopping, men prefer taking responsibilities for maintenance work, like painting, repairing, exterior cleaning, and lawn and car care (Nyquist et al., 1985, p. 23).

Also, child care remains largely an area of female responsibility. While 52 % of women have sole responsibility for their children, only 4 % of Austrian men look after their children without the help of a partner.[18] However, those who do more actively engage in child-raising usually find it rewarding (e.g. Donaldson, 1993). A special manifestation of active male involvement in child care is spending some months in parental leave. For some years Austrian men been given this possibility. Nonetheless, men's enthusiasm for this opportunity seems to be very limited. Only 2 % of Austrian men choose this option – compared to 38 % in Sweden and even 68 % in 1999 in Norway[19] – although 37 % say they would want to.[20] This discrepancy can be explained threefold: firstly, the still-prevalent earning difference between men and women makes it impossible for many families to do without the salary of the husband. Secondly, the idea of men on parental leave still does not seem to be wholly accepted in society questioning the masculinity of those men who do choose parental leave. Thirdly, the idea is very unpopular with a large majority of employers – and less accepted among male employees than among female employees. The discrepancy in numbers to Sweden can be largely explained by different socio-political circumstances. However, the fact that a large proportion of males have at least a positive attitude towards this alternative is encouraging. Another heartening number comes from Canada where in single earner families in

---

[18] Source: Bundesministerium für Soziale Sicherheit und Generationen, 2002 (cf. Weinzinger & Wagner, 2004).
[19] Source: Oftung, Knut: Fathers and Parental Leave in Norway
[20] Source: Ludwig Boltzmann Institut für Werteforschung (cf. Die Presse, 7.6.2003). For more information on parental leave for fathers in Austria the webpage of "Väterkarenz Consulting" (www. vaterkarenz.at) is recommended.

1976 only 1.000 dads stayed at home, compared to three million women. In 2001, however, there were already 77.000 men staying at home.[21]

In conclusion, there is extensive evidence for changing women's sex roles and some visible manifestations of men's. The shift in the labor market has been documented and some changes in household and child-rearing responsibilities, traditionally assigned to women, can be observed. It must still be noted that the documented evidence refers to western cultures (i.e. Europe, USA, Canada, Australia & New Zealand) only. In different cultural context, such as eastern cultures or countries with a different religious background, change patterns might be weaker, different, or even not observable at all.

However, in a first evaluation, claims for changes in sex roles seem to possess substance, provided that demographic shifts indeed result in such changes – what is judged to be probable. But the gap between the sexes is, though narrowing, still prevalent. Additional and more precise support for altered sex roles can be found in the studies examining attitudes and traits which are reported in the next section.

2.1.2 Psychographic Evidence

Over time general agreement in the literature has emerged that sex-related traits and behaviors are not fixed but rather situation-dependent (e.g. Deaux, 1985). In a broader context this means that men and women also adapt their behaviors not only to specific situations but also over time as the current state of society can be viewed as a single large "situation" which is quite different from what it used to be 20 or 30 years ago. Some aspects of changing personality patterns were already addressed above in the chapter on sex differences between males and females. Overall, there is general agreement in the literature that sex differences are not necessarily constant over time (e.g. Rosenthal & Rubin, 1982), but rather that they "ebb and flow with changes in situational forces and stereotypes [...] and vary to some degree across both time and culture" (Deaux, 1985, p. 69). The argument in this section builds on three pillars: an assessment of changes in sex differences which provides evidence for changing behavioral and personality patterns; an examination of attitude changes; and a presentation of a study on actual masculine and feminine personality shifts in the sexes.

---

[21] Source: Webpage of Today's Parent (www.todaysparent.com, accessed 13.10.2004).

2.1.2.1 Diminishing Sex Differences

Some evidence for diminishing sex differences has already been mentioned above. Sex differences in cognitive skills, such as mathematical or linguistic ability, were found to grow smaller between 1962 and 1982 (Rosenthal & Rubin, 1982). More recent studies (e.g. Hyde, 1990, p. 71) point to similar developments. It can be speculated that this might also be due to the fact that women increasingly benefit from higher level education. With regards to personality traits aggression is often cited as a major discriminator between men and women (e.g. Maccoby & Jacklin, 1972). Aggression is very strongly associated with men and but is considered one of the most undesirable traits for women (e.g. Pedhazur & Tetenbaum, 1979, p. 1006). But even here Hyde (1990, p. 70) reported diminishing differences between males and females. It is quite possible that men's and women's scores on other personality traits which are not so strongly sex-linked and whose desirability for one or the other sex is not so clearly defined are converging even more. A study by Deaux and Ullman (1983) investigated blue-collar workers, thus targeting the less-educated social strata, and found no evidence for sex differences in self-evaluations, aspirations, likes, and dislikes. All together these studies covered a broad range of social environments and age groups. Most of the studies were conducted in the United States. Reviews, such as the one by Maccoby and Jacklin (1972), cover results from different countries though usually within a Western context. However, this study is set in such a context, therefore the above mentioned results are valid for the given purpose: differences between males and females are declining and personality characteristics and abilities are thus proving their responsiveness to the environment.

2.1.2.2 Attitude Change and Related Indicators

A substantial number of studies examine attitudes towards sex roles and come to very similar conclusions. Generally studies report a significant shift of attitudes towards an egalitarian direction. Today both men and women hold more favorable attitudes towards working women. Such observations were already made during the 1970s and 1980s of the last century in the United States (e.g. Mason et al., 1976; Helmreich et al., 1982), though the earlier study by Mason et al. (1976) investigated only women's attitudes which might have changed earlier than men's. It is not surprising that more recent studies do not yield results very different from those obtained 20 years ago. Zuo (1997, p. 809) specifically examined males' sex role attitudes during the 1980s and 1990s and found a considerable shift towards egalitarian attitudes. However, he also found that men still prefer occupying the family provider role and furthermore that attitudes show rather large individuals differences depending on a number of factors. Also he points out the existence of a gap between attitude and actual behavior. Ciabattari (2001) investigates an even larger time period using attitude data ranging from 1974 to 1998 from different western countries. She provides deeper insight into the "why" and "how" of attitude change by separately examining cohort effects – the character of an individual birth cohort that reflects the circumstances of its unique history and experience – and period effects – society-wide shifts that influence all groups at the same time. In general she reports decreasing conservativism among men about women's roles. In this manner, cohort and period effects interact. The 1970s were the decade bringing about most of the change, whereas differences between the later decades were more modest. Within each period, the oldest cohort generally holds the most conservative sex role beliefs.

Naturally, sex role beliefs and attitudes are not only influenced by time – be it cohort or period influence – but also by a number of other factors. Egalitarian sex role attitudes are positively associated with the level of education of an individual (Zuo, 1997, p. 804) although the influence of education has become less important as the liberal movement has become more widespread (Ciabattari, 2001, p. 587). Family context (marital status, employment status of the spouse) and the number of children are also related with conservative attitudes as are conservative political and religious ideologies (Ciabattari, 2001, p. 584-585). Age and breadwinner status – the extent to which men are and have the need to be the family provider – have a negative impact on egalitarianism as well. High income of men relative to their spouses' income negatively influences their attitudes (Zuo, 1997, p. 813). Figure 12 summarizes factors influencing sex role attitudes. Thereby egalitarian attitudes are positively valued (e.g. high educational level has a positive influence on attitudes, so it leads to more egalitarian attitudes).

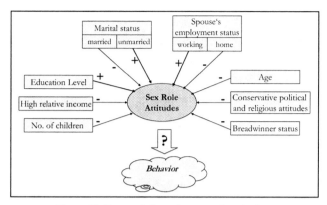

Figure 12: Factors influencing sex role attitudes

Zuo (1997, p. 803-804) also reports some interesting results on how men can benefit from holding egalitarian role attitudes. Men with less conservative sex role attitudes find child care more rewarding and enjoy higher marital quality. Conservative men also encounter more stress concerning whether they will be able to live up to society's expectations of men, namely in being the family provider. They therefore experience greater frustration when they fail (e.g. become unemployed; see Zuo, 1997, for further references). Or as Bereska (2003) puts it: "Although women are negatively affected by patriarchy in a more obvious way, the power of patriarchy has a negative impact on many men's lives as well" (p. 158).

Additional evidence for alteration of sex roles shall be given by a European study on the shifting power balance by Smits, Mulder, and Hooimeijer (2003). They investigated couples' propensity to move for job-related reasons and compared results from 1977 and 1996. In 1977 the male partner's employment situation was the determining factor and the woman's situation hardly played a role. By 1996, power distribution between the partners was more equal based on the earning capacities of each partner. Thus, unequal earning capacity for one partner enhances this partner's power regardless of their sex. Similar results were found for age influence. Whereas in 1977 the age of the male partner but not that of the female partner contributed significantly to his power, in 1996 age effects could be observed for both sexes. The authors interpret their results as pointing to a rising equality of the sexes. Now the power distribution in relationships seems to be determined by other factors than only the sex of the partner.

As may already have been noted by the reader, studies almost exclusively examine attitudes towards women's roles, although they use both men and/or women as subjects. This discrepancy in research interest is prevalent in most areas of sex or gender related study.[22] The small amount of surveys identified examining male roles will be reported below in the chapter on masculinity and the male role.

2.1.2.3 Masculinity and Femininity – Are They Subject to Change?

Data on women work force participation, men's household responsibilities, diminishing sex differences and shifted sex role attitudes provide support and encouragement to reexamine psychological and marketing issues based on masculine-feminine personality measures rather than on the male-female sex dichotomy. In this context it is of particular interest whether personalities per se (as described through standard measures of masculinity and femininity) have been subject to change as well. A meta-analytic study (Twenge, 1997) examining shifts in scores of men and women on the Bem Sex Role Inventory (BSRI) and the Personal Attributes Questionnaire (PAQ) between 1973 and 1994 sheds some light on this question.

For women, the increase in masculinity scores was significantly related to the year of administration of the questionnaire where the year accounted for over 50 % of the variance in masculinity scores. No correlation was found for female femininity. For males both masculinity and femininity scores increased slightly over time. A German study even found men rating themselves higher in feminine than in masculine characteristics (Schultze, Knussmann, & Christiansen, 1991, p. 211). Twenge (1997) also examined sex differences in scores. She found a decrease in differences between men and women's BSRI-masculinity scores and a small, though insignificant correlation between year and difference in BSRI-femininity scores. Comparing older with younger studies she concludes that "men and women's scores on the BSRI have become more similar over the last 20 years" (Twenge, 1997, p. 311). The results are in line with general suggestions that females move in a masculine direction rather than the other way round (e.g. Bellizzi & Milner, 1991, p.73). It also supports the contention that change observed in women is usually larger than that observed in men (e.g. Nyquist et al., 1985, p. 32). Although these results are not very encouraging from a viewpoint of sex equality, individual differences within the sexes are quite possibly present and can serve as potential explanations for differences in attitudes and behaviors. And the question whether there is any change in personality scores occurring at all can nevertheless be answered positively. A study by Ballard-Reisch and Elton (1992, p. 297) found that 75 % of respondents perceived only 2 of the items of the BSRI as specifically

---

[22] See section 2.1.4 "A Double Men-Women Discrepancy".

masculine and feminine, which were the specific items "masculine" and "feminine". However, as mentioned, some authors argue that BSRI or PAQ items have never reflected masculinity and femininity but only instrumentality and expressiveness. These orientations are still rather well defined by approved trait scales (e.g. Palan et al., 1999, p. 375). As indicated by the study by Ballard-Reisch and Elton (1992), the dimensions of instrumentality and expressiveness seem to loose their link to either one sex or the other.

In the context of masculinity and femininity scores another point shall be mentioned potentially indicating changes in sex role perceptions, namely shifts in the perceived masculinity and femininity of products. Just as definitions of masculinity and femininity themselves, perceptions of products are subject to change, too (Gentry & Doering, 1979, p. 107). Many products previously tied to one sex or the other have become unisex (e.g. Kahle & Homer, 1985, p. 243: blue jeans and hair dryers; Gentry et al., 1978, p. 331: cigarettes, jeans, shampoo). Apparently, men are now "allowed" to use hair dryers without being labeled effeminate.

Documenting observed changes in different fields related to sex and gender of course does not at all answer the question of why these changes occur. This issue shall be briefly addressed in the next section.

2.1.3 Why Roles Change

The basic assumption underlying the change in sex roles is that they are actually shaped by society. If pre-determinism of any form were responsible for human behavior, change would hardly be observed at all. However, the dispute on nature versus nurture is far from being settled. In the context of this chapter it can be reasonably assumed that society explains most of the variance in question. It is very likely that society influences to a large extent female work force participation, male household responsibilities, power distribution in relationships, and product perceptions. Probably some degree of biological influence could be argued for personality traits and for sex differences in cognitive abilities. Nevertheless, for good reason explanation of sex role changes focuses on social causes.

These explanations usually build on one main phenomenon, though it can take different forms: the rising economic power of women. Graham, Stendardi, Myers, and Graham (2002, p. 2) hold the changes in the financial power of women responsible, while others rephrase it and see the shift as caused be the rising number of working women (e.g. Jaffe and Berger, 1994, p. 32; Coltrane, 1994).

Studies confirm the relationship between economic power of women and changing gender roles (e.g. Smits et al., 2003). Change is therefore mostly attributed to changing female roles and not male roles, another manifestation of the imbalance between change in females and males. Figure 13 depicts a simplified picture of the antecedents of change as suggested in the literature.

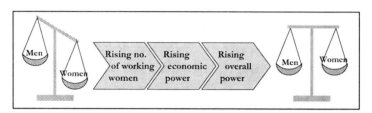

Figure 13: Antecedents of shifting power balance and consequently sex roles

Social Role Theory (Eagly, 1987) provides some explanations for this sequence of events suggesting that individuals develop traits because they enact in roles in the society which require these traits. This theory explains why personalities change as a result of different functions taken in society (e.g. mother versus working women). It also suggests that men start developing expressive (feminine-associated) traits when they enter husband and father's roles (Twenge, 1997, p. 315). This suggestion should be viewed as complementing rather than contradicting findings that younger men generally exhibit more egalitarian attitudes.

Research points out factors especially influencing sex role attitudes, where the change is probably most clearly visible. Also factors such as a broader offering of higher education facilities (especially for women) might have contributed to more egalitarian attitudes. A certain social readiness and climate seems to be needed to induce changes in sex role perceptions (e.g. Bem, 1981, p. 362; Kimmel, 1988, p. 9-10). The 1970s, in particular, with the start of and high enthusiasm for the feminist movement proved to be a fruitful decade for gender shifts. In more recent decades, however, change has become weaker again (Ciabattari, 2001, p. 575).

2.1.4 A Double Men-Women Discrepancy

When examining research on changes in sex roles two main discrepancies between the sexes emerge. Firstly, the extent of change in women is larger and more visible than that in men. Secondly, women are the far better researched sex.

Changes in role ideologies and role attitudes are observable to different degrees within the two sexes. Men did, and still do, have more traditional sex role ideologies than women (Gould & Weil, 1991, p. 635). Also Ciabattari (2001, p. 575)

notes that men tend to express more conservative attitudes and the pace of attitude change has been slower with men than with women, thus leading to a widening gap between men and women's attitudes. This is an interesting finding, as most other authors argue that the sexes are getting more and more alike, though with women shifting in a masculine direction rather than the other way round. Deaux (1985, p. 65) cites a number of studies which document a shift in attitudes with regards to the roles of women, and to a lesser concerning the roles of men. Males generally tend to hold more traditional gender ideologies than women and conformity to gender stereotypes is still more important for males than for females (Aube & Koestner, 1992, p. 490). This imbalance between the sexes is partly explained when considering that women are more likely and also allowed to show both masculine and feminine patterns than men (Twenge, 1997, p. 316).

Carlson (1971, p. 271) documents this greater psychological bisexuality[23] of females, first postulated by Bakan (1966). Hoffman (2001, p. 475) found college women were becoming more feminine and masculine at the same time, but reported no results for men. Concrete manifestations of this gradient between males and females can be found in household responsibilities: men adopt female responsibilities (e.g. cleaning, kitchen work) to a lesser extent than women adopt traditionally male responsibilities (e.g. maintenance work; Nyquist et al., 1985, p. 26). Stuteville (1971) hypothesized that this discrepancy could also apply to the acceptance of sex-linked products, meaning that women are more ready to adopt products with a masculine image than are men to adopt products classified as feminine. Parents tend to accept boyish behavior in girls more than girlish behavior in boys (Maccoby, 1998, p. 145). Aube and Koestner (1992, p. 491) explain these phenomena by pointing out that expanding male behavior to include traditional female items as well means embracing new roles that are generally less powerful and less valued. In Western society instrumental traits are generally more valued and approved than expressive traits (Jones, Chernovetz, & Hansson, 1978), although trying to comply with traditional male role norms can lead to significant role stress for males.[24] Nonetheless, since the publication of this study, considerable changes have taken place. It is quite possible that today society finds it more desirable for men to possess expressive personality traits than it was 20 years ago.

---

[23] The term bisexuality which is used by Carlson might be misleading in the present context. The way it is used here does not relate to "sexual" bisexuality as the term is used in everyday language but to what might be described by the word "bi-genderedness", namely the tendency and capability to exhibit both masculine and feminine personality traits. To emphasize this distinctive meaning and avoid confusion the word "psychological" was added to the original term.

[24] See section 2.2.2 "Masculinity in Research".

Therefore, the distance between the amount and pace of men's and women's changes should be diminishing.

Studies on gender roles and their changes have focused to a large extent on women only (e.g. Jaffe, 1991; Goughlin & O'Connor, 1985), or on women and men, but rarely on men only. Three explanations for this imbalance in research focus can be found:

- Interest in gender issues was fuelled by the feminist movement in the 1970s. Therefore the main focus and objective of academics in this research stream was the female being in an attempt to make up for centuries of male predominance.

- As women's roles and attitudes were experiencing changes which were faster and more radical than those observed in men it might have been more interesting to examine women then men (e.g. Gentry & Doering, 1979, p. 103; Nyquist et al., 1985, p. 26-27).

- Women generally exhibit greater psychological bisexuality (e.g. Bakan, 1966; Carlson, 1971, p. 271), they are thus more likely to show masculine and feminine patterns in personality and behavior. Therefore research might have been perceived as more interesting and fruitful.

However, considering these three points the development of men's studies – studying masculinity – comes as a logical consequence of reported societal changes also increasingly observed in men. Responding to the feminist movement, a masculinist movement emerged during recent years. Men started to change, though later than women, but also to a considerable extent over time as demonstrated in the studies reported above. Because this goes along with exhibiting feminine patterns parallel with masculine ones instead of replacing them (e.g. Kimmel, 1988, p. 9) men have gradually become more psychologically bisexual. Work in this already established field – men's studies – is consequently reported in the next section.

Summing up, there is enough evidence to document a considerable shift in society away from clearly distinguished male and female roles to blurring concepts of being male and femininity and achieving a more egalitarian perspective. The change can take different forms: In the area of sex differences even "differences found in [...] cognitive domains are likely not immutable" (Fischer & Arnold, 1994, p.165), which supports the use of gender- rather than sex-dependent information processing styles made in this study. Attitude change is particularly well documented, although is does not manifest itself to the same extent in actual behavioral change, for instance male household participation. Also personality variables, such as measured masculine and feminine traits, are now less tied to sex than a couple of years ago. These findings provide encouragement for testing and re-testing sex and gender related phenomena, such as responses to role portrayals in advertising or sex-related information processing strategies.

2.2 The Male Gender Role

As mentioned, the male gender role has not received much attention in the literature. Males have long been viewed as "the social norm" (Stern, 2003, p. 215) or the "benchmark gender" (Kimmel, 1988, p. 11), while women were simply the other sex. Probably one of the reasons for lack of research on men is that it is usually more interesting to examine deviations than norms, development and changes than standards. Then, in the late 1970s a new research discipline emerged: *men's studies*. This rising attention has not only been documented in an increasing number of articles in academic journals and also in separate journals dedicated to men's studies that have been established (e.g. *Men and Masculinity*, first issue published in 1995, *Journal of Men's Studies*, 1992, *Men and Masculinities*, 1998, and recently, *The International Journal of Men's Health*, 2002, and *Fathering*, 2003).[25] Additionally, as already shown above for gender in general, a rising interest in maleness and masculinity and new constructions of it are manifest in popular culture. Magazines such as *Men's Journal, Men's Health* (the German version already started in 1987) or *Men's Fitness* target males exclusively with topics ranging from fitness, health, and leisure activities to traveling.

This study follows this current research trend, but the subject of study is not masculinity itself, because masculinity is defined as a potentially moderating variable. Nevertheless, the part on perception of male images in advertising might provide additional hints on how male role models are perceived today and therefore give some insight into prevalent constructions of masculinity.

2.2.1 What is Masculinity?

The idea of maleness and masculinity has of course not been the same for all time and role models have always been subject to change. Prior to the nineteenth century, for example, men were considered the fashionable sex and young male bodies were eroticized as much as female ones (Tseelon, 1995).

---

[25] See the Homepage of Men's Studies Press (www.mensstudies.com) for more academic publications in the field on men's studies.

Self-categorizations – in this case, masculinity – usually need to be established in contrast to some other class (Maldonado, Tansuhaj, & Muehling, 2003, p. 6), so masculinity needs to be defined in contrast to femininity, or, as Bordo (1993) put it: "Masculinity and femininity […] have been constructed through a process of mutual exclusion" (p. 174). These two definitions depend on each other (Kimmel, 1988, p. 14); those of masculinity have always been responsive to those of femininity and vice-versa (Stern, 2003, p. 215). Therefore, blurring female roles will logically provoke the blurring of male roles, too. The development of "the women's movement […] has suggested that the traditional enactments of masculinity are in desperate need of overhaul" (Kimmel, 1988, p. 9). Although the change from old definitions of masculinity to the new ones stipulated surely will not come to pass smoothly and still seems to be a long process. Because not only does modern masculinity need to be redefined to differentiate itself from femininity, but also to clearly demarcate against male countertypes (e.g. homosexuality; Stern, 2003, p. 220). This is one reason why masculinity is more important to men than femininity is to women (Hacker, 1957), but possibly also because in Western societies more social advantages are associated with being masculine than feminine. Moreover, new role models have never replaced older ones but have grown alongside them taking away even more clarity from the definition of masculinity (Kimmel, 1988, p. 9).

2.2.1.1 Literary Images

Traditional role models and stereotypical definitions of masculinity are very well illustrated by Bereska's (2003) analysis of recommended novels for adolescent boys with their publication dates ranging from 1942 to 1997. In these novels the classical form of masculinity and maleness is still overtly present even in the more recent books. Thus, it gives a good overall impression of the construction of male roles, complementing scientific attempts to define masculinity and femininity. Bereska (2003, p. 162) found that heterosexuality is an indispensable part of manhood, as is the physical body – preferably strong and athletic – which serves as a means of identifying as male and masculine.[26] Consistently, manhood has to reject all sign of "sissy stuff" (i.e. to cry easily) and be adventurous. Bereska notes that men may exhibit some female-attributed qualities and be esteemed for them but that as soon as they show these non-male emotions and behaviors too frequently, they are

---

[26] Interestingly, a study by Schultze, Knussmann and Christiansen (1991, p. 212) found that males with large bodies show particularly high scores of masculinity. They speculate that the lower testosterone level in such men causes a need to make up for this lack of "masculinity" by particularly embracing traditionally masculine characteristics.

excluded from male society. Emotional expression is generally considered inappropriate for boys. Aggressiveness is the only allowed legitimate feeling allowed according to societal standards. Also does manhood imply having strict principles and pursuing them even in the face of difficulties. Collectivity – the male group – is an important component of masculinity, as are the existing hierarchies in these groups, which are defined through competitive processes (see Prakash, 1992, for an advertising application). This is interesting given that masculinity is commonly associated with independence rather than group membership. However, collectivity as a component of the male role does not mean caring and close interpersonal relationships as does female interdependence. Bereska's findings are summarized in Figure 15.

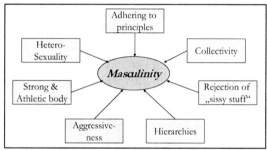

Figure 15: Components of masculinity in recommended readings for adolescent boys (Bereska, 1997)

The example of Bereska's (2003) analysis shows what ideals are presented to maturing boys and why change in men's role models and attitudes might be slower because of society's still traditional reflections of role norms, especially regarding masculinity.

2.2.1.2 Advertising Images

Books are not the only medium to present reflections of male roles and masculinity. Important influence on stereotyping and role modeling can surely be exercised by advertising as well. Kolbe and Albanese (1997) examined sole male images (males appearing on their own) in magazine advertisements. The most popular role depictions met male stereotypes, portraying athletes, outdoorsmen, and cowboys. However, the study included mostly male-directed magazines, such as *Business Week*, *Playboy*, and *Sports Illustrated*. Also, the range of role descriptions used did not include expressive roles, such as fatherhood. Males tend to favor magazines where males are depicted in occupational rather than model or consumer roles (Vigorito & Curry, 1998, p. 144). Consequently, the use of the stereotypical role descriptions was weaker in a more sex-neutral music magazine (*The Rolling Stone*), where men were most often portrayed as a typical user. Because of the biased selection of magazines, not much can be said about prevalent advertising stereotypes. Still, it seems as if advertisers are carefully adapting role portrayals to the target audience, as male images in men's magazines were found to be very different from men's images in women's magazines (Vigorito & Curry, 1998, p. 149). Thus, if males turn to the media for help in defining their masculinity they may find reassurance of accepted traditional models rather than modern role definitions (Vigorito & Curry, 1998, p. 150). The media does not seem to be very involved in establishing new forms of masculinity but rather responding to what they believe to be the favored form of masculinity of their target audience.

2.2.1.3 Men's Movements

Academics have made various efforts to find a definition for masculinity but have not always been very successful. Barak and Stern (1986, p. 207) simply define masculinity as self-assurance but also see femininity as incorporated in the definition of masculinity. Stern (2003) advocates for a "fluid, evolving, and dialectically progressive" (p. 216) definition of masculinity without making any attempt to actually define it. A comprehensive definition of masculinity is still lacking and it is questionable whether it will ever be found at all. Some effort has been made by Clatterbaugh (1996) who identified eight "men's movements" which probably best illustrate the multiple meaning and widely different concepts of masculinity. These eight movements have to be understood as responses to the feminist movement. (As already mentioned, masculinity has only started to define and redefine itself when forced to do so by changes in the definition of femininity.) A short summary follows.

1. *Conservative*: This early response to the feminist movement aims at preserving the status quo prevalent before the feminist upheaval.
2. *Profeminist*: This movement supports feminism and postulates that both men and women need to move out of their restrictive roles for achieve self-actualization.
3. *Men's Rights*: Men are viewed as the oppressed group.
4. *Socialist*: The capitalist society is inevitably patriarchal with men functioning as the producers who control the production factors.
5. *Spiritual (mythic) "Iron Men"*: This movement claims that men have become overly feminized in response to women's demands and tries to reestablish masculinity by focusing on masculine myths and archetypes.

6. *Gay Rights:* Gays view themselves as an oppressed group and question traditional definitions of masculinity and femininity. They claim that the traditional concept of masculinity was derived from homophobia.

7. *African-American Rights:* Black men define themselves as an oppressed group, arguing that Black men are historically emasculated by the institution of slavery.

8. *Evangelical Christian Movement – The Promise Keepers:* This religiously based return to conservatism promotes the traditional sex roles with men being the family providers.

Although this model is clearly tailored to an American background, it illustrates another viewpoint on masculinity, here from a political rather than a social-science or psychological perspective. Thus, it is an interesting supplement to other illustrations cited in this section.

The eight movements are again summarized in Figure 16, where also a classification into modern (progressive) and traditional (conservative) movements is attempted and their approximate temporal order of appearance is shown.

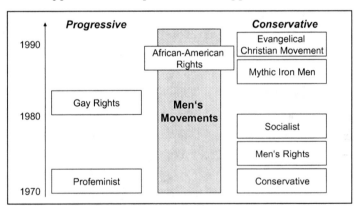

Figure 16: Eight Men's Movements

It is obvious from the figure that most men's movements – being masculinist reactions to feminism – aimed at conserving the status quo role models rather than responding in a "new man" manner. However, none of these responses have been overly successful. The question of how to construct a new masculinity was not convincingly solved by any of them.

2.2.1.4 Masculinity Measures

For the sake of completeness it is necessary to include here a short reference here to how masculinity is constructed in social science and psychology research, and more specifically in scales aimed at measuring masculinity. Masculinity is defined as an agentic orientation specified through personality traits, such as assertiveness, ambition, competitiveness, and dominance for example. Thereby stereotypic notions of male (and female) qualities are taken to define masculinity.[27]

2.2.1.5 Conclusion

If roles are blurring, then members of a group who were previously based their living on these role definitions and expectations need to reexamine of what they actually are and what standards they should follow. The more heavily questioned these old stereotypes become, the more numerous the demands made for a change in male self-perceptions and role behaviors and also the more insecure men probably become on what it means to be a man and what masculinity is all about. The fact that there is no society-wide agreement on the meaning of masculinity makes it even more difficult. What should men do with answers such as "the meaning of masculinity is that it changes" (Stern, 2003, p. 215)? Concurring models of masculinity may expose men to considerable role stress and provoke inner conflicts. Men have meanwhile become repulsive to stereotypical constraints (Horrocks, 1994). They have realized by now that traditional models are not socially valued to the extent they used to be and thus understand the necessity for change. Nevertheless, feminine traits in males are still undervalued if not already considered inadequate by certain social groups. Therefore men are still reluctant to openly embrace feminine traits and behaviors. The fear of homosexuality held by many men is one manifestation of this anxiety and their increasing sense of vulnerability and inadequacy (Kacen, 2000, p. 351).

The current questioning and ongoing reevaluations of masculinity and its meaning and implications have led researchers to call for a masculinity crisis (e.g. Pollack, 1999; Seidler, 1997). Although a standard definition might not be desirable because it would restrict the number of role models available to individuals, the lack of it on the other hand poses problems to men themselves. What remains is the need to find an individual answer to one's own personal sense of masculinity and a social environment which does not restrict masculinity to one single definition but permits and accepts different forms.

---

[27] It is referred to the sections 1.2.4 "Measuring Gender" and 1.2.5 "Conclusion: Conceptualizing Gender" which go into further detail on this scientific and operational definition of masculinity.

2.2.2 Masculinity in Research

Researchers largely acknowledged the female bias in the studies performed (e.g. Golden et al., 1979) and often proposed future research examining men's roles. Jaffe (1990, p. 878), for example, suggests that future studies should examine the relationship between male role portrayal and men's responses to advertising which will be done in this study. Zuo (p. 800) still complained in 1997 that very few studies have so far examined beliefs and attitudes towards the male sex role. In fact, attitudes were surely not the only field being neglected while women's studies were thriving. However, with time there has been an increasingly greater amount of research conducted focusing on male roles, including male role attitudes, male reference group identity dependence, masculine ideologies, masculine role stress and men's gender role conflict (O'Neil, Helms, Gable, David, & Wrightsman, 1986; see Hoffman, 2001, for further references on masculinity research). This section shall present selected areas of men's studies which are of interest to the study at hand.

Studying males is not meant to rival women's studies. In the end it was the growing research on women and evidence for changes in female sex roles that provoked the start of the masculinist research stream.

2.2.2.1 *Masculinity, Well Being and Sex Role Conflict*

Masculinity, as measured by instrumental personality traits,[28] generally seems to favor psychological well-being indicated through the positive correlations of masculinity traits scores and indicators for psychological well-being, such as self-esteem, healthy ego identity, and global measures of psychological adjustment (e.g. Bem, 1977, p. 200; see Sharpe & Heppner, 1991, for further references). High femininity is related negatively to adjustment measures for both men and women (Aube & Koestner, 1992, p. 489), though low masculinity for males seems to have a more severe negative impact on their psychological well-being than a lack of femininity does for females (Aube & Koestner, 1992, p. 487). This supports previous arguments that it is more difficult for men not to be masculine than for women not to be feminine. However, Koestner and Aube (1995, p. 696) propose that masculine traits are not related in the same way to all aspects of psychological adjustment but that certain masculine attributes may actually undermine well-being.

---

[28] For sake of simplicity here instrumental personality traits shall be referred to by the term *masculinity*, although this is not totally correct from a multifactorial gender perspective. However, no studies have been identified examining the effect of other components of gender on well-being, such as attitudes or global self-concept. Therefore, the findings are better interpreted with limitation to personality traits (Aube & Koestner, 1992).

This view is supported by a number of researchers. The traditional male role and the related patriarchic system is not only *not* beneficiary to men themselves (Bereska, 2003, p. 169); on the contrary, certain masculine characteristics prescribed by social role norm standards are highly dysfunctional (Kimmel, 1988, p. 9). Davis and Walsh (1988) report that self-esteem in men is negatively correlated with restrictive emotionality and restrictive affectionate behavior between men, since both emotionality and affective behavior are personality traits prohibited by traditional masculinity models. Not surprisingly, studies indicate that feminine traits adopted by men may actually facilitate effective social functioning (e.g. Spence, 1984) as these traits involve dedicating more attention to others.

Traditional male-role socialization provides contradictory and unrealistic messages, resulting in a considerable internal conflict (O'Neil, 1990). Zuo (1997, p. 801) also recognizes some inconsistencies in men's gender role attitudes indicating a fuzzy definition of their masculinity and ultimately their self-concept. Subsequently, O'Neil et al. (1986) developed the Gender Role Conflict Scale (GRCS) to measure men's gender role conflict and fear of femininity. The term *male gender role conflict* describes the stress resulting from the belief that one is unable to meet the societal demands of the male role. Sharpe and Heppner (1991, p. 329) found that masculinity is still responsible for a certain amount of psychological well-being but that femininity and gender role conflict also account for a substantial portion of variation in well-being (see Figure 17).

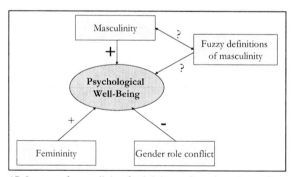

Figure 17: Impact of masculinity, femininity, and gender role conflict on well-being

It has already been argued above that the lack of a clear definition of masculinity exposes men to considerable role stress. Studies show that deviation from sex role norms still has greater consequences for men than for women (Aube & Koestner, 1992, p. 487). The discrepancy between aspired-to and actual behavior, the rising tendency of men to incorporate feminine qualities in their behavior and the stress and anxiety they encounter when doing so is well illustrated in a study by Jaffe and her colleagues (Jaffe, Lee, Huang, & Oshagan, 1995): They found that men tended to express greater social interdependence – as opposed to classic masculine autonomy – when they were protected by the use of pseudonyms on the internet. Jaffe et al. (1995) concluded "that what we consider to be a feminine pattern [...] might be an essentially human style" but that only men seemingly experience some reservations against openly behaving in such a manner.

So wrongly understood masculinity, and in particular male gender role conflict, does not only cause negative psychological consequences but it also clearly impacts physical well-being. Possible results of a psychologically unhealthy definition of maleness are depression, suicide, alcohol use, behavioral problems, declining school performance and violence (Bereska, 2003, p. 169). Stern (2003, p. 221) reports relations between a too strict concept of masculinity and anxiety, depression (and not seeking treatment), feelings of loneliness and early death.

Summing up, a masculine personality does have some positive impact on an individual's psychological health. However, if the definitions of masculinity are too limiting in today's changing world and meet an already large number of fuzzy masculinity concepts, men may experience substantial gender role conflicts. This can negatively impact psychological well-being as well as substantially affect physical health. It has been suggested that males could benefit from integrating feminine traits into their character (e.g. Spence, 1984). In the light of sex role changes in society such "intergrations" should become more accepted and therefore more widely spread. These considerations provide further support for the study at hand.

2.2.2.2 Feminine Males – A Very Special Masculinity

A field which has up to now received particularly little research interest is the special group of *feminine males* (e.g. Lobel, Rothman, Abramovizt, & Maayan, 1999). These individuals should be of special interest to researchers as they are part of the small group showing psychological gender patterns opposite to their biological sex. Consistent with the line of reasoning above that women are more likely to move in a masculine direction than are men to move in a feminine direction, this phenomenon is particularly rare in males. According to Lobel et al. (1999, p. 580) feminine males comprise approximately five to eight percent of the population. However, there is more evidence available which contrasts Lobel's experience because it indicates that approximately equally-sized gender groups can be expected for samples (e.g. Jaffe & Berger, 1988, p. 264). Also, Gentry and Haley (1985, p.

261) document a masculine-feminine sample distribution that justifies expectations of an almost equal distribution of feminine and masculine individuals in the population. Possibly, Lobel's et al. (1999, p. 580) very low estimate is due to the specific cultural context in the country where the study was conducted (Israel). For this study it is reasonable to expect that men make use of most of the spectrum of the measurement scales and furthermore, it is not only the absolute scale values that are important but also the differences between subjects which are interesting. Independent of its actual size, the uniqueness of this group promises the exhibition of very special psychological and behavioral patterns.

This contention was supported by two studies by Lobel (1994) and Lobel et al. (1999). In the first study (Lobel, 1994) respondents had to make inferences about a target subject behaving either in a sex-appropriate or a sex-inappropriate way. In this manner, feminine males showed emotional and motivational judgments different from all the other gender groups. Lobel (1994, p. 384) found that although feminine males seemed to be aware of the social appropriateness or inappropriateness, respectively, of the behavior in question, they still showed regard and personal preference for the target behaving counter-stereotypically. Also they express particularly egalitarian gender ideologies. Lobel concluded that affective responses towards people's behavior seemed to be guided by gender. In a follow-up study Lobel et al. (1999) investigated deceptive behavior in masculine, feminine and neutral tasks. They discovered that feminine men were the only ones to pretend to know significantly more about feminine topics. They then concluded that for feminine males failing in a feminine task was experienced as incongruent with an inner feeling of femininity

Somewhat surprising is the fact that the respondents of these two studies obviously had no difficulties displaying counter-stereotypical emotions. Part of this might be due to the age of the subjects who were all elementary level students, but studies do indicate that children develop a sense of their own maleness or femaleness early in life (e.g. Maccoby & Jacklin, 1982). Sex differences can already be observed at the age of five (Tieger, 1980; Maccoby & Jacklin, 1982). As these studies were only recently conducted the relative openness of the children could also be caused from growing up in a changed environment where it is valued and even expected that men and women possess both masculine and feminine characteristics (e.g. Eagly & Mladinic, 1989).

Unfortunately, no other studies could be identified examining special psychological patterns in feminine males. This group appears to be lacking the most attention in academic research. Nevertheless, this group is of particular relevance to this study. Differences in male behavior are investigated in relation to their masculinity and femininity scores. Thus it is hoped that feminine males will exhibit special patterns of attitude and behavior regarding the questions at hand just as they did in the research by Lobel and her colleagues.

2.3 Conclusion: Where Are We Going?

In this chapter an array of evidence for shifts in society with respect to male and female roles, behaviors, and personality patterns has been reviewed. Of course the database of evidence is far too large to be completely covered. However, the evidence at hand also strongly suggests that male/female differences are not stable but ever-changing, resulting in new role models especially for women and to a lesser extent for men. As Darley and Smith (1995, p. 55) proposed, socialization differences between the genders must be assessed, as these ultimately cause differences in information processing styles. Such differences may then diminish if gender neutral roles eventuate as has been demonstrated above. There is evidence that men are gradually moving towards egalitarianism and away from the traditionally defined masculine-feminine dichotomy. The behavioral repertoires of men and women are basically the same (Deaux, 1984, p. 114). Thus, indeed "the time may have arrived when distinctions between what is considered masculine and what is considered feminine have faded" (Hoffman, 2001, p. 478). From this point of view, reexamining information processing differences on the basis of gender seems justified. It has also been shown that the change in men is especially visible in their attitudes which are moving from conservatism to egalitarianism, though this is still not strongly noticeable in their behavior. This might influence men's liking of advertisements depicting different role portrayals. Modern role portrayals may become preferred over traditional ones though men might still be reluctant to buy the product. Especially with public products the attitude-behavior link might be questionable since buying them would include openly stating some degree of femininity.

These changes imply, as demonstrated, changing definitions of masculinity or femininity itself. The definition of masculinity is currently particularly vague – or rather non-existent – ranging from very traditional to extremely feminine role models.

Changes in definitions of masculinity and femininity can possibly impact the results of gender measurement scales of gender in different ways. When comparing a standard measurement scale of masculinity and femininity, such as the BSRI which is based on the possession of certain pre-defined personality traits, and a global self-assessment measure (where respondents indicate their masculinity and femininity on a single scale without a definition given by the researcher), four effects can be identified:

- The definition of masculinity or femininity, respectively, has not changed to a large extent, but men indeed report the possession of more feminine personality traits (true personality change).

- Men report the same degree of masculinity and/or femininity for themselves as they did years ago. Neither the definition nor the personality has changed.

- Men still report the same degree of masculinity and/or femininity on global measures for themselves as they did years ago but now the definition of masculinity itself has become more feminine. Men see themselves as masculine as before but still exhibit more of the personality traits formerly classified as feminine (true personality change).

- Respondents have a greater willingness to describe themselves using masculine or feminine terms (Twenge, 1997, p. 316) or feel the social pressure to do so (no personality change).

As can be seen from Table 2, personality change can best be assessed by comparing standard measurement scores from different years (as done, for example, by Twenge, 1997) as standard measurements are irresponsive to changes in definitions. If individuals' scores on a standard measure are different from those some years ago, then the reason for this difference can only be due to a true personality change (see Table 3).

	Definition of masc/fem has changed	*Definition of masc/fem has not changed*
Personality has changed	Respondents report personality traits different from those in the past	
Personality has not changed	Respondents report personality traits equal to those in the past	

Table 3: Effects of change of personality and change in definitions
of masculinity and femininity when using a **standard measure.**

If only scores of global measures are compared, the effects of "definition change/personality change" and "no definition change/no personality change" cannot be distinguished easily (see Table 4). Therefore, we hypothesize that changes take place in the egalitarian direction, i.e. that men show more egalitarian attitudes and more feminine personality traits. The effect observable in the "definition change/no personality change" condition depends on the individual responsiveness to and perception of social pressure. These different effects should be taken into account when interpreting the results.

	Definition of masc/fem has changed	Definition of masc/fem has not changed
Personality has changed	Respondents report approximately the same values of masc. or femininity.	Respondents report higher values of femininity and lower values of masculinity.
Personality has not changed	Respondents report higher masculinity and lower femininity. Social pressure!	Respondents report approximately the same values for masculinity and femininity.

Table 4: Effects of change of personality and change in definitions of masculinity and femininity when using a global self-assessment measure.

To summarize, it can be said that sex role orientations might have significantly more explanatory power than they did some decades ago because society is now more flexible in its male and female stereotypes. If the studies once published without significant results about the effects of gender on some dependent variables would yielded different conclusions today, this would be a very powerful proof that our society and its sex role models are indeed changing.

As change up to the present day has been extensively documented in research, literature of course continues to speculate on the further development of sex and gender in society. Kacen (2000, p. 352-353) points out two main possible consequences emerging for gender identity:

- Gender becomes superfluous because in the emerging virtual world individuals hold a large variety of different identities.
- Traditional gender ideologies are revived, which provide safe ports for individuals to adhere to, though this precludes individuals from knowing and using the wide range of desires, perspectives, and styles they are capable of.

From a more straight-thinking point of view, Gentry and Doering (1979) proposed very early that "there is an androgynous society coming, so there may be sufficient impetus for marketers [...] to become less interested in the male-female dichotomy and more interested in the level of masculinity or femininity" (p.103). Hoffman (2001) concludes that "neither do men have feminine sides, nor women masculine sides. [...] Both sexes are highly capable of a full range of human emotions and qualities." (p. 481) The point at which both sexes take full advantage of the "range of human emotions and qualities" they are capable of might not have been reached yet but it seems that at least a portion of society is on its way. Paralleling Barak and Stern's (1986, p. 208) picture of the future women –

"aggressive, forceful, competitive, and ambitious and not losing one bit of their femininity" – the future man might be interdependent, emotional, and sensitive, without loosing a bit of his masculinity.

3 Gender in Advertising

In this chapter I will review academic research on gender, role portrayals and advertising effectiveness. An overview of sex role portrayals in the media serves as a starting point.

3.1 Role Portrayals and Stereotyping in Advertising

The media helps to "promote and mold gender identity" (Kacen, 2000, p. 346). More precisely, by showing men and women in different occupations and roles, the media provide a general picture of standard male and female roles in society. Instead of a one-way road an interdependent relationship exists between media and society, as advertising "plays a critical role in both reflecting and shaping this distinctly gendered view of men and women" (Kacen, 2000, p. 347). Some aspects of this duality are briefly presented in the next section.

3.1.1 Stereotyping and the Media – An Ambivalent Relationship

Advertising both responds to and has the potential to shape a society's definition of masculinity and femininity. Naturally, marketers are very sensitive to what their prospective customers want to see or hear and likewise do not want to repulse consumers by showing them portraits of men and women they cannot identify with or may even dislike. The basic process of marketing – segmentation, targeting, and positioning – is built on the effort to give the customer exactly what he or she wants, not only in terms of products and services but also in terms of advertising formats. Thus, analyzing media role portrayals might provide good insight into a society's definition of what is appropriate for women and men (e.g., Hurtz & Durkin, 1997, p. 112). On the other hand, if the media extends its scope beyond what is to be considered standard stereotypes it may have the power to influence people's opinions and thus to shape sex roles (e.g. Vigorito & Curry, 1998, p. 136; Kacen, 2000, p. 347).

Although these two opposing effects may seem intuitive, they are not very well documented in research. While analyses of media content "contribute to our understanding of the social context of gender" (Hurtz & Durkin, 1997, p. 112) and help to document the relationship of sex roles in the media, there are not many studies examining the opposite relationship, namely the effect of role portrayals on sex specific role perceptions and behavior and the development of these role perceptions (see Hurtz & Durkin, 1997, for references). Even more difficult is finding the answer to what extent these two effects counterbalance each other – in other words, whether advertising is more likely to create sex role attitudes or rather almost exclusively responds to existing ones. Based on some empirical attempts to measure advertising effects (Durkin, 1985; 1986) the latter effect seems to be by far the more important (see Figure 18).

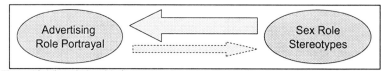

Figure 18: The relationship between role portrayals in advertising and sex role stereotypes

Generally, many factors influence gender role development (for an extensive list of references see Hurtz & Durkin, 1997) and there are many other sources excluding media which support children's modeling of their sex role perceptions and perceived sex-adequate behaviors. Particularly personal or direct sources, i.e. daily family or other social environment examples might have even more influence than television images, as children are exposed to the same behavioral models often and for long periods of time.

Still, it cannot be negated that there is a relationship between role portrayals and society's representation of sex roles. Commercials tend to be selectively responsive to aspects of the surrounding culture (Neto & Pinto, 1998, p. 154). Conversely, there is evidence that television can and does profoundly influence both children and adults' perception of their and others' sex roles (McGhee & Frueh, 1975) and that television does have the potential to shape attitudes (Kolbe & Langefeld, 1993, p. 393). Kolbe and Langefeld (1993) examine literature on the subject and conclude that "the nature of gender roles might have a powerful impact on viewers and their perceptions of others" (p. 395). Napoli, Murgolo-Poore and Boudville (2003) report effects of male and female images on self-esteem, especially for women. Advertisements establish images of the ideal woman or man and thus set standards for comparison of one's own self-perception with the ideal image. Often, these images are far from reachable which leaves women in particular with low self-esteem and eating disorders (Napoli et al., 2003, p. 64). Figure 19 shows a simplified picture of these complex interaction processes.

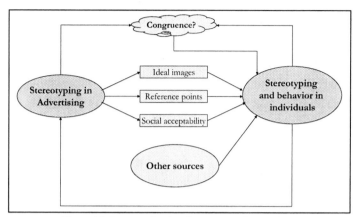

Figure 19: Stereotyping in advertising and individual
stereotypic behavior – an interdependent relationship

If marketers' perception of what role types are preferred by consumers is not completely accurate or they decide to construct non-stereotypical advertisements on purpose, these advertisements will not sufficiently meet the stereotypes of the target group. In turn, if advertisements are outside what is considered to be appropriate they can lead to a rejection of the ad by the consumer and have no effect at all on stereotyping or on consumers' attitudes and purchase probabilities.[29] Should ads deviate only slightly, to the extent in which they are not rejected, then they may be able to slowly change existing stereotypes. This can occur for the following reasons:

- People often do not use the whole range of behaviors they want to because they doubt the social acceptability of traits and behaviors for a specific sex. Advertising can *influence the standard of social acceptability* if it manages to confirm the positive effects of behaviors previously considered inappropriate for stereotypical reasons only and thus encourages men and women to go beyond their standard behavioral repertoire.

- Drawing from identity theory, shared meanings such as how the male or female role is defined are constructed through interaction. Advertising, or

---

[29] Some advertisements that have caused resentments among consumers might still be effective because they are more heavily debated and therefore better memorized (for example, Bennetton or Humanic). However, most models of advertisement effectiveness found some form of positive attitude or liking preceding purchase (e.g. the AIDA model).

more generally, media consumption can be seen as one way of interaction with the environment. Therefore the process of the construction of shared meanings is activated in part when people consume media content. Individuals use others and the media as sources of information and *reference points* to construct and maintain identities and as sources of *validation for existing identities* (Snow, 1983). If modern roles are shown in advertisements this can encourage people to acquire and exhibit more non-role conforming behavior.

On the other hand, if role portrayals continue to reflect traditional stereotypes, it may become increasingly difficult for individuals to maintain their own non-traditional identities that they have already acquired through change processes. Identities are reinforced through communication, including mass communication. In examining this element inferences about sex roles and stereotypes can be made. If role portrayals really reflect society's current standing, then there is still a considerable amount of stereotyping going on in today's society, as will be shown below.

However, it is worth noting that there are some companies which have started altering their advertising practices towards the integration of more contemporary sex roles (see Hupfer, 2002, p. 4-5, for a list of examples). This should therefore confirm and reinforce the exercise of non-stereotypic behavior. Also, according to the relationship "stereotypes → advertising portrayal", an increasing diversity in male roles specifically might lead to very different advertising styles and role depictions in the future. Quite possibly, future studies on stereotyping will find more evidence for change than past ones. However, the question of the amount of interdependence between society's standards and advertising images and the extent of imbalance between to two opposing effects remains very difficult to answer.

3.1.2 Studying Role Portrayals

There is a large amount of studies investigating some aspects of male and female role portrayals in advertisements. Because of this abundance of literature only a selection of studies can be included in the following paragraphs. Intriguingly, the studies are set in different time and cultural contexts ranging from countries as far apart as Portugal (Neto & Pinto, 1998) and Australia (Mazzella, Durkin, Cerini, & Buralli, 1992) and as culturally diverse as Malaysia (Bresnahan, Inoue, Liu, & Nishida, 2001) and Great Britain (Furnham & Bitar, 1993), yet they all report similar results. Literature reviews by the authors in the course of these studies do not point to any other existing studies reporting very different or surprising results.

The worldwide advertising industry seems to be rather consistent in its use of male and female stereotypes. This is why even the rather small sample reported here is considered to provide a reasonably good insight into the topic.

Most studies use the method developed by McArthur and Resko (1975). This classification scheme was extended by Manstead and McCulloch (1981), Furnham and Schofield (1986), and Furnham and Voli (1989). The scheme evaluates an advertisement along different categories, the attributes of which are linked to the representation of male or female stereotypes. An extensive version of the scheme's category and pertaining attributes is shown in Table 4. Attributes written in the same line indicate that these attributes have been assessed separately but were combined later for further analysis. Of course, not all criteria are used in every study.

Criterion	Attributes
Central figure	Male, female
Mode of Presentation	Voice-over (disembodied) Visual/silence, visual/voice, visual/music
Credibility basis	User, authority, others
Role	Dependent (parent, spouse, partner, gender object, home maker) Professional Interviewer/narrator, other
Location	Home, occupation, leisure, unknown
Age	Young, middle-age, old
Type of argument	Factual, opinion, none
Reward type	Social approval Self-enhancement Practical Pleasure, other
Product type	Body, home, food, auto, sports, other
Background	Mostly female Mostly male Mixed Mostly children None (no other human beings around)
End comment	Present, Absent

Table 5: Criteria and attributes for the assessment of stereotypes in advertising
(own tabulation, based on Furnham & Bitar, 1993)

The criteria and their mode of realization described in this table will be used to develop stereotyped and non-stereotyped advertisements as stimuli for the present studies. It will also serve as a guideline for interpreting the results obtained in previous studies on advertising sex role stereotyping.

3.1.3 Role Portrayals in Advertising

The criteria most often used for evaluating stereotyping and classifying role portrayals include (see also Table 5)

- the central figure in the ad (male or female)
- the mode of presentation (voice-over or visual)
- the credibility basis (user, authority, or others)
- the role (dependent, professional, narrator, or others)
- the location (home, occupation, or leisure)
- age (young, middle-age, or old)
- arguments presented (factual or opinion)
- reward type emphasized (social approval, self-enhancement, practical or pleasure)
- product type (body, home, food, auto, sports or others)
- background (mostly female, mostly male, mostly children, mixed or none)

Others less frequently used (and not included in the systematics of McArthur & Resko, 1975) are whether an end comment is spoken or not, which accent the spokespersons exhibited, or the relationship between the price of the advertised product and its endorser.

The results reported in the following paragraphs are a summary of the studies by Mazzella et al. (1992), Furnham and Bitar (1993), and Hurtz and Durkin (1997). These authors also report that their results are similar to those obtained by previous studies.

- Regarding the *mode of presentation*, males are largely presented as voice over, while females are mostly presented only visually. Females function thus as objects rather than as subjects of the ad. Also, without speech it is tough to represent some degree of expertise and authority.
- Consequently males mostly base their *credibility* on representing authority figures.
- Men appear in independent and narrator *roles,* where females mostly picture product users and are more often shown in dependent roles.
- Females are also usually portrayed in a home *setting*, whereas males can mostly be seen in an occupational setting. This depicts the classical division of labor and ignores the fact that an increasing number of women are entering the workplace.

- Additionally, females tend to be of younger *age*, while male product endorsers generally belong to the middle-age category. Speculations about underlying reasons for observed age differences are: external appearance is more crucial for females than for men, i.e. it is more important for a woman to be attractive than for a man. Since the current definition of beauty undoubtedly includes youth, this would explain the use of younger females as compared to men of more advanced age. Age could add to the perceived competence of the spokesperson due to the supposed experience and knowledge associated with increasing age, which would then be more important to men who are more often concerned with representing authority figures and experts.

These findings are consistent across studies and clearly point to a regular use of role clichés in advertising. There are, however, also a number of criteria where reported results are less unanimous and sometimes indicate a change in advertising strategy among companies and a lower degree of stereotyping in advertising and possibly in society as well. A summary is reported in the next few paragraphs.

- Furnham and Bitar (1993, p. 304) and Hurtz and Durkin (1997, p. 109) found no or only slight differences regarding the *type of argument* (factual vs. opinion) presented depending on the sex of the person featured. On the contrary, both Neto and Pinto (1998, p. 158) and Mazzella et al. (1992, p. 254) report men as more likely to present scientific or factual arguments while women often do not present any arguments at all.
- Results on which sex is most likely to present which *product type* conclusions are different. Some studies find no significant differences (e.g. Furnham & Bitar, 1993, p. 304), while others report stereotypical role divisions with men speaking for automotive, sports and technology products and women presenting body, food and household merchandise (e.g. Bresnahan et al., 2001, p. 122-125; Neto & Pinto, 1998, p. 159; Mazzella et al., 1992, p. 254).
- Interesting from a theoretical perspective are findings relating the *reward type emphasized* with the sex of the person featured. Mazzella et al. (1992, p. 254) report that ads portraying females mostly emphasize social approval as a reward. This is consistent with the agency-communion hypothesis (Bakan, 1966). In contrast, Neto and Pinto (1998, p. 158) report self-enhancement which is classified as a stereotypically agentic motive as the most often

presented reward type for females –an indication for changing women's roles.[30]

- The *background* setting is also consistent with the theory of male separateness and female connectedness. Studies find males to be set either in a male background or to have no background at all (no people around) and females to be set in either a female or mixed background (e.g. Neto & Pinto, 1998, p. 159). Mazzella and his colleagues (1992, p. 252) report that women typically occupy roles which are defined in relation to other people, whereas men are more often portrayed as being autonomous. According to Mazzella et al. this patterns can be observed in a large number of other studies as well.

Disagreeing, Furnham and Bitar (1993, p. 309) conclude that stereotypical differences are not as strong as they used to be in previous studies. They base their reasoning on their findings that women are mostly portrayed without a background. Women are also as likely as men to give factual arguments, and less likely to give no arguments at all compared to previous studies. Table 6 summarizes again the findings of role portrayal studies. Criteria highlighted in grey indicates where evidence for changing roles of either men or women or both were found.

Criterium	Men	Women
Mode of Presentation	Voice over	Visual
Credibility basis	Authority	---
Role	Independent, narrator	Dependent, product user
Location	Occupational	Home
Age	Middle-age	Young
Type of argument	Scientific, factual vs. No Difference	None vs. No Difference
Reward type	---	Social Approvement vs. Self Enhancement
Product type	Automotive, sports, technology vs. No Difference	Body, food, household vs. No Difference
Background	Male or no background	Female or mixed background

Table 6: Male and female role stereotyping in advertising

The above findings indicate that some stereotypes in advertising portrayals of men and women are continuing but also give evidence to changing patterns in some fields. However, role depictions are not only dependent on time but also on culture. A few studies examine role portrayals in a cross-cultural context. For example, Bresnahan et al. (2001) compare role portrayals in Malaysia, Japan,

---

[30] These implications of course only make sense under the contention that ads portraying females are also targeting females. Although this is definitely not always the case, the assumption on this relationship is made out of lack of information in the studies in question.

Taiwan, and the United States. Their findings support the results of previous studies regarding the mode of presentation and the location of the ad. They also group the role portrayals into stereotypical and non-stereotypical categories and compare them across countries. Surprisingly, while in Taiwan stereotypical and non-stereotypical role portrayals of both males and females were balanced (about 50 % stereotyped and non-stereotyped, respectively) and in Japan predominantly non-stereotypical role portrayals were found, the US advertisers relied primarily on stereotypical depictions of masculinity and femininity. More change and flexibility in male and female role perceptions seems to be present in Taiwan and Japan than in the United States. Such findings emphasize cultural dependency of the topic, though no relationship could be found between the degree of stereotyping in advertising and a country's masculinity as assessed by Hofstede's classic cultural dimensions (Odekerken-Schroeder, De Wulf & Hofstee, 2002, p. 416).

Moreover it shall be noted that results differ by the type of media under investigation: stereotypes in radio commercials are not present as often when compared to TV commercials (Hurtz and Durkin, 1997, p. 111). Hurtz and Durkin speculate that one of the reasons might be the absence of visual cues in radio, as women are often used only as visual objects. Another possible explanation might be the difference between radio producer's perceptions of audience preferences and television producers. The latter explanation does not appear easily supported, however.

Despite the large amount of research dealing with role portrayals in the media, studies focus to a large extent on women's role (e.g. Napoli et al., 2003; see Kolbe & Albanese, 1997, for an extensive list of references) – a bias which has already been documented for gender studies in general. Few studies so far have put men under examination. In 1997 Kolbe and Albanese found only two studies focusing solely on men's images (Skelly & Lundstrom, 1981; Wolheter & Lammers, 1980).[31] Examples of male images have already been given above while trying to find some current definitions and depictions of masculinity.

Kolbe and Albanese (1997) examine the group of sole male images, namely commercials where a man is the only human figure depicted. The authors argue that this group is particularly subject to stereotyping, as it includes "American icons, such as the lone pioneer, cowboy, and athlete" that "are heralded for their individual accomplishments" (Kolbe & Albanese, 1997, p. 815). These stereotypes seem to be exceptionally resistant to change. Men are portrayed primarily as

---

[31] There is, however, a considerable body of research examining both men's and women's role portrayals.

athletes, cowboys, and outdoorsmen. Thus, advertisers obviously believe that men feel attracted by this kind of role. This assumption might indeed be very valid, however, on average only 21 % of the ads examined contained a sole male image.

Vigorito and Curry (1998, p. 148) found that there is a relationship between advertising images of males and the audience towards which the magazine is directed. Generally, depictions of men in magazines feature the classical definition of masculinity: dominance, control and unemotional relationships. Vigorito and Curry note that representations of males in male-oriented magazines vary a lot from male images in female-directed magazines where males are portrayed much more often in nurturing roles. This discrepancy may lead to a problematic imbalance between men and women's expectations of male role behavior.

Peevers (1979) examined male role portrayals and connected them to masculinity ratings of the portrayed person. He reported that males depicted in commercials tended to be rated as highly masculine, despite the fact that this orientation is only held by a small portion of the general population. Advertising seems to work best with role depictions allocated mostly at the extreme points of masculinity and femininity instead of more balanced "androgynous" pictures. Audiences holding such acute role perceptions are not usually present in society. Kolbe and Langefeld (1993, p. 408) showed that counter-stereotypical and stereotypical role portrayals are indeed related to the perceived masculinity and femininity of the spokesperson as measured by the BSRI. Significant differences in masculinity and femininity scores were found for the two different role portrayals with women assigning higher femininity values than men. These findings suggest that ads are indeed perceived and evaluated as masculine or feminine by consumers.

In conclusions, although many broadcasters and advertisers continue to transmit predominantly traditionally stereotyped images, there is some evidence for change (see especially Bresnahan et al., 2001, p. 129-130) and new, less stereotyped advertising strategies, even if the change in men's depiction is especially slow and dubious. As studies show that "gender role orientation of subjects is related to their appraisal of ad characters" (Kolbe & Langefeld, 1993, p. 395), gender changes can cause different perceptions of stereotyped advertisements. Researchers have already suggested that "a substantial proportion of the audience – especially, though not only, the female audience – is offended by what are perceived as sexist advertising materials" (Adams, 1991, cited after Hurtz & Durkin, 1997, p. 113). If advertising strategists continue to stereotype they "may be pursuing strategies that are counterproductive to even their own goals" (Hurtz & Durkin, 1997, p. 113). Even men could one day start to feel offended by portraits of lonely cowboys and rough outdoorsmen.

3.2 Gendered Responses to Advertising

Though individuals might not consciously notice every single ad they see, they might still process them and react in some way. Their liking of the ad, or attitude towards the ad and towards the product, their purchase probability and finally the affected purchase of a product are reactions to advertising and will thus be influenced by the way the advertisement is designed. Therefore, marketers are concerned about which type of advertisement appeals to consumers or more precisely – in an age where segmentation is a key component of marketing – which type of ad appeals to which type of consumers. One important characteristic often defined for a target group is its sex and increasingly, though still less frequently, its gender.[32] Over the years researchers and practitioners tried to establish rules on how to best address men or women. Blurring sex roles now question the validity of these rules, so researchers are suggesting that new conventions will be established building on psychological gender rather than on sex (e.g. Hupfer, 2002, p. 2). Following these two different concepts the second part of this section will report studies where advertising effectiveness was investigated separately for men and women. These studies mostly examine the effects of stereotyping and compare different role portrayals leading to different reactions among males and females. But in contrast to the bundle of research presented in part three of this section, these studies do not include gender as an explanatory variable. Before these two groups of research are analyzed some general notes shall be made on the measurement of advertising effectiveness and problems associated with this popular area of research.

3.2.1 Measuring Advertising Effectiveness

Generally, for advertising to be effective the receiver has to notice, process, and favorably relate the content to his or her existing memory structure (Gentry & Haley, 1984, p. 259). The problem with measuring advertising effectiveness is that there is no single measure available but rather a diversity of indicators varying in

---

[32] Often parts of the gender model, such as modern sex-role attitudes, are included in target group definitions. Ads targeting the "new generation women" (Widgery & McGaugh, 1993) or showing men in fatherly roles already make use of the gender concept – although they might not be explicitly aware of it.

their implications. Generically, for evaluating an advertisement campaign a company has several possibilities (Brassington & Pettitt, 2003, p. 642):

- Aided or unaided recall
- Attitude tests (towards the product, before and after the campaign)
- Enquiry tests (number of requests for information, increase in sales visits)
- Sales tests (campaign is run in a part of the market, sales increase is monitored)

For the study in question recall measures do not make much sense as respondents are asked immediately after seeing the ad and also see only one ad at a time. Enquiry tests are similar to Jaffe's measure of information interest (Jaffe, 1994, p. 472). What remains is attitude assessment and sales performance which has to be modified to assess purchase intention rather than actual sales increase in the context of the study without industry participation. These were also the dimensions commonly assessed in past research. If we look only at the operationalizations of advertising effectiveness in the studies on sex and gender related advertising, we end up with a number of different possibilities – usually a combination of measurement categories. Table 7 summarizes the measure used in studies examining advertising effectiveness in this context. The main constructs are highlighted in bold. Their specific operational variables can be found in the lines below them. The lines highlighted in gray point out the two measures used most often (attitude and purchase interest).

Criterion \ Study	Coughlin & O'Connor, 1985	Leigh, Rethans, & Reichenbach-Whitney, 1987	Prakash 1992	Jaffe, 1994	Jaffe & Berger, 1994	Orth & Holancova, 2004
Emotional response					X	X
Disapproval-approval scale						X
Semantic differential scale					X	
Attitude towards the ad/brand/model		X	X			X
Semantic differential scale		X	X			X
Purchase intention	X		X	X	X	X
Rating scales				X		X
Semantic differential scale	X		X		X	
Cognitive responses		X				
Open assessment of thoughts		X				
Information interest				X		
Semantic differential scale				X		

Table 7: Examples for operationalizing advertising effectiveness in studies examining either sex or gender influence

Some trends are visible even from this small selection of studies.

- First, advertising effectiveness is usually measured by different values rather than by a single score. The dimensions of the composite, however, differ across studies. Mostly a combination of attitude and purchase intention measures is used.
- Second, the semantic differential scales seem to be particularly favored by researchers in order to assess any kind of value, from purchase intention to emotional response.

The process of how advertising works is not clearly observable, as most sub-processes take place inside the consumer. However, a number of models exist which try to explain these invisible processes. A fairly general one will be used for founding this study (Prakash, 1992, p. 45; see Figure 20).

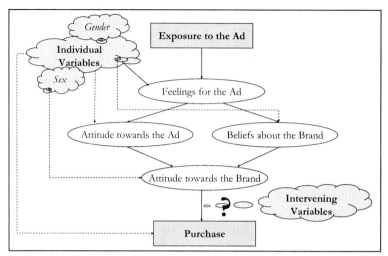

Figure 20: Modeling advertising effectiveness and sex and gender influences:
Exposure – Attitude – Purchase (cf. Prakash, 1992; extended)

When consumers are exposed to advertising they first develop feelings towards the ad determining whether they like it or not. The reasons for their like or dislike of the ad lie in the characteristics of the ad and the individual consumer personality – or more precisely, in the combination of both, a specific ad and a specific consumer. In this study the characteristics of the ad refer to the role portrayal depicted (traditional or modern), while the consumer personality refers to the respondent's gender (cf. Oliver, Sargent, & Weaver, 1998). The match of the two then triggers a reaction to the advertisement where effects of sex (or gender) are hypothesized to affect in essence the feelings developed about the ad (e.g. liking, resentment, degree of identification, etc.).

The developed feelings about the ad lead to an attitude towards the ad as well as to beliefs about the brand. Both are then integrated to form a single attitude towards the brand. A positive attitude will then lead to a purchase of the brand. Sex and gender consequently also influence attitude towards the ad, the brand, and purchase intention, though mainly through influencing feelings about the ad. They may as well do so directly, however, because for the conceptualization of the study the difference between direct, indirect or combined influence is not of importance and is thus neglected in this context.

The attitude-behavior relationship is questionable on a number of points. First of all, it is not self-evident that a positive attitude indeed leads to a purchase of the brand as there are a number of factors that can intervene (e.g., price of the brand, reference group influence, situational availability of the brand, etc.). Also, social desirability might play a special role in the socially sensitive context of gender. Secondly, it is often questioned if attitude indeed precedes purchase or if purchase is actually effectuated first and in consequence leads to a positive brand attitude provided that the customer is satisfied with the product. This is usually the case with low-involvement goods. When examining the whole process "advertisement → attitude → purchase", it is quite possible that consumers have some attitude towards the product before buying it which can be caused by advertising exposure (e.g. Kotler, 2003; Brassington & Pettitt, 2003, p. 642).

It seems useful to employ attitude measures when investigating advertising effectiveness. On the other hand, at least purchase intention measures should be integrated to assess actual impact of advertising on sales. Especially in a gendered context individuals might exhibit in fact positive attitudes towards an advertisement and a brand but still be reluctant to buy it because they fear that the possession and use of this product might undermine their masculinity (cf. Morris & Cundiff, 1971, p. 374).

3.2.2 Advertising Response Differences in Men and Women

A number of studies investigate the effects different role portrayals and advertising appeals exert on men and women. In that they are very much like the studies focusing on gender instead of sex as an individual difference variable. In both groups of research, the studies show a similar design. Usually advertisements are constructed representing the defined appeals or roles. Subjects are then exposed to the ad for some time. Afterwards, they answer questions regarding their perception of the ad using variables believed to capture advertising effectiveness. Researchers then try to find evidence for hypothesized relationships between advertising effectiveness, role portrayal, type of appeal, and sex or gender, respectively.

Some studies have been published on individual male-female differences regarding the receptiveness of both sexes for ads. Females were found to be more easily persuaded and more readily influenced (see Widgery & McGaugh, 1993, for references). But as is the case with other sex differences these ones might have also changed between the 1070s and the turn of the millenium due to changing sex roles in society, especially for those women who have already grown up in a different environment (Widgery & McGaugh, 1993, p. 37).

Studies can be classified according to whether they rely exclusively on sex as an explanatory variable or if they also consider individual difference or personality variables. This has already been accounted for by dividing this chapter into two parts (differences in men and women versus differences in masculine and feminine individuals). In Figure 21 the classification is illustrated graphically. The clouds attached to the different studies show the main independent variable examined. The results of these studies are then reported below. The studies investigating gender effects are reported in the next section. Tables 8 and 9 summarize the studies and their findings.

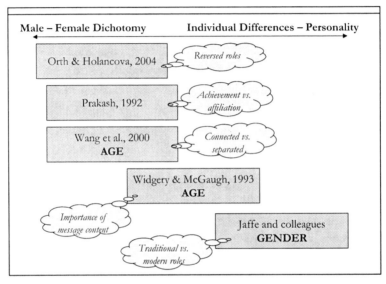

Figure 21: Classification of studies on advertising response
based on the independent variables considered

Study	Sample	Findings
Orth & Holancova, 2004	120 M and F	Males and Females differ in their reactions to different roles portrayed in advertising. Across genders, responses are affected by consumer's a priori attitude towards sex role portrayals.
Prakash, 1992	43 M 42 F	Males prefer an ad depicting competition with others, while females are indifferent between competitive and non-competitive situations. Men also prefer large-group socialization. When advertising to women, advertisers should provide more detailed and complete information.
Wang, Bristol, Mowen, & Chakraborty, 2000	201 M and F	Connected advertising appeals result in more favorable advertising appeals for women, while separate appeals do so for male consumers.
Widgery & McGaugh, 1993	1 740 M and F	Men and women are different in their perceptions of message content importance. This difference is diminishing with younger age of the people questioned.

Table 8: Studies investigating differences in male and female responses to advertising

Orth and Holancova (2004, p. 86) found that sex role portrayals in general elicit strong emotional and attitudinal responses from consumers which supports the application of the advertising effectiveness framework described above. This study exclusively examines role portrayals where the male and the female role are conformed to stereotypes in the first case and are reversed in the other. The authors found that role portrayals that were most favored by women were least favored by men and vice versa.

Prakash (1992) took a similar approach but selected two variables for manipulating advertisement content which reflect the psychological achievement-affiliation distinction[33] assumed to exist among men and women. This was done by varying the level of competition shown in the advertisement and the group size. Although Prakash acknowledged these psychological dimensions he does not go further by conceptualizing them as independent from biological sex. His results show that males prefer an ad format depicting competition with others, whereas females are indifferent between competitive and non-competitive situations. Similarly, men like large-group socialization better, whereas for females both large and small group situations are effective. Similarly, Wang, Bristol, Mowen and Chakraborty (2000) examine the effect of connected versus separated advertising appeals but also use sex as the only independent variable.

The results of the last two studies reflect some of the hypotheses proposed in theory. Prakash's (1992) results are in line with the greater behavioral and personality bandwidth reported for females (e.g. Carlson, 1971, p. 271). Additionally, they might also be an indicator that women have already bid farewell to stereotypical personality constraints whereas men are only partly on their way. They as well support the traditional definition of men as showing rather competitive and assertive behavior and women inclining towards more interaction and acting in both a self- and other-oriented manner. Also the findings of Wang et al. (2000, p. 113) are consistent with theory in that they report more positive attitudes in women for connected appeals and better persuasion of males by separated appeals.

However, the difference calculations in the reported studies were generally based on mean attitude scores of the sexes, thus neglecting individual differences within the male or the female segment. This comparison of means obscures

---

[33] Achievement-affiliation is another pair in the row of men-women dichotomies such as instrumentality-expressiveness or agency-communion, contending that males show need for achievement whereas women primarily show need for affiliation (see section 1.2.3 "Rethinking Sex and Gender").

potential differences within groups, which might be larger than actual differences between groups (Hyde, 1990, p. 62).

Widgery and McGaugh (1993) make a step in this direction when examining advertising message appeals for cars. They divided the female part of their sample into age groups. By doing so they were able to examine differences to some extent within the same-sex group, although they relied on demographic instead of psychographic data. Widgery and McGaugh (1993, p. 40) found significant differences between men and women in their importance perception of different message content. Interestingly, this difference was not present anymore among the younger age group. The authors suggest that different role programming of women who have grown up within the last 25 years is responsible for this effect.

Concluding, differentiated role portrayals seem to be necessary in general, depending on whether the ad is targeting men or women (Orth & Holancova, 2004, p. 86). When examining reactions of men and women separately, results still point to substantial differences between the male and the female sex. Sex is still an important explanatory variable in research (e.g. Prakash & Flores, 1985) and studies continue to detect a number of differences between male and female responses to advertising. However, these results are proven to be relative when taking into account differences among same-sex groups as done by Widgery and McGaugh (1993). Assuming that the sexes are internally homogenous is not justified (Hyde, 1990, p. 61) and might lead to diluted results because of the omission of important influencing variables. Considering gender as a moderating variable yields promising results in explaining differences in advertising response. Corresponding research is reported in the next section.

3.2.3 Response Differences in Masculine and Feminine Individuals

First there is the need for a brief introduction to a concept which provides one way of explaining why gender potentially has an impact on advertising response: the product-image self-image congruence hypothesis. After that the analysis will enter the research field providing the exact theoretical framework for testing research question number one. A special section will be dedicated to the pioneering and extensive work of Jaffe and her colleagues (Jaffe, 1990, 1991, 1994; Jaffe & Berger, 1988, 1994; Jaffe et al., 1992a; Jaffe et al., 1992b) as the present research is in part an adaptation of their studies. One major difference, however, is that Jaffe included only women in her sample, whereas this research will focus on men.

3.2.3.1 *Product-Image, Self-Image, and Reference Group Influence*

Sirgy (1982, p. 297) suggested that self-concept is an integral part of attitude research. Although self-concept encompasses more than only gendered self-concept, as sex and gender are both recognized as important parts of the self-concept. If one uses the term sex-role self-concept instead of gender (e.g. Golden et al., 1979; Allison et al., 1980) the connection between the two is clearly visible. The relevance of self-concept for consumer research is based on a positive correlation between the congruence of product and self image and purchase probability (e.g. Sirgy, 1982, p. 289). Applied in an advertising context this relationship can be reformulated as such: the better an advertisement depicts an image congruent with the self-image, the more likely the consumer is to develop positive feelings toward the ad. This in turn leads to a positive attitude towards the advertisement and the brand and the consumer is more likely to finally buy the brand (see the model explained in the previous section). The matching model is graphically displayed in Figure 22.

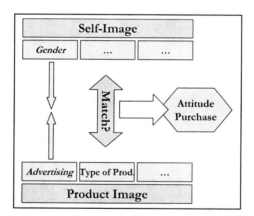

Figure 22: Relationship of product-image and self-image
and congruence effects on attitude and purchase

As can be seen from Figure 22, gender is one component of the self-image, just as advertising is partly responsible for the product image. The match or mismatch of product image and self-image – or in this specific case, advertising format in connection with gender self-perception – influences the favorability of the attitude towards the ad as well as towards the brand and finally the purchase probability. Thus, of the various components constituting both self-image and product-image the assumption underlying this study is that the match between gender (sex-role self-concept) and the transmittance of product image through advertising has a positive effect on attitudes and purchase intention. Other both self-image and product image builders are not considered in the current context.

The contentions made in Figure 22 are supported by research (e.g. Sirgy, 1982, p. 289). Brannon and Brock (1994) state that "people are more persuaded by messages geared to their self-schemas than by schema-irrelevant messages" (p. 174). Based on the results of their own study, Martin and Bellizzi (1982) proposed "that careful consideration should be given to the relationship between consumer self-image and brand image *especially when product positioning is primarily based upon promotional tools*" (p. 485, italics added). This suggests that the congruence question is crucial when advertising is used to build brand image (which is they case for most consumer goods). Therefore, image congruency might have a strong impact on consumers' attitudes in an advertising context. Congruency also seems to be more important for privately consumed products, whereas reference group influence is stronger for socially consumed products (Martin & Bellizzi, 1982, p. 476). Brannon and Brock (1994, p. 177) suggest that a threefold congruence of product (or brand) schema, advertising appeal and the recipient is necessary for advertising effectiveness. They conclude that congruence between appeal and product is particularly important for prototypical products, i.e. products matching their category schema closely. For less stereotyped products advertising appeals should instead try to match the individual's self-schema. This provides some guidelines for the selection of products to serve as stimulus material and the possible associated implications. Specifically, the use of a neutral product is recommended when the category schema is not predefined as masculine or feminine.

But not only image congruency but also reference group influence might play a role in the current study. Although this factor will not be tested, some notes on it might be useful. Generally, positively valued reference groups can exert considerable influence on consumers independent of whether the consumer is member of the group or not. Advertising can make use of this potential by portraying products being consumed in socially pleasant situations or using prominent spokespersons for promoting products. As a reaction consumers may try to resemble the reference group or form an attachment or liking towards the group (Bearden & Etzel, 1982, p. 184). This theory may explain why it is possible for men to hold favorable attitudes towards an ad depicting a modern male role even if they do not possess feminine-valued traits themselves. In this case, the congruence hypothesis would fail by predicting unfavorable attitudes towards the ad because of a mismatch between the spokesperson's and the consumer's personalities. Taking the attitude dimension of gender into account, a match can be identified between the spokesperson's the consumer attitudes and thus reference person can favorably influence buyers' attitudes towards the ad and the brand.

3.2.3.2 Gender and Advertising Effectiveness

Table 9 presents a selection of studies examining masculinity and femininity effects in advertising.

Field	Study	Sample	Findings
Psychology	Oliver, Sargent, & Weaver, 1998	193 M 207 F	Both sex and gender influence individuals' affective reactions to films. The gender influence is stronger for males than for females.
Advertising Research	Gentry & Haley, 1984	168 M and F	Biological sex may be a better predictor of ad recall and ease of recall than gender identity. Gender identity differences within sexes are more interesting than between-sex differences.
	Renn & Calvert, 1993	80 M and F	Gender aschematic individuals recall more counterstereotypical information than gender schematic adults.
Gender, Role Portrayal & Advertising Response	Coughlin & O'Connor, 1985	420 M and F Non-students	Masculine gender identity explains more differences in purchase intention as a reaction to female role portrayals in ads than does biological sex.
	Leigh, Rethans, & Reichenbach-Whitney (1987)	87 F	Women's reactions to female role portrayals in advertising differ according to their own gender role orientation.
	Bellizi & Milner, 1991	69 M 45 F	A feminine framing of a masculine product leads to better responses for women than a masculine framing, independent if their career orientation.
	Jaffe & Berger, 1988	100 F	Gender identity is significantly related to preferences for sex role positioning in advertising, but the relationship differs by product category.
	Jaffe, 1990; 1991	200 F Non-students	Modern portrayal of sex roles in advertising improves advertising response to and purchase intention for financial services; positioning is more essential for high masculine females than for lesser masculine women.
	Jaffe, 1994	200 F Non-students	Sex role identity is a useful predictor of women's responses to advertising. Thereby masculinity is the driving force.
	Jaffe & Berger, 1994	140 F	An egalitarian positioning is favored over both a superwomen and a traditional positioning. Individual gender ideology is useful in explaining these effects.
	Jaffe, Jamieson & Berger, 1992	200 F Non-stud.	The comprehension of a positioning has significant impact on advertising effectiveness.

Table 9: Studies investigating differences in masculine and feminine individuals' responses to advertising

Generally, gender – as measured by the communal and agentic orientation of individuals – can influence emotional reactions. This has been shown in a non-advertising context by Oliver et al. (1998, p. 54-58): communal and agentic individuals exhibited different emotional reactions towards various types of films. Gender was found to be a particularly influential factor on male's responses compared to female responses. The authors explain this finding with an especially strong tendency in sex-typed males not to show sex-inappropriate emotions (cf. Bem & Lenney, 1976). From these findings it can be concluded that also advertisements also evoke different emotional reactions (feelings towards the ad) in masculine versus feminine individuals and thus lead to ad and brand attitudes which are differentiated on the basis of gender.

Upon entering the field of advertising related research, the studies by Gentry and Haley (1985) and Renn and Calvert (1993) are worth mentioning, though they do not belong to the field of attitude-purchase intention research. Instead, they examine the effect of gender on ad recall. Recall is one method to measure advertising effectiveness, though it does not take the quality of the response into account (i.e. liking of the ad, attitude formation). Gentry and Haley (1985) varied the gender of products and the model presenting it and found that on average masculine individuals are more likely to recall masculine ads (masculine image, male model). They noted that the sex of the model presenting a product plays a crucial role in shaping the respondent's perception of masculinity and femininity of an advertisement. Their results indicated that it is possible to change the gender of a product by using a model whose sex is inconsistent with traditional product perception.[34]

Renn and Calvert (1993, p. 457) found that androgynous and undifferentiated individuals were more likely to recall counter-stereotypical information than were masculine and feminine individuals, regardless of their sex. Also, men high in femininity recalled counter-stereotypical information better as well. These results point to a significant influence of gender on the extent to which people recall advertising information. This will be of special relevance when examining information processing further.

In short, a significant influence of gender on advertising response (in a broad sense) has been documented for

▪ Ad recall (masculine individuals recall masculine ads; Gentry & Haley, 1984, p. 262);

---

[34] This finding again supports the importance of using a neutral product in the current study.

- Type of information recalled (aschematic individuals better recall counter-stereotypical information; Renn & Calvert, 1993, p. 457).

Again, more specific evidence supporting the study at hand is given in research examining the interaction of gender and role portrayals as well as their effect on advertising response.

3.2.3.3   Gender, Role Portrayals, and Advertising Response

In 1984 Coughlin and O'Connor examined reactions to traditional and non-traditional role portrayals of women. Within females they found significant differences in purchase intent depending on the role portrayed and their own gender. However, no significant differences – based on personality characteristics – emerged among men. It might be, though, that men are rather indifferent towards women's roles but are a lot more sensitive when their own sex is shown in advertising. Confirming, Leigh, Rethans, and Reichenbach-Whitney (1987, p. 59) found significant differences in women's reaction to depiction of female roles depending on their own role orientation. Modern women were shown to be more sensitive on this matter than traditionally oriented women. Bellizzi and Milner (1991) showed a traditionally male product (car care) once in a feminine and once in a masculine framing. Their results point to a better performance of the feminine framing with women, although no differences were found for women with different career orientations. However, career orientations, though related to the modern female sex role, might not be the best variable to capture gender issues. Nevertheless it is interesting that both men and women reacted similarly to a masculine-framed positioning.

In 1988 Jaffe and Berger started a series of studies aimed at examining such relationships, as they found that there was a lack of studies in the marketing literature which examine the effects of modern versus traditional role portrayals on advertising response. They investigated gender, as measured by the BSRI, as a moderating variable.

The first study (Jaffe & Berger, 1988) examined the interaction between advertising effectiveness and gender in two low involvement product categories: food and cleaners. This is the main study to build on, as this research will also be situated in a low involvement product category. Because advertising interest and the degree of processing might be different when individuals are highly involved with a product category as compared to low involvement products, this differentiation could be of importance (Jaffe, 1991, p. 63; Tolley & Bogart, 1994, p. 76). Neither high nor low involvement results may thus be generalized across product categories. The procedure, however, is similar for all studies. The sample of this first investigation consisted of 100 female individuals who completed the short form of the BSRI (Bem, 1981), resulting in three (masculine, feminine, androgynous[35]) gender groups of approximately equal size. They were then each shown four different stimuli (print ads) and eventually indicated purchase intent on a seven-point scale. The results confirmed the expectations of the researchers (see Figure 23 for an illustration of the findings: the picture shown (modern – business women – or traditional – woman with child doing housework) is the picture preferred by the gender group. The size of the picture roughly corresponds to the strength of preference with larger pictures signifying a stronger preference):

- Women with a masculine sex-role identity preferred the modern positioning above the traditional one, whereas women with a feminine sex-role identity chose the traditional positioning.
- Androgynous females also favored the modern positioning, but to a lesser extent than masculine individuals.

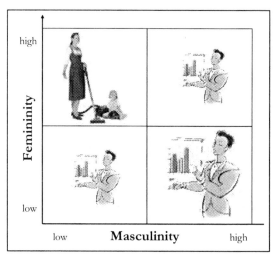

Figure 23: Impact of gender on preference of traditional vs. modern role positioning in women (Jaffe & Berger, 1988) [36]

However, these preferences were not as clear for the cleaner category as they were for the food category. Jaffe and Berger (1988, p. 268) hypothesize that the modern cleaning portrayal was to extreme to be believable. Another explanation

---

[35] Jaffe and Berger (1988) did obviously not distinguish between androgynous and undifferentiated individuals as suggested by Spence et al. (1975).

[36] As Jaffe and Berger did not distinguish between androgynous and undifferentiated individuals, the results reported for „androgynous" also apply for the „undifferentiated" group, although differences between these two groups might be present in a closer examination.

might be that cleaning products are seen as a lot more feminine than food products, so as a consequence the modern portrayal looses a certain amount of its modernity. In her 1990 study, Jaffe also votes for a category influence on the relationship between gender segment and positioning.

The second study conducted by Jaffe (1990) served as a basis for following in-depth analyses of the relationship between gender and advertising effectiveness. It was conducted among 200 women in a high-involvement category (financial services). Sex role identity was again measured by the short form of the BSRI (Bem, 1981). Each respondent was presented a block of four different advertisements, out of 16 treatments which varied in

- positioning (modern vs. traditional)
- product category (two different financial products)
- the financial institution advertised
- the execution of the ad.

Respondents then again indicated purchase probability. The results obtained are as follows:

- On average, modern positioning enhances advertising response, therefore leading to greater purchase probability for ads portraying modern roles than for ads portraying traditional roles (The modern minus the traditional positioning differential is further on referred to as the "modern positioning advantage"; MPA).
- Modern positioning is particularly critical and effective for the high masculinity segment (the modern positioning advantage is larger for high masculinity women), but both positionings are of equal attractiveness to women low in masculinity.
- Considering femininity, the modern role portrayal enhances advertising response for both the high and low femininity segment as compared to the traditional depiction, though the modern positioning advantage is greater for low femininity women compared to high femininity women.

The concept of the modern positioning advantage is graphically explained in Figure 24:

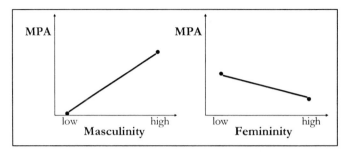

Figure 24: Relationship of masculinity and femininity in women to
modern positioning advantage of advertisements (Jaffe, 1990)

As can be seen from Figure 24 the impact of masculinity is stronger than that of
femininity. It seems to be that not only are females less extreme in their behaviors
and capable of a larger range of behaviors (e.g. Carlson, 1971, p. 271), but that this
is possibly also true for feminine individuals. Combining the effects of masculinity
and femininity[37] as shown in Figure 24 and putting them into Bem's gender
framework we obtain the following results (see Figure 25):

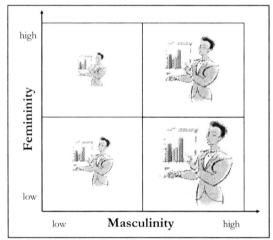

Figure 25: Combined effects of masculinity and femininity of
preferred role portrayals in advertising for women (Jaffe, 1990)

As can be seen from Figure 25, modern positioning is always at least slightly
preferred above traditional positioning (Jaffe, 1990, p. 877), though to a different
extent by the various gender groups (masculine women favor it most, while
feminine women favor it least). The results thus correspond with the expectations
made in theory.

---

[37] As this was not done by Jaffe and her colleagues the calculation here is based on the data available in the studies
and was carefully executed by the author of the current study.

Subsequent studies (Jaffe, 1991, 1994; Jaffe et al., 1992a; Jaffe at al., 1992b; Jaffe & Berger, 1994) extended the previous findings. The most important points are summarized below:

- The above findings are also true when using information interest instead of purchase intention or probability as a dependent variable (Jaffe, 1991, p. 62; 1994, p. 476).
- Comprehension of the intended positioning further increases purchase probability (Jaffe et al., 1992a, p. 56; Jaffe et al., 1992b, p. 31).
- Masculinity is particularly important as a predictor of women's responses to advertising, whereas androgyny does not add any incremental predictive ability (Jaffe, 1994, p. 477).

A third study was conducted by Jaffe and Berger in 1994 where they exposed 140 women to six different advertisements of a food product and then measured affective response and purchase interest. Contrary to the two other studies, role portrayals were classified into three categories: traditional, super-women and egalitarian. The most important new result in this study was that women generally prefer an egalitarian positioning over a super-women positioning. Thus equality seems to be preferred over extremes, no matter which side they favor.

3.3 Gender Does Matter

A brief analysis of prevalent role portrayals of women and, to a lesser extent, of men has given some impression of how role models and stereotypes are constructed in our society and to what extent they are still present. These studies are not only interesting in that they reflect society's perception of male and female roles and possible inherent changes, but they are also useful for constructing the stimulus material for the present study where two ads must be developed reflecting either a modern role or a traditional role. The above findings provide help in determining what depictions are associated with male or female roles, respectively.

In the second part of the chapter, a simple model of advertising effects was developed, which underlies the assumptions made about measuring advertising effectiveness. An overview on these measures has been given. Some possible explanations for gender influences on the perception of advertisements have been analyzed in brief, most importantly the relationship between product image and self-image, where congruence between the two has been shown to favor purchase probability.

A selective review of research on men and women's responses to advertising has been conducted. This research usually reaches conclusions which are consistent with standard theories of male-female personality differences (e.g. separateness-connectedness, Wang et al., 2000). However, these studies do not investigate the question of possibly prevalent differences within each sex and therefore seem to miss out on a number of explanatory variables and interesting findings. Research that actually takes gender into account does indeed point to considerable differences within the sexes based on their gender, usually described in terms of masculine and feminine personality traits. However, the object under examination is generally women's roles. That is why for the present study it was important to examine male roles and men's corresponding advertising responses. The extensive work by Jaffe and her colleagues which examined women has yielded very promising results and will thus serve as a basis for conducting the study. Specific research hypothesis are stated in the next section.

3.4 Hypotheses: Part One

The first research question addresses the assessment of the impact of a certain type of role depicted in an advertisement has on advertising effectiveness. The formulation of the hypotheses builds on those proposed in the studies of Jaffe and Berger (1988) and Leigh et al. (1987) as these match the conditions of the present study most closely in examining low involvement products. It needs to be taken into account, however, that the issue examined is male roles and men rather than female roles and women as in the previously cited studies.

The hypotheses stated by Jaffe and Berger (1988, p. 261-262) were:
- masculine women will prefer the modern positioning over the traditional one.
- geminine women will have the least preference for the modern positioning and they may even prefer the traditional positioning
- androgynous women will fall in between these two groups.

The hypothesis stated by Leigh et al. (1987, p. 55-56) was
- consistency of the role portrayed and one's own role orientation should yield more favorable attitudes

Jaffe and Berger (1988) used Bem's (1973) method to divide the respondents into the four gender groups of masculine, feminine, undifferentiated and androgynous individuals. However, the usefulness of this approach has been questioned and it has been suggested that working with the raw scores on masculinity and femininity scales will produce better results (e.g. Kelly et al., 1978, p. 1576). Nevertheless, the available data does allow for both possibilities, so that an ex-post comparison of the two methods could deliver interesting insight, but it is assumed that masculinity and femininity scores per se are the better alternative at first.

Masculinity was found to be the driving factor in the evaluation of advertisements for women (Jaffe, 1990, p. 877). It might seem plausible then, to propose that it would be the opposite for men – in other words, that men's femininity is the factor determining advertising response for men. However, several facts speak against such an easily-reached assumption:
- Masculinity and femininity are simply not opposing ends of a continuum (e.g. Constantinople, 1973, p. 405; Bem, 1974, p. 155) but rather form an orthogonal framework where the two dimensions exist independent of each other.

- Masculinity and femininity are not equal from the point of social desirability and valuation (e.g. Gill et al., 1987, p. 496; Kacen, 2000, p. 347). Qualities stereotyped as masculine are more highly valued and more socially accepted in Western societies.
- Males are more reluctant to embrace feminine qualities than women are to adopt masculine qualities (e.g. Aube & Koestner, 1992; Nyquist et al., 1985). This is partly the consequence of the lower social desirability attributed to feminine qualities.

Therefore, it is hypothesized that femininity in males does not considerably impact attitudes towards advertisements and purchase intent. On the contrary, it is expected that the results are similar to those obtained for women, namely that masculinity is responsible for different attitudes. Masculinity represents the degree to which a person adheres to traditional sex roles and also incorporates the possession of a certain amount of "courage" to deviate from stereotypically assigned sex roles. All hypotheses build on the contention that ad liking is enhanced by congruence of the role depicted with one's own gender (e.g. Leigh et al., 1987, p. 60). Preference of the modern or the traditional role portrayal always refers to both attitudinal preference and higher purchase intent.

H1: High masculinity males will have a more favorable attitude towards the traditional role portrayal as compared to low masculinity males.

Put another way, high masculinity males will prefer the traditional role portrayal. Accordingly, should high femininity males then prefer the modern role portrayal? Taking into account what was said above about the driving force of masculinity for attitude towards women's role portrayals and considering the specific definition of femininity this conclusion is not imperative. Femininity is associated with a greater tendency for integration and connectedness (e.g. Lang-Takac & Osterweil, 1992), therefore it can be expected that the preference for traditional role portrayals in high masculinity males is stronger than the preference for modern role portrayals in high femininity males. Additionally the usual way of portraying men in advertising is the traditional way (e.g. Kolbe & Albanese, 1997) which men are accustomed to. It can also be safely assumed that men do not feel as offended by traditional male role portrayals as women do by traditional female role portrayals, because the male picture usually represents an independent, socially accepted authority figure (e.g. Mazzella et al., 1992; Furnham & Bitar, 1993). Taking all this together, one can presume that males – independent of their degree of femininity – still do not go so far as to *prefer* modern over traditional role portrayals, though they might like them equally. Hypothesis 2 thus runs as follows:

H2: Compared to low femininity males, high femininity males will not show a specific preference for the modern portrayal.

For analyzing gender group differences, based on the framework by Bem (1973), the effects of masculinity and femininity need to be combined. The following effects are expected as stated in Hypothesis 3. It is important to note that the terms *masculine* and *feminine* now indicate an individual's gender group membership whereas in Hypotheses 1 and 2 they referred to the scale scores for the different gender dimensions.

H3: Gender group members will differ in their preference for the two role portrayals.

H3a: Masculine males will prefer the traditional over the modern role portrayal.
H3b: Feminine males will prefer the modern over the traditional role portrayal.
H3c: Undifferentiated males will be indifferent between the two role portrayals.
H3d: Androgynous males will prefer the traditional over the modern role portrayal.

As undifferentiated males are characterized by being neither masculine nor feminine it is not expected that they show any specific preference based on the role portrayed in the ad. On the other hand, androgynous males are expected to react to a gendered portrayal by exhibiting some preference, but because they are equally masculine and feminine the direction of this preference is difficult to predict. For previously explained reasons, it is expected that their masculinity has a somewhat stronger impact on their attitude than their femininity. Therefore, a slight preference for the traditional role portrayal is expected. These expected preferences by gender group are illustrated in Figure 26. (Just as in Figure 25, the drawings represent the portrayal which is expected to be preferred by the different gender groups. The man in business dress thereby stands for the traditional portrayal and the father with his son for the modern portrayal. Different relative sizes of the pictures again indicate the strength of preference, with larger pictures representing stronger preferences.)

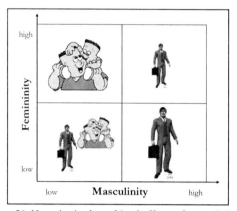

Figure 26: Hypothesized combined effects of masculinity and femininity in males on their responses to advertisements

The view that sex differences in processing originate from the inculcation of agentic and communal values in males and females, leads to the question of how persistent these differences are likely to be in the light of recent societal changes.
(Meyers-Levy, 1989, p. 254)

4 Gender and Information Processing

The claim that advertising messages should be developed with the target group in mind does seem intuitive not only to marketing or advertising specialists. One important aspect in this field is the target's style of information processing (e.g. Graham et al., 2002, p. 8). A number of models have been developed on how individuals acquire, store and retrieve information and research has shown how these processes can be disturbed or enhanced, respectively. In marketing, information processing plays an important role in the field of advertising and product evaluation. The goal of advertising is to transport product information to consumers and get them to notice, process, and favorably relate that information it to existing memory structure (Gentry & Haley, 1984, p. 259) so that it will eventually result in positive judgments and preferences in consumers' minds. However, a considerable growth in the amount of available information (and not only advertising information) renders this task increasingly difficult.

This chapter gives first a brief introduction to information processing theory. Following, theoretical work on how gender might impact information processing will be presented. The selectivity hypothesis by Meyers-Levy (1989) probably provides thereby the most comprehensive framework for explaining sex differences through different information processing strategies.

4.1 Introduction to Information Processing

As already indicated, the research in information processing of human beings is ample, not only in consumer behavior but also in research areas related to brain organization and functioning. For the purpose of this study a short summary of findings was deemed to be sufficient in order to provide the necessary background.

4.1.1 Cognitive Processes

The term *cognitive processes* summarizes the activities of reception of information, perception and judgment, and learning and memory. According to Kroeber-Riel and Weinberg (1999, p. 224) cognitive processes can be grouped into:

- reception of information
- processing of information
- storage of information.

The first step, reception of information, is influenced primarily by an individual's interest in a topic. This interest is determined by a variety of factors such as personal involvement, involvement with the product and the situation, perceived risk and possibly resulting cognitive conflicts. Also the perceived relevance of the information for the individual, which might be influenced by the extent of genderedness of both the situation and the individual, is likely to play a role.

Processing of information is done in the short-term memory and includes perception, because perception is already done in the ultra short-term memory. Perception is subjective, active, and selective. Selective perception refers to an individual's tendency to avoid displeasing stimuli and process mainly only the information that is consistent with existing schemas and current needs. As a certain degree of agreeableness quite possibly is inherent in incongruent information, schema-incongruent (and gender-incongruent) information is more likely to be avoided than schema (gender)-congruent information.

Information is finally stored in the long-term memory where new information is connected to existing knowledge structures.

4.1.2 Semantic Networks, Schemata, and the Gender Schema[38]

Notwithstanding other attempts to model knowledge structures[39] the notion of semantic networks and schemata as a way of human brain organization is still largely popular (e.g. Grunert, 1990; 1996; see Kroeber-Riel & Weinberg, 1999, for more references). A semantic network depicts knowledge in the form of items linked to each other (see Figure 27 for a simple example of a network centered on

---

[38] The terms schemas and schemata are used interchangeably throughout the book.
[39] Another theory in the context would be the theory of Embodied Cognition which has received some attention recently (see Malter, 1996, for an introduction). However, the debate of all available theories would be outside the range of this book, therefore discussion is limited to the standard model of semantic networks.

the term *car*). If one of these items is activated through an either external or internal stimulus, the activation spreads on through the knots to other parts of the network, the sequence of which depends on how closely linked the individual knots are.

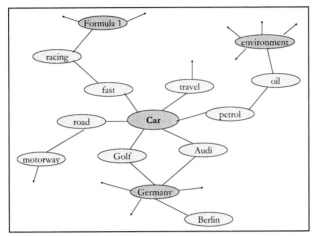

Figure 27: Example of a Semantic Network

As can be seen from Figure 27, the term car is related to a number of terms which are in turn connected to other items. Some items in the network will also represent a schema. For example, an individual might have a car schema or a road schema.

A schema (or knowledge structure) is

"any cognitive structure that specifies the general properties of a type of object or event and leaves out any specification of details that are irrelevant to the type. A schema is an abstraction that allows particular objects or events to be assigned in general categories. General knowledge of the category can then be applied to the particular case." (Stillings, Feinstein, Garfield, Rissland, et al., 1987, p. 30).

An alternative definition is given by Gentry and Haley (1984): "[Schemas are] large sets of well structured cognitions that have been learned over time as experience accumulates. [They] determine the readiness to search for and to assimilate incoming information" (p. 259).

Schemas are hierarchically organized in categories. Higher categories are more general than the more specific schemas of hierarchically lower levels which are more specific. The characteristics of hierarchically higher schemas are then transmitted to more specific schemas. An actual occurrence of the characteristics of specific object is then determined based on the individual case. If the new information does not comply with the schema it leads to perceived incongruency. The effects of it will be examined in the next section.

In short, a schema

- represents the most important characteristics of a object
- is more or less abstract (or concrete, respectively)
- is hierarchically organized
- is useful because it economizes information processing
- simplifies thinking processes
- organizes information storage
- controls perception as individuals tend to process mainly schema-consistent information (Kroeber-Riel & Weinberg, 1999, p. 232-234).

Possibly the most important schema we have is our self-schema (cf. Sirgy, 1982). As already argued above, gender schema is a central part of self-schema as sex and/or gender is one of the most easily distinguishing variables among individuals. Indeed there seems to be "no other dichotomy in human experience with as many entities assimilated to it as the distinction between male and female" (Bem, 1981, p. 354). Being gender schematic contends that "the gender connotations of both masculine and feminine stimuli will be especially salient" (Bem, 1982, p. 1193). Therefore, in the hierarchical organization of schemata, gender schema is probably one of the most essential ones for the majority of individuals. It is much more general than, for example, a car schema or a beer schema and as such shapes a large part of our information processing. Because gender schema stands high in the schema hierarchy, it could be called a meta-schema as it provides a basis for organizing large parts of other more specific knowledge structures. Gender schema not only relates to whether we perceive ourselves as masculine or feminine but also generalizes on our overall perception of and attitude towards what it means to be masculine or feminine. Thus, the term gender self-schema is being introduced at this point and will be later on used for an individual's self-perception of masculinity and femininity (i.e. gender) to distinguish it from gender schema which relates to the self and others at the same time.

The readiness with which an individual accesses one schema rather than another when processing information is referred to as the cognitive availability of the schema. Given the importance of one's sexual self-concept it is likely that the gender schema is readily available (Markus et al., 1982, p. 39; Gentry & Haley, 1984, p. 259). Theory on gender schema should provide insights into how people process both gendered information and non-gendered information on the basis of their gender schema. In a consumer behavior and advertising context such theory should explain how people process gendered ads and why they respond to them differently (Alreck, Settle, & Bench, 1982).

4.2 Influence of Schemata on Information Processing – A Gender Perspective

Most models of consumer behavior hypothesize that personality affects information processing variables rather than the actual "outputs" of processing, such as attitudes, intentions, or purchase behavior (Gentry & Haley, 1993). Moreover, Markus and Oyserman (1989, p. 101) suggest that the self-concept may influence information processing and affect emotional responses (see Brannon & Brock, 1994, for a good summary of self-schema influence on information processing). Thus gender self-schema as an important part of the individual personality might have substantial impact on information processing. This influence has been conceptualized in two seemingly similar models which nevertheless have very different assumptions and implications. They will be analyzed in the first part of this section, in order to provide some theoretical framework. Next, part two will be dedicated to the special question of how congruity or rather non-congruity of information and gender self-schema affect information processing.

4.2.1 A Theoretical Framework

Two main theories have been presented modeling the influence of gender (self-schema) on the way men and women process information. The first one, Gender Schema Theory, was proposed by Bem in 1981, followed a year later by Self-Schema Theory (Markus et al., 1982; Crane & Markus, 1982).

4.2.1.1 Gender Schema Theory

Gender Schema Theory (Bem, 1981) contends that
"individuals differ in their readiness to search for and to assimilate incoming information in gender-related terms, with sex-typed individuals having a greater readiness than non-sex-typed individuals to encode and to organize information on the basis of gender, despite the existence of other dimensions that could serve equally well as an organizing principle" (Frable & Bem, 1985, p. 459).

In other words, masculine males or feminine females have a tendency to organize and structure information in relation to gender – to simply perceive, process and store information guided by a gender bias. This is not the case for androgynous, undifferentiated, and cross-sex typed individuals according to Bem (1981, p. 355),. The functions of the BSRI are amplified from a personality measure to an instrument which can assess "whether or not [...] self concepts and behaviors are organized on the basis of gender" (Payne, Connor, & Colletti, 1987, p. 938). The theory implies that the gender schema is more easily accessible in sex-typed individuals than non sex-typed individuals. Therefore tasks such as recognition or recall of gender-related information are facilitated.

Bem (1981) tests the theory on a number of hypotheses: Sex-typed individuals showed more gender-based clustering of items in free recall and they were faster than the other groups to render schema-consistent judgments about themselves. Also, sex-typed individuals appeared to be more likely than non-sex-typed individuals to categorize people on the basis of their own gender (Frable & Bem, 1985, p. 466). The results by Bem and her colleagues (Bem, 1981; Frable & Bem, 1985) thus seem to confirm that gender-related information is more easily accessible because incoming information is organized on the basis of gender in masculine males and feminine females but not in androgynous, undifferentiated and cross sex-typed subjects.

4.2.1.2 *Self-Schema Theory*

Similar to Gender Schema Theory Self-Schema Theory builds on the basic notion that "differential processing of information about the self in various behavioral domains is associated with differences in self-schemas" (Markus et al., 1982, p. 38). However, the authors criticize Bem's aggregation of masculine and feminine subjects into a single group of sex-typed individuals. They argue that the gender schema may be different for masculine sex-typed subjects as compared to feminine sex-typed subjects (Crane & Markus, 1982, p. 1196). As a result they proposed distinguishing between gender schematic and gender aschematic individuals. The former "think of themselves as distinctly masculine and/or feminine and [...] have a large network of schema-relevant cognitions" (Markus et al., 1982, p. 40). Contradictory to Bem's assumptions, androgynous individuals are classified as highly gender schematic as they may exhibit both masculine and feminine gender schemas depending on the situation (Crane & Markus, 1982, p. 1196). Undifferentiated individuals are the only ones to be considered truly aschematic. For these subjects features of masculinity and femininity have not been incorporated into the self-concept. It is important to note, however, that according to Self-Schema Theory the group of masculine (or feminine) schematics can consist of both men and women, thus that gender schematicity occurs independent of biological sex.

Results of experiments conducted by Markus and her colleagues (Markus et al., 1982) supported Self-Schema Theory. They found that masculine schematics recall substantially more masculine words than feminine words and that the opposite is true for feminine schematics. Also gender schematic individuals cluster masculine and feminine words more than neutral words. From their results Markus et al. conclude that individuals seem to have either masculine or feminine schemas but not schemas relevant to gender as a whole. This is the main difference of Bem's Gender Schema Theory which proposes that people either have or do not have a general gender schema. Furthermore, their findings suggest that "important differences among individuals in how gender-relevant knowledge may be organized in memory" (Markus et al., 1982, p. 50) are present. Thus, gendered advertisements (ads which activate the gender schema) may elicit different responses with viewers depending upon their gender orientation. Consequently, the research aim of this study is thus further supported.

Naturally, both Bem and Markus report experimental results supporting their own theories. However, when examining follow-up research the picture becomes more differentiated and thus allows at least some conclusions to be drawn on which theory better reflects actual behavior.

4.2.1.3 *Comparison and Conclusion*

There is one main difference between the two theories: For Bem being gender schematic means that the gender dimension is highly salient and is actively used as a basis for decision making and information processing. Markus et al. (1982) support this contention in its fundamental meaning but add that gender schematicity includes having a well-developed understanding of the characteristic. When taking the latter definition into account the suggested existence of a difference between masculine and feminine schematics becomes very plausible: masculine schematics most likely exhibit a very well-developed understanding of masculinity whereas their notion of femininity is quite possibly less precise. For this reason Markus and her colleagues find it necessary to distinguish between masculine and feminine gender schemas. It shall be noted that according to Self-Schema Theory more individuals use gender as a basis for information processing as compared to Gender Schema Theory: Following Bem's contention only sex-typed individuals, i.e. those who exhibit the traits considered stereotypically desirable for their sex, are theorized to use gender as a basic variable for organizing their information processing, whereas in Self-Schema Theory, however, all but undifferentiated individuals are supposed to show some degree of gender influence on processing. For better understanding, the assumptions of the two theories are compared in Table 10.

Gender Schema Theory			Self-Schema Theory		
Gender / Sex	Men	Women	Gender / Sex	Men	Women
Masculine	MASC	None	Masculine	MASC	MASC
Feminine	None	FEM	Feminine	FEM	FEM
Androgynous	None	None	Androgynous	MASC + FEM	MASC + FEM
Undifferentiated	None	None	Undifferentiated	None	None

Table 10: Gender Schema Theory and Self-Schema Theory compared: Which group is schematic for which type of information (adapted from Payne et al., 1987)

Groups where gender schematic processing is supposed to occur are highlighted. The abbreviations *MASC* (masculine) and *FEM* (feminine) stand for the type of information for which this group is considered to be schematic. It is now clearly visible that in Gender Schema Theory schematic processing occurs only for a specific combination of sex and gender (male – masculine, female – feminine) although it is acknowledged that these two groups might still represent a large part of the population. The conclusion that follows is that in Gender Schema Theory, biological sex is still a factor that influences gender schematicity, whereas in Self-Schema Theory, masculine, feminine and androgynous individuals are considered gender schematic – independent of whether they are men or women.

Both theories receive mixed support in the literature. Surprisingly, there are almost no studies replicating the contentions of Gender Schema Theory, while most find at least partial support for Self-Schema Theory. Spence and Helmreich (1981) criticize Bem for the general assumption that the BSRI measures both gender and the tendency to process information on the basis of gender (i.e. gender schematicity). They conclude that with the help of the BSRI it is only possible to assess instrumental and expressive personality traits but neither of the two constructs which it is used to measure by Bem. Further, Schmitt et al. (1988) examine whether sex-typed subjects show more positive attitudes towards sex-role conformist advertisements than non sex-typed subjects. They find no support for their hypothesis. However, although they claim to test Gender Schema Theory because they distinguish between sex-typed and non sex-typed respondents, they leave aside the fact that Gender Schema Theory is essentially an information processing theory or more precisely, that it assumes that "encoding and recall are [...] facilitated as a function of the activation of schemas" (Payne et al., 1987, p. 937). Thus, Schmitt's et al. (1988) claim that advertising response can serve to test Gender Schema Theory might simply not be justified. The researchers believe that they can test Gender Schema Theory when they examine recall, clustering in recall, and response latencies. However, they find no differences between the groups on these dimensions either. Thus the results of their study do not actually support Gender Schema Theory in any way.

Payne and her colleagues (1987) investigated ratings of objects, recall, and recognition tasks replicating studies originally conducted by Bem and Markus to test their theories. Their results also fail to support the contentions made by Gender Schema Theory but they do replicate most of the findings of Markus and her colleagues. Additionally, Payne et al. (1987) found strong evidence for substantial differences between androgynous and undifferentiated individuals, further disqualifying the practice of combining them into a single group of non sex-typed people. Gentry and Haley (1984) examined advertisement attitudes and recall measures and also found no support for Bem's contentions but their findings did substantiate the results of Markus et al. (1982). Only Edwards and Spence (1987, p. 146) found non sex-typed individuals to be relatively unresponsive to stereotypically masculine or feminine message cues thus providing at least partial support for Bem's theory.

Despite the results of Edwards and Spence it seems that Gender Schema Theory is not a particularly good framework for predicting differences in information processing between masculine and feminine subjects. On the contrary, the contentions made by Self-Schema Theory have mostly received support in follow-up examinations (e.g. Kempf et al., 1997, p. 444). Thus Self-Schema Theory might provide a more useful basis for analyzing processing differences between masculine and feminine males in the current study which leads to the dropping of Gender Schema Theory without further examination. In Self-Schema Theory, the fact that biological sex seems to have no influence on the individual propensity to organize information on the basis of gender and that Self-schema Theory receives more support in the literature, is encouraging for the present study. However, neither theory will be tested in this study.

4.2.2 The Effect of Schema Congruity on Information Processing

Besides relying on theoretical conceptualizations some logical reasoning might also lead to worthwhile hypotheses about individual differences in the processing of information and more specifically about the influence gender self-schema exerts in this context (e.g. Gentry & Haley, 1984, p. 259-260). One aspect of information processing which could be of importance in the present research context is the degree of congruity between the content of information and the personality of its receiver.

In reference to the study at hand it is safe to assume that the degree of stereotyping of male and female schemas is different in sex-typed individuals as compared to non sex-typed individuals. Specifically, masculine men should possess a masculine schema of a male with more masculine traits being connected to the male identity, whereas the male schema of feminine men would instead emphasize their feminine qualities. (cf. Crane & Markus, 1982, p. 1195).[40]

Thus also the congruence of new information with existing knowledge structures might vary with personality and the type of information presented. The existence or non-existence of such congruity and their implications on the processing of information has already received some attention in the literature and provides useful ground for explaining information processing differences between individuals.

When new information is acquired it is usually incorporated into existing knowledge structures. If this new information is found to be inconsistent with existing structures – a finding generally displeasing for an individual – he or she can react in two ways (cf. Kroeber-Riel & Weinberg, p. 181-184 and 334-337):

- he or she can ignore new information, devalue it or take some other form of precaution, so that there is not need to integrate the information into existing knowledge structures;
- he or she can nevertheless incorporate it into existing frameworks, thus amplifying and changing schemas or even forming completely new ones.

Which reaction is chosen depends on a number of variables, such as the degree of disagreeableness evoked by inconsistency or the importance of the schema in question, and thus the centrality of this schema to the self. Because an individual's gender schema is closely related to his or her self-schema, gender incongruent information might therefore result in a considerably uncomfortable feeling and a

---

[40] The same – only vice versa – would be true for women.

tendency to reject the new information. The source of information (specifically their credibility) will also play a role, as will personality and sex. Interestingly, males are more likely to change existing schemas than women (Block, 1984). A possible explanation for this finding could be that men's schemas were found to be broader and more general than those of women (see Meyers-Levy, 1989, for a list of references), therefore it might be easier for men to integrate moderately incongruent information into existing knowledge structures.

Incongruity has been found to lead to enhanced attention and perception (e.g. Rojahn and Pettigrew, 1992) and possibly even to more intensive processing (cf. Mandler, 1982, cited in Meyers-Levy & Tybout, 1989, p. 1). Also, people are more easily persuaded by messages geared to their self-schemas than by schema-irrelevant messages (Brock, Brannon, & Bridgwater, 1990). Zajonc (1980) emphasizes that schemas often have an emotional component and that emotional processes can disturb or enhance information processing. Self-schema consistent and thus pleasing stimuli should therefore have a positive effect on memory performance. Disagreeable stimuli are usually avoided. Consequently, individuals may find the observation of schema-inconsistent pictures displeasing and try not to notice them. Existing product or brand schemas also influence to a large extent the perception of new information regarding a product or a brand.

If role portrayals, varying in their degree of male role stereotypes, are presented to men with different gender identities there will be matches between gender self-schema and information for some individuals but mismatches, or incongruity, for others. Moreover, gender self-schema will have some degree of (positive) emotionality (cf. Zajonc, 1980). Congruity of stimulus and gender self-schema should therefore also trigger positive emotions and enhance liking of the advertisement. Drawing on the above reported effects of schema congruity on information processing the following propositions can be made:

1. Enhanced information processing can be expected for the combinations "feminine stimulus – masculine gender schema" and "masculine stimulus – feminine gender schema" because of the perceived incongruity between the stimulus and existing schemas (e.g. Hogg & Garrow, 2003, p. 169).

2. The depiction of a man in a feminine role is in itself already incongruent. Therefore this combination can be expected to lead to increased information processing. However, this effect might be stronger for masculine individuals than for feminine individuals as the incongruity between stereotypical roles and depicted roles might be more obvious for the former. Nevertheless, this contention might possibly provoke the strongest effects.

3. Enhanced information processing can also possibly be expected because of the liking of/preference for a gender schema congruent advertisement (for feminine stimulus – feminine gender schema and for masculine stimulus – masculine gender schema; e.g. Wang et al., 2000, p. 114)

Research results partly support the contentions on the influence of congruity on processing: Payne et al. (1987, p. 937), for example, report that the high-stereotyped group recognized more gender-consistent pictures than gender-inconsistent pictures. Thus, the high-stereotyped group seemed to better process information consistent with their self-schema (Proposition 3). Also Maldonado et al. (2003, p. 8) report that a match between the product and the category prototype enhances free recall, which would again maintain Proposition 3. Another study, however, by Renn and Calvert (1993) provided only partial, but still support for Proposition 3. Now, it is not clear whether better recall is also a sign of more intensive information processing. It might simply be a matter of easier classification and connection to existing networks which would then enhance accessibility of the newly acquired information and in turn foster recall. In turn, Meyers-Levy and Tybout (1989, p. 8) found evidence that moderate incongruity of a product with its prototypical category schema leads to enhanced cognitive elaboration – a result which in general upholds Propositions 1 and 2. However, this was true for a moderate quantity of incongruity, but not for cases that had a high amount of incongruity. Meyers-Levy and Tybout hypothesize that individuals do not see any way to successfully resolve the inconsistency if incongruity is too high and have therefore refrained from trying. This of course leads to a forth proposition that is equally plausible:

4. For highly masculine men the incongruity between a male person and a shown feminine gender identity is too high to engage in detailed processing of the ad. Also, because of a potential dislike towards the ad, this group might not be motivated to engage in more intensive cognitive elaboration. However, in an advertising context, and especially in a low-involvement context it is at least questionable whether consumers dedicate enough attention to the ads to be able to *realize* the prevailing incongruity.

The degree of perceived incongruity itself might also depend on gender. Hogg and Garrow (2003, p. 169) suggest that females perceive incongruity more easily than males since they pay more attention to more specific and detailed cues. However, their results did not find convincing evidence for this idea.

In conclusion, the influence of schema congruity on information processing is complex and not clear. Available literature does not point clearly in a certain direction. Incongruity seems to nevertheless be an important factor affecting individual manners of information processing. The results of the present study should shed some more light on this matter.

The above paragraphs apply to the influence of gender (gender self-schema) on information processing and thus take a personality perspective which is basically independent of biological sex. Although, most research so far undertaken in this area has focused on differences between males and females. The results obtained might provide additional insights and as such, will be the topic of the next section.

Congruity and incongruity of stimulus, gender identity, and the picture itself is then one argument used for supporting the hypotheses stated at the end of this chapter. Congruency theory might also help later in explaining the results. However, it can only be one part of the answer to this research question. Apart from congruity and incongruity effects, the area of sex difference in processing to be considered as well for hypothesizing about gender effects and will complement the mechanisms described above. A synthesis of the two fields is then attempted when formulating the research hypotheses.

4.3 Processing Differences Between Men and Women

Although research on information processing differences between men and women is only a small fraction of the ample research on sex differences which has been discussed above, the amount of research is still extensive. A large number of studies examine multiple aspects of information processing ranging from processing strategies to confidence in one's own ability to analyze information. Meyers-Levy proposed a well-fitting framework for explaining gender differences in 1989 which builds on specific differences in processing strategies between men and women – the selectivity hypothesis. Based on her findings some interesting implications can be uncovered on male-female processing differences can be deducted which will be of importance in the course of the present study.

4.3.1 Gender Differences: A Selectivity Interpretation

Differences between men and women have been the subject of extensive research and a number of different explanations for these differences have been examined. In 1989 Meyers-Levy proposed a comprehensive framework, the selectivity hypothesis, which was intended to explain gender differences on the ground of different information processing strategies employed by males and females. Meyers-Levy (1989, p. 220-223) contended that males do not engage in comprehensive processing of all available information as a basis for judgment. Instead they employ various heuristic devices – typically ones that involve the use of single cues or cues that imply a single inference. Cues used are usually highly available and particularly salient. Also, the selectivity hypothesis holds that males focus on self-related information. On the other hand females can be characterized as comprehensive information processors who attempt to assimilate all available cues, although the limits of human processing capacity may keep females from always accomplishing such an objective. Also females concentrate on both self- and other-relevant information.

Thus, *selectivity* is conceptualized threefold by Meyers-Levy (1989):
- as using a single cue
- as using single or multiple cues but which imply a single inference
- as the tendency to employ heuristic-based processing.

Although they worked with a male-female dichotomy Meyers-Levy ascribed these differences in processing strategies not directly to sex but to different sex roles, namely the agentic role which was attributed to men and the communal role which was supposedly common among females (Meyers-Levy, 1988, p. 522). However, she did not question the dependence of these roles on biological sex which is surprising given her questioning of "how persistent these differences are likely to be in the light of recent societal changes" (Meyers-Levy, 1988, p. 254).

Meyers-Levy (1989) then examines a large set of literature on gender differences in the light of the selectivity hypothesis. She analyzes literature on the prevalence of differences between boys and girl, the development of sex differences, and the manifestations of those differences among adults. Meyers-Levy's (1989) investigation of sex difference in the structural organization of information is especially interesting: The selectivity hypothesis proposed that males possess rather simple, widely-encompassing knowledge structures while females should organize information in a more differentiated manner. Previous literature on structural organization seems to support the predictions made by the selectivity hypothesis.

The proposal of the selectivity hypothesis provoked a considerable amount of research on the subject. Also Meyers-Levy and her colleagues conducted studies for empirical validation of the suggested framework. The findings of these studies are listed below. These results will allow some conclusions to be made about the most important male-female differences regarding information processing strategies. The largest part of the research focuses on the number of message cues used for judgments and the general intensity of information processing. The following results were obtained:

- Men have the propensity to base responses on a rather selective consideration of available cues, females consider a variety of cues (Meyers-Levy, 1988, p. 528).
- Females engage in more detailed elaboration of specific message content while males' processing is driven by overall message themes or schemas (Meyers-Levy & Maheswaran, 1991, p. 68).
- Women exhibit greater sensitivity to details of relevant information when forming judgments (Meyers-Levy & Sternthal, 1991, p. 93).
- Women engage in greater elaboration of stimuli when given enough time to do so (DePaulo & Rosenthal, 1979).
- Women evoke a greater number of thoughts about judgment-relevant cues (Meyers-Levy & Sternthal, 1991, p. 91-92).
- Females consider both subjective and objective claims (Darley & Smith, 1995, p. 52-53).

- Males use self-information cues, females employ both self- and other-information cues when forming judgments (Meyers-Levy, 1988, p. 523). This is consistent with theorizing that women are more connected and men are more separated.
- Women often have a lower threshold for elaborating message cues (Meyers-Levy & Sternthal, 1991, p. 93).
- Women are superior in encoding and decoding nonverbal cues (Hall, 1978).
- Females are better at understanding nonverbal cues, recognizing faces and expressing emotions verbally (Hyde, 1990, p. 69).
- Males conceptualize in terms of physical attributes, females use evaluative concepts (Darley & Smith, 1995, p. 42).

The studies by Hall (1978) and Hyde (1990) can be interpreted in that females seem to be able and willing to process both verbal and nonverbal messages, as opposed to men who concentrate on the more salient verbal content. The last finding (Darley & Smith, 1995, p. 42) could be integrated in the selectivity framework by the plausible suggestion that evaluation might require more intensive processing and the use of more information than reliance only on factual attributes.

Other studies examine differences in the general use of processing strategies:

- Females change processing strategies when necessary (e.g. they employ more extensive processing when the situational risk increases; Darley & Smith, 1995, p. 53).
- If consumers are motivated to engage in detailed processing, males will drop their usually favored schema-based processing (Kempf et al., 1997, p. 444).

Because these two results are somewhat contradicting to each other, they leave a conflict which yet needs to be resolved. However, as indicated by Meyers-Levy and Maheswaran (1991, p. 68), there are a number of factors determining when men and women decide to switch from schema-based processing to more detailed elaboration. Table 11 provides an overview on male and female information processing differences.

	Males	Females
Number of cues used	Few	Many
Type of cues used	Self-information	Self- and other-information
Threshold for elaborating cues	Moderate	Low
Number of thoughts about cues	Few	Many
Object of processing	Overall message theme or schema	Specific message content
Detail sensitivity	Not sensitive	Sensitive
Claims considered	Objective	Subjective and objective
Change of processing strategy when necessary	If motivated	Yes
Conceptualization	Physical attributes	Evaluative concepts
Understanding of nonverbal cues	Poor to moderate	Good

Table 11: Processing differences between males and females

In short, it can be concluded that women generally exhibit more extensive information processing, pay more attention to details, and are less driven by schemes. As they engage in greater elaboration of ads (this is true for equal interest situations between men and women), they generate more thoughts about judgment relevant cues. Even more compact, there are two main points where men's and women's information processing strategies seem to differ:

- *The number of message cues used:* whereas men tend to focus on cues which are highly available, females consider a larger number of cues. This can be interpreted in the light of results showing that the threshold a cue needs to cross to be evaluated is lower for females.
- *The type of message cues used:* whereas for men self-relevant cues are of greatest importance, for women it is information relevant for the self *and* others.

It is less clear whether females are more flexible in their information processing strategies. Darley and Smith (1995, p. 53) argue that females adapt their strategies according to situational changes. Kempf et al. (1997, p. 444) found that both sexes will switch to more elaborated processing when either a message factor (e.g. highly incongruent information) or a task factor (e.g. recall) strongly recommends a specific processing strategy. The selectivity hypothesis seems to be nevertheless useful in describing differences in information processing strategies (Putrevu, 2001, p. 9).

The current study will not go into information processing details (e.g. those mentioned in table 12), but will focus on the general difference between a detailed (or extensive; "female") and a schema-based general ("male") information processing strategy.

4.3.2 Additional Findings

A number of studies both explicitly or implicitly tested the selectivity hypothesis and mostly found results supporting its contentions, although they did not always examine exactly the same constructs. The most interesting studies will be reported below and will thus illustrate and enhance understanding of male-female differences in information processing.

Laroche, Saad, Cleveland, and Browne (2000, p. 10-11) examine information search behavior and found that males are less comprehensive searchers whereas females are more likely to undertake both general and specific information searches. Males tended to rely more on sales clerk assistance. Women often consulted sales clerks but used them only as an additional source of information whereas men mostly turned to sales clerks as a result of an abundance of information. These findings thus support the contention of the selectivity hypothesis that men tend to focus on a single, highly available cue whereas women use multiple cues for forming judgments. Another note can be made regarding information processing confidence which is generally higher in males than in females (Kempf et al., 1997, p. 446).

McGivern, Robert, Huston, Byrd, King, et al. (1997, p. 332) found that female performance in visual recognition memory exceeded that of males on all stimuli except for where the nature of the stimuli increased males attention. In line with the general hypothesis this can be explained in such that visual recognition of a larger number of objects requires rather intensive processing. Males were seemingly not willing to encounter this effort. Contradicting the selectivity model equal, however, performance was observed when the presented stimuli were self-oriented. Self-referential strategy, usually associated with the male sex role, was also evident in girls. McGivern et al. interpreted their findings in the light of changing cultural and environmental influence.

Other studies investigated the role of risk in information processing and also found differences between men and women. Graham et al. (2002) reported that women investors had a distinct profile and tended to consider all relevant investment factors. Consistently, Sneath, Kennett, & Megehee (2002) found that men were likely to make decisions based on the objective level of risk while women were likely to consider both objective and subjective risk dimensions. Their results are, however, not entirely consistent with respect to sex differences. The authors suggested that this is "indicative of diminishing differences in the socialization of men and women" (Sneath et al., 2002, paragraph 38). Results from Darley and Smith (1995, p. 53) further suggested that females adapted to changing risk situations by changing their processing strategies. Males were shown to be less sensitive to the level of risk, possibly because the "risk cue" was not salient enough to enter the considerations of males. Such results are mostly in line with the selectivity model.[41]

Martin (2003) investigated the interaction of sad versus happy mood and sex in the perception of advertisements. Attitude towards the ad was moderated by mood effects but attitude towards the brand was not. However, self-discrepancy (which is, according to Martin, 2003, p. 266, prevalent in cross sex-typed subjects) was found to be a significant predictor of sad mood. It is interesting from an information processing perspective that sad mood leads to higher involvement (Bagozzi, Gopinath, & Nyer, 1999) which would in turn foster elaborative information processing. To conclude that cross sex-typed individuals generally engage in more intensive processing seems nevertheless a hypothesis which is a little farfetched.

Another area of research focuses on how individuals actively use the concept of sex or gender when receiving information such as when encoding or retrieving information. A study by Skitka and Maslach (1990) delivered some interesting results: Sex strongly affected how people remembered and processed information about social interactions. Advertising – a prestep in the consumption process – can be seen as a special form of social interaction. Many people also use sex as a semantic category to encode information. Sex thus influenced processing and recall of information. Skitka and Maslach (1990, p. 146-149) hypothesized that there were two levels of information processing: sex-based processing operates at the surface level whereas gender-based processing is a more complex process and operates in a less obvious way.

---

[41] See Sneath et al. (2002) for a large number of references in support of the selectivity model.

4.4 Gender Differences in Information Processing

So far, research has focused on sex differences in information processing. The purpose of this study is to investigate the relation between information processing and gender and to determine whether an individual's gender influences the way he or she processes information. As mentioned, not many studies have investigated this question so far. A recent attempt to do so is the study by Hogg and Garrow (2003). However, in their references there is no study listed either examining the proposed relationship.

At least for information processing *confidence* differences were found not only between the sexes but also between the genders. Kempf et al. (1997, p. 446) reported that masculine schematics[42] and androgynous individuals showed significantly higher general information processing confidence than feminine schematics and undifferentiated individuals. As Kempf and her colleagues also found this pattern in male and female subjects they were interested in determining the relative strength of these two effects. Interestingly, gender explained more variance of information processing confidence than sex. The question now inherent is if these observed sex differences are indeed sex differences or not rather gender differences. As a large proportion of the population still exhibits stereotypical attitudes and personality traits – i.e. their gender is equal to their sex – it is possible that actual *gender* differences also lead to discrepancies which are then observable between the *sexes*.

Conway (2000, p. 693) found that higher masculinity led to lower complexity in representations of emotional awareness which might be due to a less complex information processing. Greater emotional awareness includes the ability to identify numerous specific emotional reactions with oneself and other people in different situations. This would stereotypically be rated a feminine quality. Conway's (2000) findings suggest that gender could have some relevance for determining the degree of elaborateness of representations and brain networks.

At least the type of information recalled (and processed) is influenced by gender, as it was shown in a study by Renn and Calvert (1993, p. 457) where undifferentiated and androgynous individuals were found to recall significantly more counter-stereotypical information than their masculine or feminine counterparts.

---

[42] The term *masculine schematics* is used in the meaning of Self-Schema Theory (i.e. both masculine and feminine individuals with a masculine gender).

In the mentioned small scale study Hogg and Garrow (2003) related the manner of processing of advertisements to gender (measured by the BSRI). Results indicated a gender influence on the *threshold* that needed be reached in order for individuals to engage in detailed information processing. While this threshold was rather low for feminine individuals who then more often engaged in imaginative processing of the shown advertisement, it was higher for masculine individuals. However, masculine males engaged in more elaborative processing when the questions were closely related to the car shown in the advertisement – a subject which obviously aroused their interest so that they were processing the given information in more detail. This suggests that the influence of a gendered product can be substantial. Androgynous subjects showed information processing strategies similar to those of feminine subjects whereas undifferentiated individuals offered little opinion on the topic. Hogg and Garrow (2003, p. 170) concluded that masculine and feminine individuals did not differ much in their elaborative processing of information but rather in the threshold that needed to be reached to motivate them to engage in more intensive processing. They also suggested that brain organization was different in masculine individuals as compared to feminine individuals: feminine subjects established more subcategories while male individuals used a broader category definition. The results obtained reflected partly the contentions of the selectivity model, only the male-female distinction was changed into a masculine-feminine one.

Before drawing conclusions of whether it is the male-female or the masculinity-femininity distinction which is ultimately responsible for information processing differences, the explanations for these given in the literature need to be examined.

4.5 Explaining Processing Differences

If, as proposed by Meyers-Levy (1989), information processing differences are responsible for general sex differences, an explanation of how information processing strategies are developed and why this is seemingly done differently by males and females would also help explaining sex differences. Some attempts to do so can be found in the literature. None of them is totally satisfying, though.

The explanation given by Darley and Smith (1995, p. 52-53) is representative for those given in a number of studies. Darley and Smith (1995) argue that females consider both subjective and objective claims because they use more comprehensive processing strategies. While this relationship is certainly very plausible it is not very helpful for actually explaining the *origin* of processing differences as the latter is essentially just another difference. This does not foster understanding male and female processing differences.

4.5.1 Sociology or Biology?

A better attempt to explain sex differences is undertaken by Meyers-Levy (1988) and her colleagues (Meyers-Levy & Sternthal, 1991). As already mentioned, they argue that different information processing strategies can be attributed to differences in agentic or communal orientation of individuals. This seems reasonable, but still has to be criticized in that they undissolvably connect being male with agentic orientation and being female with communal orientation. Furthermore, this is questionable when considering that Meyers-Levy's herself stated that "the ontogeny of such differences can be traced back to the different socialization treatment afforded the sexes" (Meyers-Levy, 1989, p. 236). Other researchers also questioned the stability of socialization differences between the genders (e.g. Darley & Smith, 1995, p. 55).

Putrevu (2001) investigated a broad array of causes in both biological and sociological fields. The reasoning for a biological explanation is supported by the fact that some of the sex differences which the selectivity hypothesis tries to explain occur already early in life. Factors suggested in this context are hormonal differences and brain lateralization theory, namely the differential use of the right (spatial perception) and the left brain hemisphere (verbal abilities) by males and females (see Meyers-Levy, 1994, for a thorough analysis of sex differences in cortical organization). Also it was discovered that girls' brain development occured faster than boys'. Recent evidence also pointed to somewhat different forms of cerebral organization of the language function (Maccoby, 1998, p. 116). However, Putrevu (2001) concludes that "biology tells only part of the story" (p. 3). A sociological explanation is thus called for as well.

It was referred to evolution theory and evolutionary psychology previously in this book which provide an extensive framework for explaining certain sex differences.[43] Sex differences in information processing have so far only been touched in the evolutionary psychology literature and no specific reason for information processing differences has been given.

People's minds were shaped during the hunter-gatherer era in Pleistocene (Colarelli & Dettmann, 2003, p. 841). It seems plausible to propose that mechanisms that were inscribed in human brains such a long time ago are particularly difficult to change. Although this would apply to all psychological mechanisms, Collarelli & Dettmann (2003, p. 841) state that changes in mental mechanisms occur more slowly than changes of culture. In 1979 Symons predicted that we would find sex differences in the brain of every mammal, including human beings (Symons, 1979). Up to now there was no counter-evidence for his prediction (Mealey, 2000, p. 75). However, it could also be that "constraints imposed by the different functions of the two sexes in reproduction become less pervasive as cultures move away from a hunter-gatherer form of socioeconomic life" (Maccoby, 1998, p. 2). So far evolutionary psychology has mostly forgotten to link psychological mechanisms in behavior to brain structure and information processing. The only thing that research can indicate is that differences in information processing might be particularly unresponsive to social change.

Focusing again on social and psychological theory, the most thorough explanations in this field are given by Silverman (1970) and Hall (1978): Silverman traces processing differences back to different attentional styles in men and women. Hall further suggests that these differences have come from a long history of sex imbalance in society, where the less powerful group (women) developed a need to predict the behavior of the more powerful group (men). Therefore women learned to read even very subtle cues and paid attention to a wider variety of information. This is consistent with Meyers-Levy's theorizing of processing strategies being the result of different role orientations but goes that necessary step further and explains where these different orientations might actually come from.

---

[43] See section 1.2.2 "Where Do Sex Differences Come From?".

The conclusion inherent in this theory is that attentional styles, and thus information processing strategies, can be subject to change when the power disparity between the sexes is weakening.[44] The suggestion that these differences in information processing are not directly related to biological sex, but rather based on social circumstances and personality constructs, such as agency and communion, is supported. Although most researchers have not made the step of disentangling maleness and agency or femaleness and communion yet, there is no convincing evidence or logical reason available that males indeed need to be agentic and females have to be communal (e.g. Deaux, 1984, p. 112-113). On the contrary, evidence has been reported above that agency and communion of individuals, as measured through standard instruments, have been changing over the years (e.g. Twenge, 1997). Provided that the relationships between role orientation and type of processing strategy are indeed true – an assumption which seems to be justified by previous research – psychological gender might play a role in explaining differences in information processing strategies. Surprisingly – given the popularity of the selectivity hypothesis – there are not many studies which have so far examined this relationship.

4.5.2 Conclusion: So What is it?

As argued before, the question of sex or gender – or biology or sociology – is most likely not resolved as a simple either-or question. Instead, the interdependency of the two factors needs to be taken into account. Nobody denies the openness to change of human behavior in general. The question is therefore not whether social change *will* have an impact on information processing strategy, but rather how strong this impact is. The strength of this impact combined with the change-susceptibility of a specific behavior in turn determines the time that people need to adapt their behavior to different social circumstances. Following an evolutionary perspective this change-susceptibility is again a question of how necessary this change is for the human being's survival – considering not only survival in life but also "social survival".

Hogg and Garrow (2003) presented a study showing that gender can influence information processing strategy. However, this study was done with a small sample and is – so far – not supported by following research. It is thus not so much of a

---

[44] It should be remembered that also approaches more closely linked to biology, such as evolutionary psychology, do not deny the openness to change of psychological mechanisms and behavioral characteristics.

proof of existing gender differences but rather an encouragement for previous research in this field.

On the other hand, there is a large amount of studies available which document male-female differences in processing. The publication dates of these studies range from 1979 to 1997, so differences seem to have been prevalent over the last twenty years roughly. Also there was no reference found to studies with *opposed* results, namely studies finding *no* information processing difference between men and women. Plausible sociological explanations, such as those by Silverman (1970) and Hall (1978), refer to mechanisms that have been present in human society for long. On the biological side evidence for actual brain differences between men and women (e.g. Symons, 1979) also speaks against a gender influence.

When comparing research question two with research question one (advertising effectiveness effects), it must be noticed that advertising has a relatively short history in human society compared to the time from which on people have been using information processing strategies. Additionally, information processing is directly linked to the physical brain and thus at least partly a "biological construct" whereas personality traits and attitudes are psychological constructs. In conclusion, it might be plausible that social changes lead to changes in people's gender which then affects their advertising perception but it is less likely that the same social changes and gender changes also affect the preferred information processing strategy in the same way. The strength of gender effects is very likely to be weaker and its implementation is supposed to need more time. The expected results are framed in specific hypotheses, reported in the next section.

4.6 Hypotheses: Part Two

The objective covered by the second research question is to investigate whether masculine and feminine men tend to use different information processing strategies. A case was made in the last section for why it is deemed rather implausible that masculine and feminine individuals differ in the choice of their information processing strategies.[45] It is believed that gender does not influence the strategy chosen. This is further on referred to as a **direct gender effect** – where gender itself is responsible for whether a heuristic or a detailed processing strategy is employed. Hypothesis 4 examines the separate effects of masculinity and femininity and is formulated as follows:

H4:   Masculinity and femininity will have no influence on the choice of the
*   information processing strategy.*

To be able to investigate the usefulness of the Bem classification into gender groups, hypothesis 4 was reformulated to apply to gender groups, which is expressed in hypothesis 5:

H5:   Gender group members do not choose different information
*   processing strategies.*

But these were only the direct effects of gender. It is possible that gender has an **indirect effect** on information processing strategy because it evokes a feeling of congruity or incongruity – specifically a masculine personality seeing a feminine role which does not fit his expectations. It was suggested that incongruence between the consumer's gender and the role portrayed in the ad will lead to enhanced information processing and leads to the following hypotheses:

H6a: Masculine males will process ads with a feminine role more
*   extensively than ads with a masculine role.*

Again, the question is whether the same effect can be expected the other way round for feminine individuals. For the same reasons specified above in the advertising effectiveness chapter the answer is likely to be no. As feminine men are

---

[45] See section 5.5 "Explaining processing differences" for detailed references.

characterized by a greater behavioral bandwidth, they might not realize such an incongruent situation as strongly as will masculine men. Also they are used to traditional role portrayals and might not perceive them as unusual in any way. Thus such an effect is not expected for feminine men (H6b).

H6b: Feminine males will not process ads with a masculine role more extensively than ads with a feminine role.

The next chapter describes the method used for investigating the stated hypotheses. For this purpose an experiment was conducted. The experimental procedure, sampling issues, and measurement scales are outlined before the results and answers to the hypotheses are reported in Chapter 7.

5   Method

In this chapter the method for conducting the empirical research is outlined briefly in five parts: sample selection, stimuli development, operationalization of variables, pretesting, and the experimental setup.

5.1 Sample Selection

The sample consisted of male respondents only. Students were used as respondents and convenience sampling was the procedure used in choosing individual interviewees. Students were selected for the following reasons:

- A narrow age bracket helps to control effects of other personal variables that are not under consideration (Orth & Holancova, 2004, p. 81).
- Studies showed that individuals with non-stereotypical gender identities are particularly rare among people aged 40 and over (Alreck et al., 1982). Through the use of a younger sample the probability of obtaining an even distribution of gender groups was enhanced.

In their study, Gentry & Haley (1984, p. 261) reported an even distribution of gender groups and an approximately equal proportion of males and females within these groups. Since the results of Alreck et al. in 1982 change in attitudes and gender identities might have continued. In a study in a German culture context the proportion of androgynous men in the sample was around 40 % and cross-sex typing was more frequent among men than among women (Schneider-Dueker & Köhler, 1988). Thus there is reason to expect a balanced gender distribution within the sample.

The use of a males-only sample, and specifically a male student sample, does not satisfy contentions in the literature that the sample should be heterogeneous (Kempf et al., 1997, p. 448) to obtain results which can be generalized. But it has been shown before that gender, gender roles, and gender role attitudes are influenced by a large number of factors. The relatively homogenous sample in this study helps keeping such additional influencing factors (e.g. age, educational level) to a minimum and thus allows exclusive concentration on gender differences between subjects which is regarded as an advantage which is more important than sample heterogeneity.

Regarding sample size, the tradeoff between the quality of the research and the cost and time of conducting the study had to be weighed. A study by Kempf et al.

(1997) consisted only of four gender groups of approximately 10 people each. However, a sample of this size was deemed too small to obtain valid results especially as the experimental conditions (four different stimuli) had to be taken into account when determining sample size. Jaffe (1991) presented 16 different types of advertisements in four blocks to in total 200 women – a number which could serve as a baseline also for this study, as the research method and objectives are similar. Because of the four different treatments in this study a sample size of 320 individuals (80 in each experimental condition) was considered appropriate.

5.2 Developing the Stimulus Material

For testing responses to advertising, two different role portrayals had to be developed, a modern and a traditional – a feminine and a masculine – role. Some decisions had to be made in this context. First, the components of the ad needed to be selected: the person portrayed, the product advertised, and the background setting. The ad then needed to be composed. At last the advertisement text aimed at testing information processing had to be developed and integrated.

The stimulus consisted of a print ad featuring a male person presenting a product. Print ads were chosen because "the visual media – especially magazine advertisements – exert a form of cultural leadership in defining masculinity and femininity because of their ability to promote/communicate consensual images" (McCracken, 1993). Visual media is particularly effective in communicating gender stereotypes as people's responses to pictures lesser susceptive to cognitive control when compared to words. Images provoke less psychological resistance than text and people approach pictures with more security and trust compared to words (cf. Kroeber-Riel & Weinberg, 1999, p. 241). This would of course also be true for television ads, however, the effort associated with developing, pre-testing, and actually using a television ad led to preference for the print format.

5.2.1 Portraying Roles (Model & Background)

Two different pictures needed to be developed reflecting a feminine and a masculine role. Previous research provided some directions on how this could be achieved. Criteria for evaluating the degree of stereotyping in advertising were already introduced in a previous chapter (e.g. McArthur & Resko, 1975).[46] This scheme was useful for finding factors to manipulate the perceived masculinity and

---

[46] See section 3.1.2 "Studying Role Portrayals".

femininity of an ad. This is shown in Table 12. The table numbers the factors (and their attributes) identified by McArthur and Resko (1975) and following researchers and analyzes whether they can be used as manipulating factors in the present study and why or why not, respectively. Some criteria was not suitable for the present study because of the type of media used (Print). Others were excluded because they did not correspond to the previously set requirements. Criteria useful for the present study are highlighted in grey.

Criterium	Attributes	Used	Why?/Why not?
Central figure	Male Female	NO	Always male
Mode of Presentation	Voice-over (disembodied) Visual/silence, visual/voice, visual/music	NO	Visual presentation only in print ads
Credibility basis	User Authority, others	NO	Would disturb similarity of the ads
Role	Dependent (parent, spouse, partner, gender object, home maker) Professional Interviewer/narrator, other	YES	Dependent (parent, spouse) vs. professional
Location	Home Occupation Leisure, unknown	YES	Home vs. professional setting
Age	Young Middle-age Old	NO	Same person for both ads
Type of argument	Factual Opinion, none	NO	Person does not transport any arguments
Reward type	Social approval Self-enhancement Practical Pleasure, other	YES	Slogan
Product type	Body Home Food Auto, sports Other	NO	Same product used in both ads
Background	Mostly female Mostly male Mixed Mostly children None (no other human beings around)	YES	Separate vs. with others (physical of symbolic presence of other people, e.g. via pictures)

Table 12: Variables manipulating the perceived masculinity
and femininity of an ad as used in the present study

Thus the main bolts to turn for manipulating individuals' perception of masculinity and femininity were the following:

- Role (Dependent vs. professional role)
- Location (Home vs. professional setting)
- Background (separate vs. with others)
- Reward type (Social approval vs. self-enhancement)

This is consistent with Vigorito and Curry's (1998) proposal that "for a man to be too concerned with his parental or spousal roles and responsibilities is to be feminized" (p. 139). Also Coughlin and O'Connor (1985, p. 240) suggested to change background and dress to manipulate perceived masculinity and femininity, consequently dress of the person was also adapted to the setting (business vs. home dress).

The two ads still needed to be as similar as possible to ensure that they were comparable. This was obtained by portraying the model in both situations in the same posture with a similar gesture, a similar facial expression and in a similar size. Even though for a modern portrayal a background with other people would have been desirable, the same model was portrayed alone twice for reasons of similarity. Some pictures of children attached to the wall in the modern setting still conveyed an impression of connectedness without jeopardizing the comparability of the two pictures. The reward type was incorporated in the slogan. The slogan thus further enforced the pictured role.

Summing up, the traditional role portrayal (Figure 28a)
- is set in a professional background,
- portrays a person in a professional role
- in business clothes and
- cites a slogan emphasizing self-enhancement.

The modern role portrayal (Figure 28b)
- is set in a home background,
- portrays a person in a dependent role (spouse and/or father)
- wearing casual clothes and
- cites a slogan emphasizing social approval/benefit of others.

Figure 28: Stimulus advertisements

The model itself was male as specified by the research objectives of the study. Additional research on spokespersons in advertising delivered a number of other criteria for the effective use of spokespersons in advertisements. Slinker (1984) identified the following criteria for successfully using a celebrity as a spokesperson: attractiveness, honesty, age-group association, popularity, recognizability, and likeability. When using a non-celebrity product endorser we can safely omit those characteristics which are only applicable to celebrities, namely popularity and recognizability. Thus the model should be attractive, likable, honest, and fit into the age profile of the target group. Thereby attractiveness seems to more important than likeability (Kamins, 1990). The age-group match was obtained by selecting a model of student age (between 19 and 25 roughly). The attractiveness of the model was included as a control variable in the study.

5.2.2 Product

The selected product belongs to the low-involvement category. Jaffe and Berger (1988, p. 263) also chose the low-involvement category because this type of purchase decisions is rarely based on tangible attributes and thus ripe for more emotional imagery-based decisions. As the picture should be the main clue for forming attitudes, a low-involvement category was preferred over a high-involvement category.

It has been shown that some products possess distinct masculine or feminine images while others are neutral (e.g. Aiken, 1963; Allison et al., 1980). Responding

142

to suggestions that results may be different for different product categories (e.g. Jaffe & Berger, 1994, p. 40) – and thus potentially different for masculine as compared to feminine products – it was considered sensible to choose a neutral product for the present study:

- A bias could arise because one gender group might have better knowledge about the product than the other or be more familiar with it (Coughlin & O'Connor, 1985, p. 239). Vitz and Johnston (1965, p. 158) demonstrated that people who were unfamiliar with a product (or product category) based their image rating of a product primarily on the advertised image. Thus familiarity differences in respondents could affect results.
- Identification with a neutral product is supposed to be equally easy for feminine and masculine personalities (regardless of identification with the ad.) As congruence between product-image and self-image enhances liking of the ad (cf. Sirgy, 1982, p. 289), a gendered product might bias the results by favoring one or the other gender group's response.
- If stereotypic masculinity or femininity of the product does not match sex of the model, the latter can influence the gender of the product (Gentry & Haley, 1984, p. 262). This bias is largely avoided by using a neutral product.

In their study Coughlin and O'Connor (1985, p. 239) used a bogus product to reduce bias because of previous exposure to advertisements and/or previous experience with the brand. As it was expected that the sample was not perfectly homogenous in their experience with the product category and/or brand featured this strategy seemed sensible in the context of this study. A fictitious product was thus used and a fictitious brand name and logo was invented.

For choosing gender neutral products, there are different methods. Coughlin and O'Connor (1985, p. 239) recommended a product category with a balanced user ratio between men and women, as a product's gender image is usually associated with which sex is most likely to use it (Allison et al., 1980, p. 608). As well there is research assessing the gendered image of different products. The findings of these studies are summarized in Table 13.

Study	Gentry & Doering, 1977;	Gentry et al., 1978	Kahle & Homer, 1985	Allison et al., 1980
Neutral products identified	Cigarettes, mouthwash, tennis shoes	Cigarettes, jeans, shampoo	Blue jeans, hair dryers	Key ring

Table 13: Gender neutral products as identified in previous studies

Although these results were obtained some time ago, they should still be valid. It is implausible that products have acquired specific masculine or feminine images over the years, as they have rather been shown to become more unisex over the years (e.g. Kahle & Homer, 1985, p. 243). It should be noted, however, that the perception of individual brands within a product category as masculine or feminine might also vary (e.g. Vitz & Johnston, 1965, for cigarette brand images), although brands tend to be stereotyped to a lesser extent than product categories (Gentry & Doering, 1977, p. 426). This influence was eliminated by using a bogus brand, as said above.

Inspired by the mouthwash product (Gentry & Doering, 1977, p. 424) the product used in the present study was toothpaste. Toothpaste was preferred over mouthwash because it was safe to assume that all gender groups are equally familiar with it and use it on a regular basis. It is also a product category which is advertised regularly. Individuals are therefore also familiar with toothpaste advertising. Finally, the product should not totally uninteresting for respondents. It was assumed that students do have some interest in the health of their teeth.

The brand name and logo should be simple and reflect some qualities of the product (cf. Brassington & Pettitt, p. 289). Two slogans, one for each role, had to be developed.

5.3 Measuring the Variables

The main and most critical independent variable to measure is gender itself. Additionally some demographic variables were assessed. The two dependent variables measured in this study are advertising effectiveness and the employed processing strategy.

5.3.1 Gender

Gender was assessed with multiple variables following the multidimensional gender model developed by Spence (1993), which is – as reasoned above – more appropriate than a unidimensional model. It includes:

- gender identity as a global self-assessment measure,
- instrumental and expressive personality traits,
- gender related interests, role behaviors, and attitudes,
- sexual orientation.

5.3.1.1 Global Gender Self-Assessment

Following the conclusions of Hoffman (2001, p. 479) and Spence (1985, 1999) –
each individual develops their own calculus of masculinity and femininity – gender
identity was globally measured by *two* semantic differential scales (as masculinity
and femininity are assumed to form two independent dimensions) ranging from
"masculine" to "not masculine", and "feminine" to "not feminine", respectively.
Scale width was seven points, being concordant with the length of the BSRI scales
(Bem, 1974, p. 158; Schneider-Dueker & Kohler, 1988, p. 257). Comparing global
scores with those obtained by standardized instruments, such as the BSRI, might
also provide some indications on the ability of the BSRI to adequately cover
masculine and feminine personality traits in the given cultural and temporal
context.

5.3.1.2 Instrumental and Expressive Personality Traits

Personality traits were assessed using a German version of the Bem Sex Role
Inventory (BSRI; Schneider-Dueker & Kohler, 1988). Respondents rated
themselves on a seven-point scale ranging from "never or almost never true" to
"always or almost always true" – using Bem's own terminology. The BSRI was
chosen despite numerous criticisms for different reasons. Firstly, it is still the most
widely used instrument in psychology and consumer research and was used
throughout the Seventies and Eighties while the PAQ enjoyed only a short period
of popularity during the late 1970s (Stern, 1988, p. 88-91). Secondly, the results of
replication studies are far from unanimous and thus fail to indicate a sure deference
of the BSRI. Authors examining the factor structure report particularly differing
results. Therefore it cannot be concluded that the BSRI is an inadequate measure.
However, the factor structure is examined ex-post to provide additional
information when interpreting the results.

Some precautions can also be taken against the remaining two main criticisms
towards the BSRI: claims that the BSRI does not measure masculinity and
femininity per se, but rather instrumental and expressive personality traits (e.g.
Kelly et al, 1978, p. 1576; Ballard-Reisch & Elton, 1992, p. 302); and that
undesirable traits included in particular in the femininity scale of the BSRI might
bias results and favor masculine orientation (e.g. Gill et al, 1987, p. 496). In the
present study the BSRI is used to measure the personality trait dimension of gender
only, a purpose for which the use of the BSRI has never been questioned. As well,
research on the desirability of attributes included in the BSRI would allow for an

ex-post analysis omitting certain variables if they are suspected to bias the results and identify possibly diluting effects of undesirable attributes.

5.3.1.3 Gender Role Attitudes

For measuring dimension three (interests, behaviors, and attitudes) the three-dimensional Male Role Norm Scale (MRNS) by Thompson and Pleck (1988) was selected. It was shown that attitudes towards women were not related to attitudes towards men (Pleck et al., 1993), therefore a scale focusing on male roles was deemed more appropriate – given that the study is aimed at testing males' attitudes. Respondents indicated their degree of agreement to the scale statements on a seven-point rating scale labeled "I do not agree at all" and "I totally agree" – again following the original procedure by Thompson and Pleck (1988). High scores denote traditional attitudes.

As no German version of this scale or another scale assessing a similar construct was identified, the English scale was used in a translated version. To minimize translation effects the scale was translated, retranslated and compared with the original version. The fit was then assessed. The results of the translation were evaluated and improved by two people independently. Scale validity might be lower because of the application in a different cultural context than that of construction but as there is no alternative scale available this disadvantage has to be accepted. The inclusion of an attitude measure is strongly recommended in a multidimensional gender model. The transference of the BSRI into the European context did not negatively affect its validity as shown in the replication study by Schneider-Dueker and Kohler (1988). Hopefully the consequences for sex role attitudes are not so different.

All three scales as used in this study are available in the Appendix at the back of this book.

5.3.1.4 Sexual Orientation

Dimension four, sexual orientation, was omitted from the framework. A question on sexual orientation in a questionnaire might cause considerable resentment from respondents and will quite probably be only seldom answered. Additionally, the percentage of men showing homosexual preferences in the Austrian population is not high enough. It can thus be expected that only an irrelevant number of respondents will fall into this group (around 5-10%).[47] Besides, although Spence (1993) includes the variable in her gender concept, it is not clear what implications homo- or heterosexuality will have.

5.3.2 Demographics

Apart from gender several demographic variables were included in the questionnaires which were shown to be connected to gender in one or the other way. These were age, marital status, and having children.

Respondents were asked directly to state their age. In a student sample a large age range cannot be expected, it was thus not deemed sensible to form groups. Educational level – also frequently mentioned as influencing sex roles; e.g. Zuo, 1997, p. 804) – was omitted because of the homogeneity of respondents on this subjects. Marital status was assessed with three checkboxes "single", "living with a partner", and "married". Fatherhood was assessed with two boxes to check for "yes" (I have children) and "no" (I do not have children), as no great variation in the number of children was expected among students and a second or third child was not supposed to result in a considerable additional personality change as compared to the first child.

5.3.3 Advertising Effectiveness

Advertising effectiveness – i.e. the consumer's response to the ad – was assessed using an attitudinal measure on the one hand and a purchase intent measure on the other hand. The reason for including purchase intent is that every ad should ultimately lead to a purchase. Additionally, the results based on attitudinal response may be different from those based on purchase intent, as the connection between a positive attitude and an effectuated purchase is not deterministic.[48]

5.3.3.1 Attitude Towards the Ad

Attitude towards the ad is mostly assessed with the help of Semantic Differential scales (e.g. Jaffe & Berger, 1994). The scale for the present study was adapted from scales used in previous research assessing advertising responses in a gender context.

Prakash (1992) and Leigh et al. (1987) used the same items with a different wording: good/bad, like/dislike, interesting/uninteresting, irritating/not irritating.

---

[47] Source: Männergesundheitsbericht Wien 1999, retrieved June 14th, 2004, from the Webpage of the City of Vienna (www.wien.gv.at).
[48] See section 3.2.1 "Measuring Advertising Effectiveness".

Leigh et al. (1987) added a "very" in front of each adjective. Gentry and Haley (1984) additionally used appealing/unappealing and progressive/regressive and substituted uninteresting by boring.

This study measured attitude towards the ad with a seven-point semantic differential scale using the four items employed by Prakash (1992, p. 47). These items were already used successfully in previous research (e.g. Gardner, 1985; Mitchell, 1986).

Additionally, a control item was introduced to confirm that the role portrayed was indeed perceived as modern or traditional respectively (semantic differential with labels modern/traditional). Scale scores were averaged to obtain an attitude value for each person.

5.3.3.2 Attitude Towards the Product

- Because attitude towards the ad may not result in an equally favorable attitude towards the product, product attitude was examined separately. A three-item semantic differential scale was used (Whittler, 1991).

A translated version of the items was also used before (Ebster & Reisinger, 2005) and good results for internal consistency were obtained. Conforming to the other measures, scale length was seven points.

5.3.3.3 Purchase Intent

Even a favorable product attitude might not lead to the ultimate goal of advertising – getting the consumer to purchase the product. Therefore purchase intent was included as a third measure of advertising effectiveness. It is also often assessed using semantic differential scales (e.g. Coughlin & O'Connor, 1985; Jaffe, 1990; 1991). Here a multi-item semantic differential was used (Till & Busler, 2000). A translated version of this scale had also achieved good results (Ebster & Reisinger, 2005).

Although the original scale by Till and Busler (2000) was nine points in length, to be internally consistent with the measures used, only a seven-point version was used here.

All scales use for measuring the dependent variables are summarized in Table 15 (all scales were translated into German for the execution of the study). The two control variables are also summarized here (Table 16).

Variables	Original Scale	Items	Measure
Attitude Towards the Ad	Prakash (1992) α = 0,82	good – bad like – dislike interesting – uninteresting irritating – not irritating	7-point semantic differential
Attitude Towards the Product	Whittler (1991) α = 0,88 bis 0,91	good – bad satisfactory – unsatisfactory low quality – high quality	7-point semantic differential
Purchase Intent	Till & Busler (2000) α = 0,95	unlikely – likely definitely would not – definitely would improbable – probable	7-point semantic differential

Table 15: Dependent Variable: Advertising Effectiveness

	Variables	Measure
Control Variable	**Model Attractivity**	7-point rating scale
Manipulation Check	**Role Traditionality**	7-point rating scale

Table 16: Control Variable and Manipulation Check

5.3.4 Information Processing Strategy

Differences in information processing were tested building on the procedures used by Meyers-Levy and her colleagues (see especially Meyers-Levy & Maheswaran, 1991, p. 66). As explained above, the stimuli provoking advertising response were presented in form of the message picture, which left message text for use as information processing stimulus. This split is reasonable, because text is more likely to be processed consciously contrary to pictures which are often processed unconsciously (see Kroeber-Riel & Weinberg, 1999, for a list of references). Text is thus better suited for tasks which require some degree of cognitive action. It is first explained how information processing strategies will be measured, then the procedure for developing the text is outlined. This was done with a pre-survey the results of which are presented at the end of this section.

5.3.4.1 Measuring Information Processing Strategies

The two different texts used to manipulate information processing consisted of a number of adjectives describing the product. A short paragraph of advertising text was built around these adjectives to give them a context. The words were obtained by conducting a pre-survey. Students were asked for terms describing toothpaste. Eight adjectives were selected based on their frequency of mentioning, because the most often mentioned adjectives were supposed to best represent people's toothpaste product scheme.

The two texts differed in their internal congruency. For the first text exclusively adjectives found through the pre-survey were included (congruent condition). The second text contained six congruent ones and two which are not usually associated with toothpaste – words which did not appear in the pre-survey (incongruent condition). Thus the second text was not consistent with individuals' general schema of toothpaste (cf. Meyers-Levy & Tybout, 1989). Incongruent items were identified via several brainstorming sessions and then selected by the researchers. In the text, the incongruent cues should be neither at the first nor at the last position to avoid primacy or recency effects (Meyers-Levy & Sternthal, 1991, p. 90). Two tasks were then carried out by the respondents which allowed conclusions on their use of processing strategy.

- First, unaided recall of the adjectives stated was measured. After seeing the ad respondents were asked intermittent questions – they filled in the gender questionnaire – before they were administered the recall task. Subjects had to write down as many of the stated adjectives as they remembered. The number of correctly remembered adjectives was assessed in total, as well as separately for congruent and incongruent items in the incongruent condition. Thereby, the following relation holds: the higher the number of correctly recalled words, the better and more detailed the given information has been processed.

- Second, aided recall – or recognition – of the items contained in the product description was tested. Respondents were provided with a list of items, both ones that had been included in the ad and others that had not been included in the ad, and were then asked to cross those items that had been contained in the ad – according to their memory. There were shown the double amount of items contained in the ad, that is sixteen congruent, or twelve congruent and four incongruent ones, respectively. Hit rates and false alarm rates were then calculated for both congruent and incongruent items and in total. High hit rates and low false alarm rates indicate detailed processing.[49]

---

[49] In other studies, Meyers-Levy and her colleages (Meyers-Levy & Sternthal, 1991) also asked respondents to judge the brand's similarity to an existing toothpaste brand. Naturally this was the market leader or at least some other brand most of the subjects consider prototypical for the product category. Thereby, for the incongruent cue condition a high similarity value indicates heuristic processing whereas a low similarity value indicates detailed processing as the two incongruent items were hypothesized to influence detailed processors more than heuristic processors. However, it was decided not to use this third measure in this study for two main reasons: First, not all three measures can be applied at the same time as they may influence each other. Second, the difficulties associated with finding an existing toothpaste brand which truly represents the prototypical product in a differentiated market might impede reasonable results rightaway.

The results of these procedures were then related to the gender variables to see whether gender had any influence on information processing strategy.

5.3.4.2 Generating Text Messages

In a pre-survey 84 students at the Fachhochschule Eisenstadt, Austria, were asked to fill in a short written questionnaire asking for their associations about toothpaste. This procedure was already used in previous research to generate attributes which are important for describing a product (Dolnicar & Heindler, 2004). The Fachhochschule Eisenstadt was selected as to not question students twice, as students from Viennese universities were be used in the actual study. Out of the 84 submitted questionnaire, 82 were usable (98 %), two had to be eliminated because data was missing. 43 students were male, 39 female, resulting in a quite balanced sex ratio of 52 % and 48 %, respectively. Students also indicated their age; the accordant data is reported in Table 17.

Age	Men	Women	Total
Mean	22.2	20.6	21.5
Median	22	21	21
Stand. Deviation	2.6	2.0	2.4

Table 17: Age means, medians, and standard deviations for the pre-survey sample

In total 447 associations were made – 5.45 per person – in 171 different wordings which means that each association occurred on average 2.6 times on the questionnaires. In reality, the frequency of mentioning differed greatly. The associations were entered into the computer, at first without any selection, grouping only those with exactly the same wording. Mentioned brand names and advertising slogans were eliminated because they could not be used for the study at hand. After that, similar associations were summarized into groups by two independent researchers. Results were then compared and dissents discussed. A table with 55 semantic categories was obtained, the number of associations in each group was counted, and the categories sorted according to their absolute frequencies of mentioning. 20 associations could not be assigned to any group. The frequencies are shown in Figure 29.

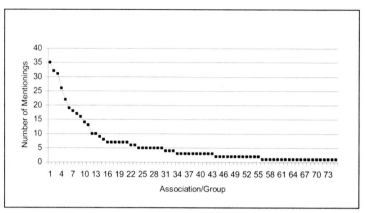

Figure 29: Number of mentionings of the grouped associations

The eight most frequently mentioned associations were selected for the study. They are listed in Table 18. The expression highlighted bold is the wording which was used in the advertising text.

No. of Mentionings	Category Name	Individual Associations
35	White	**White teeth,** tooth whitener, teeth discolorings, bleaching agent
32	Clean	**Cleanliness,** detergent, clean, neat, clean teeth, brush
31	Fresh	Fresh, **fresh feeling,** refreshing
26	Mint	**Mint,** peppermint
18	Healthy	Healthy, health, **healthy teeth,** good for your teeth
17	Tasty	Tasty, savory, **tastes good,** does not taste good, flavorsome, taste, delicious, tasteful
14	Caries	**Protects you from caries,** cariess
10	Gums	**Healthy gums,** gums, stengthens your gums, parodonthosis

Table 18: Selected associations and wording for advertising text
(associations were translated into English when writing this book)

The choice of exactly eight associations is based on the practice in previous studies (Meyers-Levy & Maheswaran, 1991, p. 65-66). As now both construction of the stimulus as well as the measurement of all variables have been explained, the last section of this chapter will describe the specific experimental procedure.

5.4 Testing Procedure

Respondents were approached between November, 9th, 2004 and November, 24th, 2004 at different universities in Vienna to achieve variety in study programs and interests. Students were informed that the research was carried out for a master's thesis which investigated the effectiveness of different advertisements. The study was carried out using computer-assisted interviewing technique. The software used was MediaLab by Empirisoft, an experimental research program. The software was easy to use and guided the respondents independently through the process. The procedure was started by the researcher who assigned the student to one of the four experimental conditions as each student saw only one of the four developed advertisements. The researcher thereby followed a list of random numbers between one and four to ensure randomization of the experiment. Respondents were instructed how to use the computer, they were told to have a good look at the advertisement and then carried out the procedure by themselves with the interviewer present in case any questions would arise. People were encouraged to ask in case of unclarity. The sequence of tasks was as follows:

1. Greeting and introduction
2. Exposure to the stimulus material for a predetermined period of time (20 sec.).
3. Control variable and manipulation check.
4. Measure of advertising effectiveness. Here the scales as well as the items within the scales were randomly ordered by the computer.
5. Assessing gender (attitude measure, BSRI, global measure). This served as a break between exposure to the ad and answering the questions relating to information processing. The individual items of the scales were rotated internally by the computer. Also, the sequence of the MRNS and the BSRI was individually selected by the computer. The global measure was always the third scale to not sensitize respondents for the underlying dimensions (masculinity/femininity) of the first two scales.
6. Measure of information processing strategy. Here the recall task is set before the recognition task.
7. Demographics.
8. Closing and Thank You.

Respondents always saw an instruction screen given them information on the next task when the task before was over. Participants also had the possibility to leave their email to receive a summary of the results once the research has been completed.

The duration of one interview lay between 10 and 20 minutes. Figure 30 depicts the experiment in a storyboard fashion; Figure 31 summarizes the four different experimental conditions: The two role portrayals and the two text conditions (congruent and incongruent) were combined into a 2x2 factorial design, resulting in total in four different conditions. The chosen experimental design was an after-only design and the testing was done in a laboratory setting.

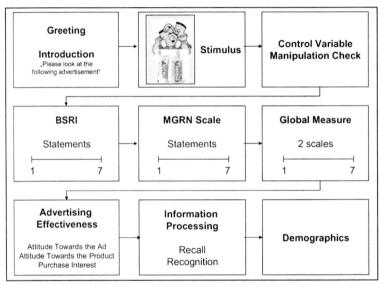

Figure 30: Storyboard: Procedure of the experiment

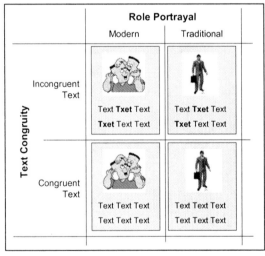

Figure 31: Four conditions of the experiment

5.5 Manipulation Check

A manipulation check was conducted to ensure that respondents perceived the two different role portrayals as modern or traditional, respectively. On a seven point scale (1 = traditional; 7 = modern), respondents gave the office setting a mean rating of 3.0 (s = 1.7), thus positioning it on the traditional side of the scale. The kitchen setting received a mean rating of 4.4 (s = 1.9) which assigned it to the modern end of the scale. With 160 respondents seeing each setting the t-test for the difference in means for independent samples indicated a significant difference in the perception of these two roles (p < 0.001). The criteria used in evaluating and designing role portrayals in the media thus proved to be valid.

To further validate the choice of the model itself his attractiveness was also evaluated. As this is also a check of the advertisement design the results are reported in this section, although it is explicitly noted that checking for model attractiveness is not a check of experimental manipulation. On a seven point scale the model was rated adequately attractive receiving a mean rating of 3.6. This not particularly high value is explained as such: men might be generally cautious when rating the attractiveness of other men, possibly because they generally do not assign too much importance to physical attractiveness for men or the rating is based on a subconscious fear to appear homosexual. A survey conducted among women (n = 17, same scale) to substantiate this speculation resulted in a better attractiveness rating (4.2, p < 0.1).

The model was rated significantly more attractive in the kitchen setting (3.9) as compared to the office setting (3.3; p < 0.001). No differences in attractiveness rating could be observed between gender groups (p = 0.393) and correlations between the different gender measures and rated model attractiveness were found to be non-significant. Summing up, it is concluded that the model chosen was adequate for the purpose of this study. Masculinity and femininity of respondents did not impact the perceived attractiveness of the model.

6 Results

6.1 Scale Check, Responses, and Interdependency

As most scales consisted of different dimensions the structure of these scales was examined using confirmatory factor analysis (Principal-components method, if more than one factor was obtained the initial solution was rotated using Varimax-rotation). Subject to analysis were the BSRI, the MRNS, and the three dimensions measuring advertising effectiveness. Empirical scores for the individual items are reported. Correlations between gender dimensions are examined as well to gain a more detailed understanding of the construct.

6.1.1 The Bem Sex Role Inventory[50]

The factor structure of the inventory is examined first, then the empirical results from this study are reported and a few results are highlighted.

6.1.1.1 *Factor Structure*

The two dimensions of the BSRI were examined both separately as well as all items together. The separate analysis of the BSRI femininity scale delivered a five-factor solution explaining 52 % of the variance in variables. For the masculinity scale a five-factor solution was generated as well which explained 57 % of the variance. For both scales factor loadings are not particularly high but satisfactory (ranging between 0.34 and 0.86 for the femininity scale and 0.39 and 0.80 for the masculinity scale). The two solutions are presented in Table 19.

---

[50] The German and the English version of the BSRI use slightly different statements. Because the German version was used in this study, the statements had to be retranslated for use in the English text..

Factor	Femininity	Masculinity
1	self-sacrificing, eager to sooth hurt feelings, sensitive, delicate, affectionate, passionate, romantic, sensual	ambitious, determined, acts as a leader, consequential, competitive, persistent
2	cheerful, happy	Assertive, defends own beliefs, has leadership abilities, athletic, authoritative, self-reliant
3	dependent, yielding, playful, soft-harted	intelligent, objective, astute, willing to take a stand
4	pay attention to my appearance, modest, flatterable, like security, seductive	fearless, willing to take risks, brave
5	do not use harsh language	criticize without unease

Table 19: Factors generated in individual analysis of the BSRI masculinity and femininity scale

The generated factors are well interpretable and the items go well together from a content perspective. However, these results jeopardize the assumption that the BSRI masculinity and femininity scales represent two independent personality dimensions. The most important purpose of this factor analysis was to verify the distinction between masculine and feminine items. Therefore a third analysis was undertaken considering masculine and feminine characteristics at the same time. Unrestricted, this analysis brought a ten-factor solution where some factors covered only two variables (58 % variance explained; α = 0.849). However, most factors consisted of either masculine or feminine items (3 masculine factors with 15 items, three feminine factors with 13 items). Running a forced two-factor analysis, masculine and feminine items were divided almost perfectly into two factors. All 20 masculine items loaded higher on factor one (masculinity factor) while 15 of the 20 feminine items loaded higher on factor two (femininity factor). This is consistent with previous results that the masculine items perform better in factor analysis as compared to the feminine items (e.g. Pedhazur & Tetenbaum, 1979, p. 1005). Five feminine items were part of the masculinity factor but two of them showed only very low loadings in general (< 0.3), the other three were: *happy*, *cheerful*, and *pay attention to my appearance*. This can be explained as such: In the age of metrosexuality and a booming male cosmetics industry paying attention to one's experience is not restricted to females (or feminine individuals) anymore. The adjectives *happy* and *cheerful* generally do not fit into the overall framework. In the initial ten-factor solution they were part of the only mixed factor. In the two-factor solution they now belong to the the masculine and not to the feminine factor. *Happy* was not contained in Bem's original (English) version of the BSRI (Bem, 1974, p. 156) either. Although the construction procedure by Schneider-Dueker and Kohler (1988) obviously resulted in the inclusion of this item, its retention in the inventory is questionable. In particular when considering that different measures of well-being (which should be related to happiness) are directly related to *masculinity* (e.g. Aube & Koestner, 1992).

Through the forced two-factor solution the variance explained was reduced to 30 %. Although the evidence still points to the existence of small subcategories in masculinity and femininity factors the analysis confirmed that masculine and feminine items are perceived as two dimensions different *from each other*. Concluding, the reproduced structure of the BSRI was not perfect enough not to warrant any further discussion of the scale which will be done in the Conclusions chapter. Still, the clear separation of masculine and feminine items indicated the existence of a masculine and a feminine dimension so that the BSRI can be used in further analysis.

6.1.1.2 Empirical Results

Table 20 lists the sample means and standard deviations for all 40 items of the BSRI obtained in this study. Minimum and maximum values are highlighted in bold. The top 25 % ($x > 5.6$) and the bottom 25 % ($x \leq 4.8$) items are shaded in light and dark grey, respectively.

It is remarkable that respondents continuously chose high values for all statements (meaning that the statement applies to them more often than not). Least applying to participants is the statement "I am dependent" ($x = 3.8$) – just slightly below the scale midpoint – whereas the statement "I am intelligent" was rated highest ($x = 6.3$). No difference could be found between participants' self-ratings on masculine and feminine items ($p = 0.592$). The highest standard deviation in ratings was found for the item "I am fearless" (mean $= 4.97$; $s = 7.9$) whereas participants were most concordant in their answers to the statement "I defend my own beliefs" ($x = 6.1$; $s = 5.3$).

Feminine Items			Masculine Items		
Statement	Mean	Stand. Dev.	Statement	Mean	Stand. Dev.
I am dependent.	3.82	5.59	I criticize without unease.	4.79	7.65
I am self-sacrificing.	4.69	5.51	I am assertive.	5.18	5.44
I pay attention to my appearance.	6.02	7.51	I am ambitious.	5.64	5.42
I do not use harsh language.	4.31	7.69	I defend my own beliefs.	6.11	5.35
I am eager to sooth hurt feelings.	5.98	7.51	I am self-reliant.	5.31	5.41
I am sensitive.	5.55	5.40	I have leadership abilities.	5.39	5.44
I am delicate.	5.63	7.54	I am fearless.	4.97	7.92
I am cheerful.	5.79	5.39	I act as a leader.	4.83	5.54
I am happy.	5.96	7.54	I am determined.	5.51	5.41
I am affectionate.	5.57	5.39	I am persistent.	5.73	7.55
I am passionate.	5.55	5.41	I am consequential.	5.60	7.56
I like security.	5.25	5.49	I am athletic.	5.20	5.42
I am modest.	4.89	7.65	I am willing to take a stand.	4.77	5.52
I am flatterable.	5.60	7.57	I am intelligent.	6.28	7.45
I am yielding.	4.63	5.49	I am brave.	4.83	5.47
I am sensual.	5.15	5.44	I am willing to take risks.	5.81	7.53
I am playful.	5.63	5.43	I am authoritative.	4.40	5.51
I am soft-hearted.	5.10	5.46	I am objective.	5.78	7.52
I am romantic.	5.48	7.57	I am astute.	5.88	7.48
I am seductive.	4.57	5.50	I am competitive.	5.06	5.52

Table 20: Mean ratings and standard deviations for BSRI items

The non-existing difference between respondents' scoring on masculine and feminine items is surprising at first. As only males were subjects of the study it would have been expected that masculine items received a higher average rating than feminine items. The result is, however, only logical when the results of the factor analysis reported above are considered. As already indicated it might be that the items of the BSRI have already lost their attribution to male or female behavior – for this particular group. Taking a look at the top and bottom items confirms such conclusions: half of the bottom 25 % items are part of the masculinity scale. From the 10 top 25 % items four belong to the femininity scale, while six belong to the masculinity scale. General conclusions on the BSRI structure and results will be drawn in the next Chapter.

6.1.2 The Male Role Norm Scale

Again, first the factor structure is examined, and then results for the individual items are reported. Further correlations between the three dimensions of the role norm scale are calculated and interpreted.

6.1.2.1 Factor Structure

Confirmatory factor analysis of the three dimensions of the role norm scale, both separately for each dimensions and all dimensions together, brought the following results (see Table 21).

Dimension	No. of factors	Eigenvalues	% variance explained	a
Status norm	2	4.12; 1.11	48 % (total)	0.826
Toughness norm	2	2.86; 1.19	51 % (total)	0.733
Anti-femininity norm	1	2.84	41 %	0.739
Gender role attitudes model (MRNS)	4	9.66; 4.60; 1.41; 1.19	65 % (total)	0.887

Table 21: Results of factor analysis for the Male Role Norm Scale

These results mostly replicate the structure found by Thompson and Pleck (1988). In the all-item-solution the status norm is most consistent, only three out of 11 factors do not load on factor 2 (status factor). Four of seven anti-femininity items are combined into one factor; only the eight toughness items are split between all factors. When examining the factors separately, for the anti-femininity norm a one-factor solution was generated as expected, for status and toughness norms two-factor solutions were calculated. Still, only very few items were assigned to the second factors and the loadings were not largely different for the two factors. The reliability measures for the factors are similar to those of Thompson and Pleck (1988). Thus the factor structure of the scale seems to be consistent enough to justify the use of the original factors for further calculations.

6.1.2.2 Empirical Results

Table 22 lists the 26 statements of the Male Role Norm Scale and the attitude ratings of respondents (means, standard deviations). High values thereby signify a high rate of agreement with the statement and thus traditional attitudes.[51] Mean ratings for the three dimensions were: 3.3 for the status norm; 3.3 for the toughness norm; and 2.7 for the anti-femininity norm. The top 25 % (strong agreement, x ≥ 3.6; dark grey) and bottom 25 % (weak agreement, x ≤ 2.6; light grey) are again highlighted as are the maximum and minimum values (bold). The overall average rating was 3.1 (s = 0.6). Men agree most strongly with the statement that "A real men enjoys some danger now and then" (x = 4.7; s = 1.9) while they do not at all bother about the masculinity of hairdressers or gourmet cooks (x = 2.4; s = 1.7).

Scale	Statement	Mean	St.Dev.
Stat1	Success in his work has to be man's central goal in life.	2.67	1.75
Stat2	The best way for a young man to get the respect of other people is to get a job, take it seriously, and do it well.	3.70	1.89
Stat3	A man owes it to his family to work at the best-paying job he can get.	2.60	1.68
Stat4	A man should generally work overtime to make more money whenever he has the chance.	2.47	1.65
Stat5	A man always deserves the respect of his wife and children.	3.11	1.97
Stat6	It is essential for a man to always have the respect and admiration of everyone who knows him.	3.10	1.84
stat7	A man should never back down in the face of trouble.	3.71	2.01
stat8	I always like a man who's totally sure of himself.	4.22	1.81
stat9	A man should always think everything out coolly and logically, and have rational reasons for everything he does.	3.57	1.96
stat10	A man should always try to project an air of confidence even if he doesn't feel confident inside.	3.82	1.89
stat11	A man must stand on his own feet and never depend on other people to help him do things.	3.59	1.92
tough1	When a man is feeling a little pain he should try not to let it show very much.	2.78	1.78
tough2	Nobody respects a man very much who frequently talks about his worries, fears, and problems.	3.75	1.98
tough3	A good motto for a man would be "When to going gets tough, the tough get going".	3.44	1.93
tough4	I think a young man should try to become physically tough, even if he's not big.	3.15	1.93
tough5	Fists are sometimes the only way to get out of a bad situation.	2.51	1.89

Table 22: Mean ratings and standard deviations for the Male Role Norm Scale

---

[51] The ratings for two statements (tough8, antifem6) were reverse scored. Thus, for example, an average value of 3,5 stands as usual for slightly modern attitudes (low score) but means that respondents degree of agreement originally was 4,5 – thus before reverse scoring high ratings meant modern attitudes for these two statements.

tough6	A real man enjoys a bit of danger now and then.	**4.74**	1.91
Tough7	In some kinds of situations a man should be ready to use his fists, even if his wife or his girlfriend would object.	2.75	1.98
tough8	A man should always refuse to get into a fight, even if there seems to be no way to avoid it.	3.50	**2.06**
afem1	It bothers me when a man does something that I consider "feminine".	2.52	**1.65**
afem2	A man whose hobbies are cooking, sewing, and going to the ballet probably wouldn't appeal to me.	2.69	1.94
afem3	It is a bit embarrassing for a man to have a job that is usually filled by a woman.	2.57	1.71
afem4	Unless he was really desperate, I would probably advise a man to keep looking rather than accept a job as a secretary.	3.13	1.90
afem5	If I heard about a man who was a hairdresser and a gourmet cook, I might wonder how masculine he was.	**2.41**	1.75
afem6	I think it's extremely good for a boy to be taught to cook, sew, clean the house, and take care of younger children.	2.98	1.77
afem7	I might find it a little silly or embarrassing if a male friend of mine cried over a sad love scene in a movie.	2.76	1.91

Table 22: Mean ratings and standard deviations for the Male Role Norm Scale (cont.)

Correlations between the three dimensions were examined and found to be substantial (see Table 23). All correlations reported were significant on the 0.01 level. As all three dimensions are supposed to measure traditionality and modernity of men's role attitudes correlations of this size were expected.

	Status Norm	*Toughness Norm*	*Anti-femininity Norm*
Status Norm	1	--	--
Toughness Norm	0.582	1	--
Anti-femininity Norm	0.561	0.557	1

Table 23: Correlations between the dimensions of the Male Role Norm Scale

In this study men rejected traditional role norm attitudes more as compared to previous results (Thompson and Pleck, 1988, p. 34) which could be due either to a different cultural context or a different social and time context or both. In both studies the anti-femininity norm was rejected strongest while status and toughness norm received approximately the same ratings. An ANOVA investigating if men give different answers to the three scales discovered a moderate difference in ratings (x_{status} = 3.3; $x_{toughness}$ = 3.3; $x_{anti-femininity}$ = 2.7; p < 0.1). When comparing two scales at a time it is revealed that this result is exclusively due to differences between anti-femininity and the two other scales. Answers to status norm and toughness norm scale are almost identical (p = 0.990), for status and anti-femininity norm the obtained p-value was < 0.01, for toughness and anti-femininity norm < 0.1. This is not completely consistent with previous results, as in Thompson and Pleck's (1988, p. 32) study all scales received different ratings.

6.1.3 Global Self-assessed Masculinity and Femininity, and Gender Relations

No factor solution can logically be reported for the two global self-assessment measures of masculinity and femininity. The mean femininity value was 4.7 (s = 1.4) and the mean masculinity value was 3 (s = 1.3). Men rated themselves slightly above the scale midpoint for femininity (rather not feminine) and a little more below the scale midpoint for masculinity (rather masculine). Self-assessed masculinity and femininity differ significantly (p < 0.001). The two scales show a significant negative correlation (r = -0.361; p < 0.001).

The question remaining is whether the three gender measures (personality scores, role norm attitudes, and global measure) are related to each other or independent concepts. As stated they do not need to be related to each other and often are not. In the empirical results some relationships have be found. The corresponding correlation coefficients (significant ones only, p < 0.001; n.s. = not significant) are reported in Table 24.

	BSRI masc.	BSRI fem.	Status norm	Toughness norm	Anti-fem. Norm	Global masc.	Global fem.
BSRI masc.	1	--	--	--	--	--	--
BSRI fem.	0.220	1	--	--	--	--	--
Status norm	0.279	n.s.	1	--	--	--	--
Toughness norm	0.230	n.s.	0.582	1	--	--	--
Anti-femininity n.	n.s.	-0.225	0.561	0.557	1	--	--
Global masc.	-0.203	n.s.	-0.113	-0.185	-0.151	1	--
Global fem.	0.187	n.s.	0.275	0.279	0.269	-0.361	1

Table 24: Correlation coefficients for measures of masculinity and femininity

A few comments can be made from above table:

- The high correlation between the three dimensions of the MRNS has already been noticed in the section above.

- There is a positive correlation between the BSRI masculinity and femininity scale, pointing to androgynous tendencies in the data. This in particularly interesting given the mentioned *negative* relation between self-assessed masculinity and femininity.

- There is a negative correlation between the BSRI femininity score and the anti-femininity role norm scale meaning that men with a higher femininity score are more likely to reject anti-feminine attitudes. This result is quite intuitive.

- There is also a positive correlation between the BSRI masculinity score and the status and toughness role norm scales meaning that men with a higher masculinity score are more likely to show traditional attitudes regarding men's status and toughness. This is again intuitive but the important result from this point and the point before is that the gender dimensions of personality characteristics and attitudes are related.

- Self-assessed masculinity and femininity also correlate with role norm attitudes. The negative correlation between masculinity and attitudes signifies that men who classify themselves as masculine have a particular tendency to show traditional role attitudes, whereas men who denote themselves as feminine show less traditional attitudes (positive correlation between self-assessed femininity and role attitudes).

There is a difference between the self-assessment ratings of masculinity and femininity and those prescribed by a standard measure such as the BSRI ($p < 0.001$). This difference is smaller for femininity compared to masculinity. Also, in this study the three gender dimensions were found to be related to some extent which is not demanded in the literature but still intuitive from a common sense perspective.

6.1.4 Clustering Respondents into Gender Groups

Following common practice respondents were then classified into four groups (four "genders") as specified by Spence et al. (1974): androgynous, feminine, masculine, and undifferentiated individuals. A median-split technique was applied to the average scores of respondents on the BSRI masculinity and femininity scales. The corresponding medians were 5.0 for masculinity and 4.85 for femininity. Table 25 shows the classification procedure and the resulting groups (see also Figure 32 below).

Masculinity	Femininity	Classification	Group size	% of sample
> 5.0	> 4.85	androgynous	95	29.7
< 5.0	> 4.85	feminine	64	20.0
> 5.0	< 4.85	masculine	67	20.9
< 5.0	< 4.85	undifferentiated	94	29.4

Table 25: Classification of respondents according to gender (based on BSRI scores)

As a control measure the same procedure was also undertaken using the global self-assessment scores of masculinity and femininity to reflect the sample's individual perspective on their masculinity and femininity (medians were 3.0 for masculinity and 5.0 for femininity; in this case a low number meant high masculinity or femininity, respectively). It has to be noted the BSRI masculinity and self-assessed masculinity were correlated as expected ($r = -0.203$, significant at the 0.01 level), but that the same was not true for BSRI femininity and self-assessed femininity. Table 26 shows the results.

Global Masculinity	Global Femininity	Classification	Group size	% of sample
< 3.0	< 5.0	androgynous	40	12.5
> 3.0	< 5.0	feminine	74	23.1
< 3.0	> 5.0	masculine	194	60.6
> 3.0	> 5.0	undifferentiated	12	3.8

Table 26: Classification of respondents according to gender (based on self-assessment)

Figure 32 compares the two classification approaches. The classification results were very different. Only 83 individuals (26 %) were assigned to the same group by both procedures.

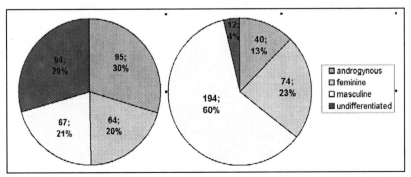

Figure 32: Gender groups compared: BSRI-based (left) and global score-based (right)

It was investigated for both classification approaches whether these four groups differed significantly in the other gender measures. An ANOVA was used to compare the group means of BSRI, MRNS, and global measure results. As most correlations between gender dimensions are significant, some concordance can be expected. Table 27 lists the p-values for gender group differences.

	BSRI classification	*Self-assessment class.*
BSRI masculinity	0.001	0.053
BSRI femininity	0.001	0.097
Status norm attitudes	0.001	0.002
Toughness norm attitudes	0.001	0.001
Anti-femininity norm attitudes	0.009	0.004
Self-assessed masculinity	0.036	0.001
Self-assessed femininity	0.045	0.001

Table 27: Significance of differences in gender measures between gender groups

As can be seen from Table 27, the four gender groups differ significantly in all gender measures at a level of at least 0.01 – no matter what factors are used to construct them. Thereby the BSRI-based classification obtains slightly better results. Following research tradition the BSRI-based classification will also be the main model used in further analyzing the present data. The self-classification grouping has not been used in previous research, but might be useful in examining the current validity of theoretically based scale classifications. However, there is no theoretical reason to believe that self-assessment can influence advertising reaction or information processing styles, while there is – as reported – evidence for differences between BSRI-based gender groups. The fact that the BSRI scores are still able to form valid gender groups despite the not-confirmed factor structure is further encouraging the use of the traditional BSRI item division.

6.1.5 Advertising Effectiveness

Advertising effectiveness was measured using three dimensions (attitude towards the ad, attitude towards the product, purchase intent) which were again surveyed with multiple-item scales. This section examines the factor structure of these scales as well as investigates relations between them.

6.1.5.1 Attitude Towards the Ad

The four statements assessing the attitude towards the ad taken from Prakash (1992) were all but one (irritating – interesting) significantly related with each other on a 0.01-level. The factor analysis resulted in a one-factor solution with all items except for item four (irritating) showing factor loading above 0.8. The factor explained 57 % of the variance in variables, the Cronbach alpha was 0.68. Because item four showed a factor loading of only 0.24, a second analysis was conducted omitting this item. Factor loadings for the other three items remained approximately the same but the three factor solution was now able to explain 75 % of the variance (+32 %) and the reliability statistic increased to 0.83 (+23 %). Average attitude towards to ad was calculated for both the four- and the three-item solution. The average scores proved to be significantly different (p < 0.001). Thus the decision for either of the two possibilities impacts results. Given above statistics the second factor solution should be preferred for conducting further analysis.

6.1.5.2 Attitude Towards the Product

The three statements covering attitudes towards the product taken from Whittler (1991) were all significantly related with correlation coefficients between 0.56 and 0.68 (p < 0.01). The factor analysis resulted in a one-factor solution with factor loadings of 0.84 and above. The factor was able to explain almost 75 % of the variance in variables and reached 0.83 in reliability (Cronbach-alpha). This scale was thus able to adequately cover the attitude construct specified as can be used for further analysis.

6.1.5.3 Purchase Intent

The three items of the purchase intent scale taken from Till and Busler (2000) were highly related. Bivariate correlation coefficients were between 0.77 and 0.89 on a 0.01-level. When the items were submitted to factor analysis, a one-factor solution was obtained explaining 88 % of the variance in variables. The factor loadings ranged from 0.92 to 0.96. The obtained reliability statistic was 0.93. The purchase intent scale represents a particularly homogenous factor whose items can be perfectly combined for further analysis.

6.1.5.4 Interconstruct Relations and Discussion

All 11 items (or 10, respectively, omitting attitude ad-item four) have been submitted again to a factor analysis which confirmed that the three scales represent different dimensions. Both approaches resulted in three-factor solutions as expected with factor loadings above 0.8. The 10-item-solution thereby achieved slightly higher loadings. Also the variance explained by the 10-item-solution was almost 80 % and the Cronbach-alpha reached 0.88 as compared to 72 % explained variance and 0.85 reliability for the 11-item solution.

Although the three scales were shown to be separate dimensions, they should still be related to a certain degree as they are all supposed to measure the construct of advertising effectiveness. This was shown to be the case. The bivariate correlations were all significant on a 0.01-level and lay between 0.465 and 0.521. They were again better for the 10-item-model as compared to the 11-item model.

Concluding, all three scales have proved to be adequate measures of advertising effectiveness. Additionally, from the data reported above all evidence points to omitting item four of the attitude towards ad-scale from the framework and not using it in subsequent analysis. This way advertising effectiveness is captured efficiently.

6.2 Sample Description & Demographics

As the sample consisted of males and students only, there is not much is to be said about sample demographics. Three demographic variables were surveyed. Because of the rather homogenous sample no large effects of these demographics were expected. However, they might indicate some trends concerning the influence of demographics on personality and attitudes, i.e. gender. The correlation of these variables with the individual gender measures was thus calculated. 320 students coming from different universities in Vienna participated in the study (Figure 33).

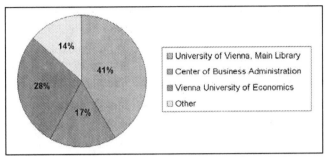

Figure 33: Sample composition by location of questioning

The largest number of participants was approached at the Main Library of the University of Vienna (132 respondents) because a considerable variety in students' subjects was available there. Students were also recruited at the Center of Business Administration of the University of Vienna (54), at the Vienna University of Economics (90), and at other locations, such as students' halls of residence (44).

6.2.1 Age

The respondents were on average 23.8 years old (s = 3.3), the youngest being 19 and the oldest 38. The age distribution is shown in Figure 34.

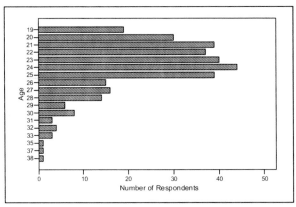

Figure 34: Age distribution of the respondents

As there is some indication in the literature that age can influence gender and sex role attitudes (e.g. Ciabattari, 2001) the data was tested for such effects. Age as well as the gender measures are metric variables, thus the relationship between the two can be assessed via correlation coefficients. Only two relationships proved to be statistically significant: the correlation between age and status norm score was -0.114 ($p < 0.05$) and the correlation between age and anti-femininity norm score was -0.126 ($p < 0.05$). This means that traditional role norm attitudes (specifically status norms and anti-femininity norms) are more likely to be rejected by older men. The degree of agreement or disagreement with such norms may also change with developing age of a person. When using regression analysis age was found to have an small influence on status norm attitudes ($b = -0.04$; $p < 0.05$) and on anti-femininity norm attitudes ($b = -0.04$; $p < 0.05$). This is consistent with the results of the correlation analysis. These results contradict the general age hypothesis which predicts that older men hold more traditional attitudes. However, modern role norm attitudes may only start developing at a certain age together with partner or father responsibilities (cf. Eagly, 1978). Thus the narrow age range in the present study might be responsible for this counter-intuitive result.

Possibly prevalent age differences between the four gender groups was assessed with ANOVA by comparing the age groups means. No significant differences were found ($p = 0.221$ for groups classified according to BSRI scores and $p = 0.611$ for groups classified according to self-assessment scores).

6.2.2 Fathership and Marital Status

As expected, only very few of the respondents had children (2.5 %). It was therefore not feasible to identify trends in this direction. A preliminary analysis showed no significant results for differences in gender measures or between gender groups. Because of the very unequal group sizes the contention that the fathering role makes feminine qualities develop in males could be neither supported nor rejected in this study.

More interesting are the results for marriage status effects on gender. Figure 35 shows the distribution of marriage status in the sample. Because the group of married men was again very small, the categories *living with a partner* and *married* were combined for subsequent analysis. After all, it should be dependent on the status of having a partner or not whether men develop feminine qualities or "appropriate" role norm attitudes and not on the formal act of marriage itself. Thus the sample was split into *men with a partner* (42 %) and *men without a partner* (58 %).

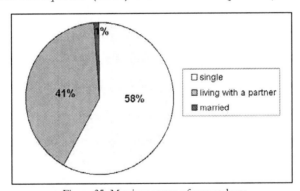

Figure 35: Marriage status of respondents

No significant effects could be observed for gender groups, both BSRI-based and self-assessment-based. But interesting results were obtained for individual gender measures. Differences between men with a partner and men without a partner were found in the following dimensions: BSRI femininity, anti-femininity norm attitudes, and status norm attitudes. Table 28 lists the details. Scale minimum and maximum were 1 (not feminine/not masculine) and 7 (feminine/ masculine).

Dimension	Mean/with partner	Mean/no partner	p-value
BSRI femininity	4,95	4,75	0,003
Status norm attitudes	3,12	3,47	0,006
Anti-femininity norm attitudes	2,46	2,91	0,001

Table 28: Gender differences between men with and without a partner

Thus, men with a partner had more feminine personality characteristics (or were more willing to openly say so). Also they showed more modern status norm and anti-femininity norm attitudes than men without a partner.

In conclusion, the sample was too homogenous to be able to observe significant age effects. Relationships between age and gender do seem occur only with a minimum sample age range which was not reached in the current study. Effects of fathering on gender could not be observed because of the too large homogeneity of the sample. On the other hand, some significant gender differences were found between men depending whether they had an existing relationship. Thereby having a partner leads to greater femininity and more modern role attitudes.

6.3 Men´s Reaction on Male Role Portrayals: Results

This section will focus on answering the first block of hypotheses and investigate the relationship between gender and advertising effectiveness for a male sample.

The overall ratings of the two different advertisements – the modern and the traditional setting – by respondents are shown in Table 29. Low values signify favorable attitudes (range: 1 to 7). The values reported refer to the average scale values of the three advertising effectiveness scales (attitude towards the ad, attitude towards the product, and purchase intent). These three scores will then be used for any subsequent analysis on advertising effectiveness.

Measure	Modern Setting		Traditional Setting		p-value
	Mean	Stand.Dev.	Mean	Stand.Dev.	
Attitude towards the ad	4,99	1,31	5,17	1,32	0,220
Attitude towards the product	4,07	1,09	3,86	1,09	0,087
Purchase intent	4,66	1,52	4,77	1,62	0,538

Table 29: Average means and standard deviations for advertising effectiveness

On average, respondents showed the same attitudes towards both ads. Significant differences between the two role portrayals were *not* observed on an average basis. Respondents rated them slightly on the negative side of the scale midpoint (4). It can only be speculated about the reasons for this: comments made by respondents during the experimental stage allow the conclusion that men do not respond particularly favorably to same-sex models in advertising but instead prefer a female model. However, the purpose of this study is not to study the effects of same-sex versus opposite-sex models but to relate advertising effectiveness to individual gender measures which is now done in the following sections. As defined by the sequence of the hypotheses stated, masculinity and femininity effects will be examined first. The value of gender groups is explaining response differences to advertising is analyzed in part three.

6.3.1 The Impact of Masculinity on Advertising Effectiveness

The impact of masculinity on attitudes and preferences was analyzed using three ways of measurement: first, bivariate correlation coefficients between the gender variables and the advertising effectiveness variables were calculated; second, regression analysis was performed with advertising effectiveness as the dependent variable; and third, respondents were split into groups of high and low masculinity individuals and the group scores compared using t-tests.

The conceptualization of masculinity follows the gender model developed in this book.[52] A masculine personality is therefore characterized by

- a high BSRI masculinity score
- a low global masculinity score
- a high score on the Male Role Norm Scale (traditional attitudes).

As low scores for attitude and purchase intent signify a positive attitude and strong purchase intent, respectively, we would expect the following correlations to occur *for the traditional setting* (Table 30):

	BSRI masc.	Global masc.	MRNS
Attitude towards the ad	–	+	–
Attitude towards the product	–	+	–
Purchase intent	–	+	–

Table 30: Expected relationships between masculinity and advertising effectiveness (traditional setting)

High BRSI masculinity would therefore result in a positive attitude, as would a high self-assessed masculinity and the belief in traditional role attitudes. The effects should be exactly vice-versa for the modern setting, with high BSRI- and high global masculinity, and traditional role norm attitudes leading to a negative attitude.

For the analysis the column MRNS needed to be split into the three corresponding dimensions: status norm, toughness norm, and antifemininity norm. Table 31 displays the observed correlations between advertising effectiveness and masculinity for the traditional role portrayal. Values significant at a 0.01-level are marked **, those significant at a 0.05-level are marked *; n.s. means *not significant*.)

	BSRI masc.	Global masc.	MRNS		
			Status	Toughness	Antifemininity
Attitude towards the ad	n.s.	n.s.	-0.379**	-0.264**	-0.239**
Attitude towards the product	n.s.	n.s.	-0.317**	-0.267**	-0.195*
Purchase intent	n.s.	n.s.	n.s.	-0.164*	n.s.

Table 31: Correlation coefficients masculinity – advertising effectiveness (traditional setting)

---

[52] See section 2.2.5 "Conclusion: Conceptualizing Gender".

For the modern setting all correlation coefficients except one (global masculinity – attitude towards product, 0.180, $p < 0.05$) were not significant. From this perspective it seems that traditional role attitudes are the important factor for determining whether men hold a positive attitude only when using a traditional positioning. The direction of the effect is as expected: men with traditional role attitudes favor the traditional role portrayal.

In step two simple regression models were calculated. The results for the traditional setting are displayed in Table 32 (standardized regression coefficients, marked ** for 0.01- and * for 0.05-level).

	BSRI masc.	Global masc.	MRNS		
			Status	Toughness	Antifemininity
Attitude towards the ad	n.s.	n.s.	-0.379**	-0.264**	-0.239**
Attitude towards the product	n.s.	n.s.	-0.317**	-0.267**	-0.195*
Purchase intent	n.s.	n.s.	n.s.	-0.164*	n.s.

Table 32: Regression models masculinity – advertising effectiveness (traditional setting)

As expected, looking at the regression models does not change the picture. Again role norm attitudes proved to be a good predictor for attitudes towards modern and traditional role portrayals while BSRI and global masculinity scores were not of relevance in this context.[53]

To get further insight into the data, in a third step respondents were split into high masculinity and low masculinity groups using the median split method for all variables (BSRI, global masculinity, and the three dimensions of the role norm scale). T-tests were used to compare high and low masculinity males. The differences *d* between the high and low masculinity groups' advertising effectiveness scores in the traditional setting are reported in Table 33.

---

[53] The non-significant effects of the BSRI and the global measure were examined a little further. The considerations undertaken and results obtained are reported in this footnote in order to preserve the clarity of the main argumentation.

Although the correlation coefficients were not significant at the specified level, they were different in size with the global measure score showing slightly more influence than the BSRI score. These coefficients are positive, meaning that less masculine males have a less favorable attitude. Importantly, this seems to be the case for both (!) settings – are men with different masculinities thus indifferent between modern and traditional role portrayals?

The average correlation for the traditional setting is stronger compared to the modern setting. The advertising effectiveness should thus be still slightly higher for traditional roles/masculine men as compared to modern ads/masculine men. In the modern setting a low self-assessed masculinity thus leads to a more favorable opinion about the product. Again, no significant correlations were observed for BSRI masculinity. These results confirm the direction of the relationship as described above but the fact that significant values were found only for the modern setting challenge the question of whether men are really indifferent between the two positionings.

	BSRI masc.	Global masc.	MRNS		
			Status	Toughness	Antifemininity
Attitude towards the ad	n.s.	n.s.	0.82**	0.68**	0.61**
Attitude towards the product	n.s.	0.47**	0.44**	0.58**	0.86**
Purchase intent	n.s.	n.s.	0.61**	0.36*	n.s.

Table 33: Differences in advertising effectiveness scores for high and low masculinity males (trad. setting)

The effects are as expected: men high in masculinity showed a better attitude towards the traditional role portrayal as compared to men low in masculinity – at least if masculinity is defined via traditional sex role attitudes. Additionally, men who rated themselves high in masculinity showed a better attitude towards the product in the traditional setting.

The results thus provide partial support but also limiting conditions for hypothesis 1. If preference patterns were observed, they followed the predicted direction. Masculine males showed a more favorable attitude towards the traditional role portrayal than males low in masculinity. However, this is the effect of attitudes rather than a personality effect. While the general suggestion of hypothesis 1 is thus supported, the implications of the discovered limitations will be discussed in detail in the Conclusions chapter.

H1:   *High masculinity males will have a more favorable attitude towards the traditional role portrayal as compared to low masculinity males.*   ☑

It must be noted that this relationship was largely true for the two attitudinal measure (attitude towards the ad, attitude towards the product) but not for the behavioral consequence (purchase intent). This discrepancy will also be analyzed in the Conclusions chapter.

6.3.2 The Impact of Femininity on Advertising Effectiveness

The analytical procedure is the same as in the preceding section. First correlation coefficients are reported, then regression models are calculated and finally the sample is split into high and low femininity males and group means are compared. Following the conceptual definition of gender a feminine personality is defined by

- a high BSRI femininity score
- a low global femininity score
- a low score on the Male Role Norm Scale (modern attitudes).

Because the hypothesis was that feminine men do not show a specific preference for the modern role portrayal, respectively that femininity does not considerable impact advertising effectiveness, we would expect the correlation and regression coefficients to be non-significant.

The bivariate correlation coefficients between advertising effectiveness and femininity were all not significant for the modern setting. They were also small in size, ranging from -0.12 to 0.11. On a first glance the hypothesis was supported. In step two regression models were calculated using advertising effectiveness as the dependent variable. In the modern setting none of these models had significant regression coefficients as it was already expected based on the results of the correlation analysis. In a third step the modern setting sample was again split into a high femininity and a low femininity group using a median split just as it was done for the masculinity values. But none of these group comparisons showed a significant difference in attitudes or purchase intent between high and low femininity males.

Given all this evidence, hypothesis 2 is fully supported.

H2: ***Compared to low femininity males, high femininity males will not show a specific preference for the modern portrayal.*** ☑

The caution in applying masculinity results vice-versa to femininity was justified. As the orthogonal model suggest, masculinity and femininity are not simply opposing ends of a continuum. Therefore the effect of the one cannot be assumed to be simply the reverse effect of the other. Masculinity and femininity are different in their implications and therefore have to be considered separately.

6.3.3 The Impact of Gender Groups on Advertising Effectiveness

The relationship between gender group classification and advertising effectiveness was assessed by conducting tests for differences in mean ad evaluation for each gender group separately. Thereby androgynous individuals showed a more positive attitude towards the product in the traditional setting as compared to the modern setting. This is consistent with the predictions made by hypothesis 4d. No effects whatsoever were observed for feminine, masculine, and undifferentiated individuals. These three groups seem to be indifferent between modern and traditional positioning, a result which was predicted only for the androgynous group. The evaluation of hypothesis 3 therefore results in the following picture:

H3a: Masculine males will prefer the traditional over the modern role portrayal. ☒

H3b: Feminine males will prefer the modern over the traditional role portrayal. ☒

H3c: Undifferentiated males will be indifferent between the two role portrayals. ☑

H3d: Androgynous males will slightly prefer the traditional over the modern role portrayal. ☑

On a whole, Hypothesis 3 was not supported. Masculine and feminine males were expected to show the strongest attitude differences compared to androgynous and undifferentiated individuals. But the effects for these two groups were zero. Given this result, it is likely that the observed indifference in undifferentiated males is not due to their being undifferentiated but rather to a general inability of gender groups to explain preferences for different role portrayals. That the expected preference pattern was observed for androgynous individuals does not significantly change the overall picture. H3 is therefore rejected.

H4: Gender group members will differ in their preference for the two portrayals. ☒

Gender group membership (as defined by BSRI scores) does not affect preference of modern or traditional role portrayals in advertising. This can be due to two different factors:

- It might indeed be that men – contrary to women – simply do not care about the type of images portrayed in advertising and that the obtained results reflect a real indifference between the two positionings.
- It might also be the classification itself – criticized for its randomness – which provokes these results.

6.4 Men's Processing of Information: Results

Two tasks were employed in the experiment to measure individuals' information processing strategy: free recall and recognition. For a systematic approach to the results this section is structured similar to that before.

6.4.1 General Results

In this section some general results for the whole sample will be reported. Also the analysis procedure and its pre-steps will be explained shortly.

6.4.1.1 Recall

Comments from respondents during the experiment allow the conclusion that they perceived especially the free recall task as difficult. Instead of entering recalled expressions some people made comments such as "I usually do not remember advertisements". Therefore the recall data had to be cleaned before analysis. In a first step the following absolute frequencies were counted for each respondent:

- total number of expressions recalled and associations made (total recall)[54]
- the total number of correctly recalled expressions from the text (correct recall)
- the number of correctly recalled congruent expressions from the text
- the number of correctly recalled incongruent expressions from the text.

The last two figures were counted for the respondents exposed to the incongruent condition only. Additionally it was assessed whether respondents recalled the brand name and the advertising slogan.[55]

On average respondents wrote down 2 expressions (text recall and associations; s = 1.8; max = 10). Counting only text expressions, they correctly remembered only 0.8 (s = 0.98; max = 4) phrases on average. 5 % stated the brand name of the toothpaste correctly and 15 % made some reference to the slogan. Figure 36 shows the frequencies of total recall and correct recall.

---

[54] This number was assessed because it is a manifest of the elaboration that occurred within the individual although it is not a measure of actual recall. Studies have shown differences between males' and females' information processing not only for recall or recognition but also for the general degree of elaboration (e.g. Meyers-Levy & Maheswaran, 1991, p. 68; DePaulo & Rosenthal, 1979).

[55] The frequency for this was very low, mainly because the task description did not ask respondents to do so as this was not its purpose.

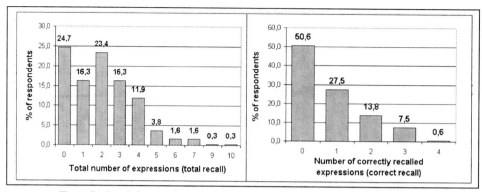

Figure 36: Recall frequencies for total (all statements) and correct recall (text recall)

No differences were found on average between the congruent and the incongruent conditions for total recall, name and slogan recall, and correct recall of expressions. Concentrating on the data for the incongruent condition it becomes clear that on average congruent items were recalled more often than incongruent items (p < 0.001; see Figure 37). However, given that respondents had only two incongruent items but six congruent ones to choose from the difference does not seem too high. Thus incongruent items were noticeable and could have had some impact on processing as compared to the congruent condition.

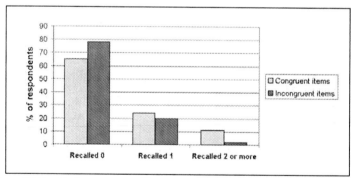

Figure 37: Recall of congruent and incongruent items in the incongruent condition

Nonetheless, what are of interest in this study are not these average results but individual differences. They will be examined in the next sections. Before that general results for the recognition tasks are reported.

6.4.1.2 Recognition

For measuring recognition the following frequencies were counted:
- the number of correctly recognized expressions (hits)

- the number of falsely recognized expressions (false alarms)
- the number of correctly recognized incongruent items (incongruent hits)
- the number of incorrectly recognized incongruent items (incongruent false alarms).

Additionally the difference between correctly and incorrectly recognized expressions was calculated to form an index of the overall goodness of recognition. The following frequencies were observed for the whole sample (see Table 34).

	Mean	*Maximum*	*Stand.Dev.*
Recognition hits	3.74	7	1.66
False alarms	1.66	7	1.40
Difference index	2.08	7	1.90
Incongruent hits	0.74	2	0.70
Incongruent false alarms	0.33	2	0.56

Table 34: Recognition results for the total sample

In general, people recognized a little less than half of the expressions, no respondent recognized all (max = 7 out of 8). Only about one third of the incongruent items was correctly recognized (x = 0.7; max = 2 out of 2). As expected, people had more recognition hits than false alarms, both for all items together and for the incongruent items separately (p < 0.001) indicating that they did remember something and not only crossed the items randomly. The frequencies for hits and false alarms for the whole sample are shown in Figure 38.

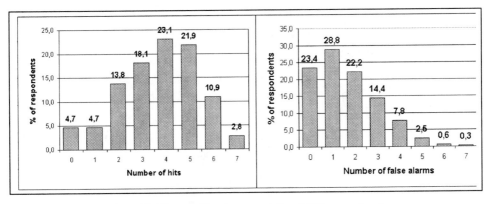

Figure 38: Hits and false alarms total (for all 320 respondents)

On average, there was also no difference in hits and false alarm frequencies for the congruent and the incongruent experimental condition.

6.4.1.3 Discussion

The findings for recognition and recall are rather consistent with each other. They also confirm that recognition was an easier task to respondents than recall. Recall and recognition results are related both within (marked in gray) as well as between each other. Table 35 lists the corresponding correlation coefficients. (All coefficients are significant on a 0.01-level, those significant on a level of 0.05 are marked *).

	Total recall	Correct recall	Congruent recall	Incongr. recall	Hits	False alarms	Diff.	Incongr. hits	Incongr. FA
Total recall	1	--	--	--	--	--	--	--	--
Correct recall	0.567	1	--	--	--	--	--	--	--
Congr. recall	0.541	0.873	1	--	--	--	--	--	--
Incongr. recall	0.345	0.661	0.229	1	--	--	--	--	--
Hits	0.173	0.310	0.241	0.271	1	--	--	--	--
False alarms	n.s.	n.s.	n.s.	n.s.	0.243	1	--	--	--
Difference	n.s.	0.248	0.207	0.292	0.695	-0.529	1	--	--
Incongr. hits	0.169*	0.473	0.264	0.560	0.479	n.s.	0.474	1	--
Incongr. FA	n.s.	n.s.	n.s.	n.s.	n.s.	0.578	-0.314	n.s.	1

Table 35: Correlation coefficients for information processing variables[56]

The following comments to Table 35 can be made:
- False alarm frequencies – both for all items and for the incongruent items separately – showed no relation to recall figures and only some to other recognition measures. False alarm statistics thus seem to be not a particularly good indicator of information processing.
- Between all different statistics positive relationships were observed (except for false alarms): this indicates that there is a clear tendency towards one or the other type of processing, either extensive or heuristic.
- Relations within recall or recognition figures were stronger than between-task relations. This was expected as the two tasks, though they both measure information processing intensity, are still different.

---

[56] The correlation coefficients were calculated using the data of all 320 respondents. Coefficients involving congruency or incongruence data could only be calculated using the data from the incongruence condition in the experiment and are therefore based on a sample size of 160 respondents.

- Those who recalled more expressions generally recalled more congruent than incongruent expressions. This can simply be explained by the fact that there were more congruent items to remember (6 as compared to 2).
- There was a strong relationship between incongruent recall and incongruent hits which indicated that respondents either actively noticed and processed incongruent words or did not pay attention to them at all.

Concluding, recall and recognition were difficult tasks to respondents and the frequencies observed for each task were not very high. Frequencies for the individual measures were reported. On average, incongruency of expressions did not lead to enhanced information processing.

6.4.2 Direct Gender Effects on Information Processing

As expressed by formulating two hypotheses (Hypotheses 4 and 5) both individual masculinity and femininity scores and gender group membership could influence information processing strategies. These two questions thus need to be researched separately.

6.4.2.1 The Impact of Masculinity and Femininity

The impact of masculinity and femininity on information processing strategy will be analyzed with regression analysis. Gender is thereby the independent variable, whereas information processing measures, such as recall frequencies, serve as the dependent variables. Table 37 shows the relationships found in the complete data set. The regression coefficients are displayed, those significant on a 0.05-level are marked *, those only weakly significant ($p < 0.1$) are not marked).

	Dependent Variables	
Independent Variables	Hits	Recall
BSRI-M	0.102	0.107
Glob-M	-0.104	
BSRI-F		0.105
Toughness Norm		-0.124*

Table 36: Regression models for gender and information processing variables (complete data set)

Table 36 is not a very convincing argument for establishing a relationship between the choice of information processing strategy and gender. First, because such a relationship has only been found for selected gender variables, and second, because the statistical significance level achieved leaves some room for doubt. If these results are nevertheless used to establish a first trend, this trend is as follows:

- High masculinity (both BSRI and Global) enhanced (!) the frequency of hits and correctly recalled expressions (the reverse algebraic sign of the regression coefficients is due to a reverse scoring of the two variables).
- The same effect was true for femininity: the higher the femininity according to the BSRI-F scale, the more expressions are correctly recalled.
- Traditional role norm attitudes, in turn, led to fewer items recalled.

Now, such a mixture of results can definitely not be called a trend per se but needs some more insight into the data at hand. The interesting question was after all, how masculine and feminine individuals would react to the incongruity prevalent in half of the messages presented. The data for this condition was thus analyzed separately.

The influence of the variables on information processing as described above generally also holds in the incongruity condition, only the effects are stronger and significance levels increase considerably. Thus, individuals responded to the incongruity and the strength of this response depended on their individual disposition to recognize and react to incongruity which is, as explained, a stereotypically female behavior. However, the results had almost nothing to do with femininity. As indicated, there were two main effects: the effect of BSRI-masculinity and the effect of role norm attitudes.

- Men high in BSRI-masculinity responded to text incongruity by employing a more intensive processing strategy. They had more recognition hits, and recalled more items, both incongruent items separately and all items taken together (see Table 39 for group comparisons between high and low masculinity/femininity males).
- Men holding modern role norm attitudes (femininity!) responded to text incongruity by employing a more intensive processing strategy and recalled more items in general, and also more congruent items (see Tables 37 and 38).
- Femininity (as measured by BSRI-F and global score) played only a weak role, however, high femininity individuals recalled more items compared to low femininity individuals.

Independent Variable	Dependent Variable	alpha-level	Group with more intensive processing
BSRI-masculinity	Hits	< 0.01	High **masculinity** males
	Recall	< 0.05	High **masculinity** males
	Incongruent recall	< 0.05	High **masculinity** males
BSRI-femininity	Recall	< 0.1	High **femininity** males
Toughness Norm	Recall	< 0.01	Men with **modern** role attitudes
	Congruent recall	< 0.01	Men with **modern** role attitudes
Antifemininity Norm	Recall	< 0.05	Men with **modern** role attitudes
	Congruent recall	< 0.05	Men with **modern** role attitudes

Table 37: Comparing high and low masculinity individuals and their choice of processing strategy

Independent Variable	Dependent Variable	Regression coefficient
Toughness Norm	Incongruent recall	-0.140
	Congruent recall	-0.195*
	Recall	-0.216**
Antifemininity Norm	Incongruent recall	-0.173*
	Congruent recall	-0.173*
	Recall	-0.199*

Table 38: Regression models for MRNS and information processing in the incongruent condition

It is obvious from Table 38, that there were no effects for status norm but only for toughness and anti-femininity norm. A logical explanation for this phenomenon is missing.

The answer to hypothesis 5 is thus difficult: the hypothesis stated that there will be no effects of gender (masculinity and femininity) on the choice of information processing strategy. In a strict sense the hypothesis was not supported. Masculinity showed a stronger effect than femininity on recall and recognition of the advertisement text. The connection was stronger when the text was incongruent, indicating that masculine men – as defined by the BSRI – responded to the incongruity while less masculine men did not. This effect is not only contradicted by empirical evidence that masculine (traditional) role norm attitude led to a less intensive processing of the incongruent text, but also by theory. According to theory, women are comprehensive processors – and thus femininity should lead to a more intensive processing strategy. From this point of view hypothesis 4 needs to be rejected, masculinity and femininity seem to have some impact on information processing.

H4:   Masculinity and femininity will have no influence on the choice of the information processing strategy.   ☒

However, there is definitely need for some further elaboration about the confusing findings presented in this section. There is one tentative explanation for these results: both high masculinity and high femininity – though to a weaker extent – led to the choice of a more intensive processing strategy. Both high masculinity and modern role attitudes had the same effects. Now, there is a psychological concept combining masculinity and femininity which was already treated to some extent in this book: androgyny.

Above, when analyzing gender group effects, androgynous individuals were found to have a slightly better processing strategy compared to the other three gender groups. In this section, considering masculinity and femininity separately, high scores in both improved recall and recognition. Is there thus some kind of *androgynous advantage* in information processing? The data at hand is not fit to answer this question, but it might be of interest for further research.

6.4.2.2   The Impact of Gender Group Membership

Differences between the four gender groups were investigated by conducting ANOVAs for both recall and recognition results. Thereby no differences were found for total recall, name recall, and correct recall of expressions. Only for slogan recall there was a weakly significant difference ($p < 0.1$) with feminine individuals showing the highest recall rates. For recall of incongruent items gender differences were found: thereby androgynous and masculine individuals tended to recall more incongruent items compared to undifferentiated individuals ($p < 0.1$). Feminine individuals recalled the lowest number.

No differences were found between the groups for overall frequencies of hits and false alarms. Only for androgynous individuals there was a slight tendency to recognize more expressions correctly than for the other groups ($p < 0,1$). Separate analysis of the individuals in the congruent condition brought no group differences. When looking only at the incongruent condition data androgynous individuals were again found to correctly recognize more expressions then the other groups ($p < 0,05$).

Table 39 summarizes the results (if significant differences were observed, the alpha-level is stated; which group showed better results is indicated next to it).

Recall		*Recognition*	
Total recall	n.s.	Hits	$p < 0.01$; Androg.
Correct recall	n.s.	False alarms	n.s.
Correct congruent recall	n.s.	Incongruent hits	$p < 0.05$; Androg.
Correct incongruent recall	$p < 0.1.$; A. & Masc	Incongruent false alarms	n.s.
Name recall	n.s.		
Slogan recall	$p < 0.1$; Fem.		

Table 39: Observed gender group differences in recall and recognition

As can be seen from Table 39 the observed differences are infrequent and those found are weak. They do not show an overly consistent tendency either, though there is a slight indication that androgynous individuals differ from the other groups. These few effects observed could be due to either some other underlying factors or be indeed first indicators of change. However, for now it cannot be concluded that gender groups differ in their preference for detailed or heuristic information processing strategies. The prediction made by Hypothesis 4 is not rejected.

H4: ☑ *Gender group members do not choose different information processing strategies.*

Just as gender groups did not help explained men's different reactions to different role portrayals, they also show a confused and unusable picture when examining information processing differences between the genders.

6.4.3 Indirect Gender Effects on Information Processing – Incongruity Effects

Hypothesis 6 builds on incongruity between the portrayed male role (masculine or feminine) and the respondent's own gender orientation. It is suggested that incongruity between the two leads to enhanced information processing. If Hypothesis 6 is true we can expect the following effects to be present in the data:

- a positive relationship between high masculinity and intensive information processing in the modern setting and
- no relationship between high femininity and intensive information processing in the traditional setting.

Table 40 summarizes these effects expected under Hypothesis 6 (left) and contrasts it with the effects observed in the experiment (right).

Independent Variable	Effects in modern setting	Effects in traditional setting
BSRI-M	+ / +	
Glob-M	– / n.s.	
BSRI-F		n.s. / n.s.
Glob-F		n.s. / +
MRNS	+ / –	n.s. / +

Table 40: Expected/observed effects between gender and information processing in both settings

As can be easily seen from Table 40 Hypothesis 6a does hold for personality traits (BSRI scale). Considering this limitation, it can be answered affirmatively. Men with masculine personality traits elaborated more about ads depicting a man in a modern role.

H6a: Masculine males will process ads with a feminine role more extensively than feminine males.   ☑

The answer to H6b is in turn clearly negative. Feminine males did not show more extensive processing when the portrayed role was a masculine one. Again it became clear the masculinity effects cannot be simply reversed into femininity effects. Hypothesis 6b was also supported.

H6b: Feminine males will not process ads with a masculine role more extensively than masculine males.   ☑

The data also indicated some other interesting effect. There was some evidence that men elaborated more about ads which were consistent with their gender. The MRNS results pointed in this direction, as did the relationship between low global femininity and more detailed processing of the traditional setting. This is again a question of interest to further researchers.

7 Concluding this Book: Key Findings

7.1 The Role of Gender

On average none of the two role portrayals were preferred over the other. This is in contrast to the results obtained for the same question with a female sample (Jaffe, 1990, p. 877). But when going into detail, moderating effects of gender on advertising effectiveness were observed.

It is safe to say that the current study indicated a certain impact on gender on advertising effectiveness also for men. It is again masculinity which impacts preferences for role portrayals more strongly than femininity. This result has been obtained for women before (e.g. Jaffe, 1994, p. 467) and it seems to be one issue where men and women are similar whereas in several other issues they are not. Still, the explanation might be different: Jaffe (1990, p. 878) argued that respondents felt that a modern woman was more trustable compared to a traditional women for the given product category (financial services). However, this explanation cannot apply to the current study as a neutral product category was used. Some speculations can be made why masculinity is more important in this context than femininity: first, femininity per definition encompasses a broader range of qualities and behaviors, thus high femininity individuals might like the modern positioning better but still be "tolerant" enough not to show extremely strong preferences. Second, masculinity should be more important to men than to women. Thus it is presumably more difficult for a man to deny his masculinity than to acknowledge his femininity. This can also lead to masculinity playing a greater role in advertising evaluation.

However, the effects observed for women were much clearer and more pronounced (cf. e.g. Jaffe, 1994). This can be explained as such: Women had a long history of being depicted in dependent roles, being objects rather than subjects in advertising while men occupied more valued and more powerful roles on posters or television. It is possible that it is due to this development that women have become particularly sensitive to how their own sex is portrayed in advertising whereas there was no need for men to pay attention to it. Such a different advertising history for the two sexes could have led to a great sensitivity for women's role but to a rather indifferent attitude towards males' roles. Male-directed advertisements most often use female subjects (cf. Saad, 2004) which might again contribute to the fact that men do not seem to feel a particular need to be sensitive about roles of same-sex models in advertising.

For practitioners it thus makes sense paying attention to their audience's gender when advertising to males with traditional attitudes. If there is doubt about the role orientation preferred by the target group it is safe to stick to traditional roles as no group showed a dislike for traditional portrayal, but some did for the modern portrayal. Though the current practice of men's roles might not be desirable from a viewpoint of sex equality, it makes sense as advertisers naturally wish their ads to be most effective.

Role norm attitudes were the gender dimensions that impacted advertising response while BSRI masculinity and global masculinity did not. Gender could thus be reduced to this dimension for advertising purposes which makes its measurement and application in a practical field easier.

For information processing it was assumed that it was more of a biological than of a psychological process. The empirical results supported this contention insofar as that there were no clear differences observed in processing strategies based on gender. However, a certain gender influence seems to have been developing over the past decades, though the direction of the relation between gender and processing strategy is not clear yet. What was obvious is that simply translating male-female effects into masculinity-femininity effects (e.g. feminine personalities employ a detailed processing strategy) is too much of a simplification.

When analyzing gender groups, androgynous and masculine individuals were found to have slightly better information processing than feminine and undifferentiated individuals. This was confirmed by analyzing BSRI masculinity scores where high masculinity again led to a better recall in the incongruent condition. Confusingly, high femininity showed a similar, though weaker effect as well, again building on BSRI scores. Contrarily, men who exhibited *modern* role norm attitudes (thus assigned to the feminine side) responded particularly to the incongruity and employed a detailed processing strategy remembering more items. An explanation for this can only be tentative: Toughness and anti-femininity scales might be more deeply rooted in the personality of men as compared to the status norm as they involve on the one hand the physical condition of the male body and on the other hand the differentiation of the male from the female sex and from homosexual men (cf. Stern, 2002, 220). Status is probably more a "social" component and thus not as critical to biologically based processes. The choice of information processing strategy might be an automatic process rooted deeper within the self. If toughness and anti-femininity attitudes are possibly also stronger bound to the self, this could explain the observed phenomenon.

Some consistent findings were also observed:

- Gender impact was generally larger on recall than on recognition. It might be that the choice of the processing strategy was more critical for the more difficult recall task. As gender does seem to have an impact of this choice effects were mostly observed in recall measures.

- The global self-assessment score was irrelevant in an information processing context. It might be "hard-fact" personality differences that impact the choice of information processing strategy. Is this intuitive? The choice of information processing strategy – at least in an advertising context – as a cognitive variable might have more ties to personality (cf. attentional styles; Silverman, 1970). In that it is likely that it is related to the characteristic formations of personality.

Concluding, this study suggests that gender as a personality dimension may function as a moderating variable for the selection of information processing strategy. However, the results do not clearly indicate in which direction the effects work. It is suggested that it might be the androgynous individual that employs a more detailed information processing strategy compared to others, as both masculinity and femininity were shown to impact recall and recognition. The data available from this study points to this direction. It will then be the task of future research to further support or invalidate this new hypothesis.

The present study indicated that there is a strong need to look closely at the data when examining gender impact. While on average no differences might be present, they may very well emerge when taking individual difference variables into account. Thereby the suggestion of forming gender groups was not proved particularly useful. Rather it makes sense to rely on the original scale scores (cf. Kelly et al., 1979, p. 1576). While an impact of gender on advertising evaluation was demonstrated, the findings remained a little fuzzy for its effects on information processing.

7.2 Learnings About Gender and Gender Research

Not only has this study investigated gender and its relationship to advertising effectiveness and information processing but it has also delivered further insight into the construct of gender itself, its conceptualization and its measurement. These general conclusions are reported in the second section of this chapter after summarizing the answers to the research questions.

At first, the frequently used grouping method for assigning respondents to the four gender group did not bring any additional insight in this study. On the contrary, by intersecting two scales on a median midpoint and combining the two measures a rather arbitrary classification was obtained which was subject to the usual problems associated with the median split technique. It is thus recommended to stick to the raw scores of scales who delivered better and more meaningful results and were more readily interpretable.

Also, a few comments on the use of personality trait scales seem appropriate: Obviously, building on the simple principles of factor analysis, a proper factor structure can only be obtained if respondents show a response behavior which is different for masculine items as compared to feminine items but similar within these dimensions. Now such a difference in responses requires two simple facts: Respondents need to be sufficiently stereotyped to

1. recognize the scale items – subconsciously – as representing two dimensions of masculinity and femininity and not as totally sex-independent and to
2. identify themselves with either one or the other dimension more.

If, as predicted, societies become more androgynous and personality traits lose their masculine or feminine connotation the two postulated dimensions of masculinity and femininity might vanish. Now, for the future the following questions are inevitable:

1. Is it still possible to define masculinity and femininity via stereotypical personality traits?
2. Are there still traits which are accepted as definitively masculine or feminine *by the whole population*?
3. Is the use of such trait inventories still adequate in an age of continuously blurring roles and changing stereotypes?

As research has shown that there is still a considerable degree of stereotyping going on, it may be premature to condemn personality trait scales. It will nevertheless be necessary to continuously evaluate their validity in a given time, cultural, and social (!) context because what is masculine or feminine behavior might not only vary across time and countries but also between social classes within a country at a given time. Thereby the degree of stereotyping occurring in the desired sample group might be an indicator whether scales such as the BSRI can lead to meaningful results at all. In a group where men and women are comparatively equal and similar they will probably deliver a fuzzier picture than in a strongly stereotyped group.

If a trait scale is to be used in studying gender:

1. it should be carefully assessed if the target population is sufficiently stereotyped to respond to such traits scales using a masculine-feminine classification scheme;

2. the scale should be carefully adapted to the circumstances of the study at hand because individuals seem to differ greatly in their responses based on their social and cultural circumstances.

Alternatively, as the BSRI schema is based on the social desirability of traits for men and women, another foundation could be developed for to substantiate the division of masculine and feminine characteristics.

Using a multidimensional gender concept provided additional knowledge in this study, as some dimensions stronger influenced information processing and some impacted more advertising effectiveness. However, it also makes the whole research design considerably more complicated. For future research it might thus make sense to carefully examine the gender dimensions which are of value for the research question at hand, which would, for example, be role norm attitudes in an advertising effectiveness context. If the investigation then concentrates on these relevant dimensions, it will not only make the questioning of respondents easier and quicker but also help in keeping the whole research design understandable.

The value of the gender concept itself was neither strongly demonstrated nor particularly invalidated in the present study. It is considered a useful concept in psychology but its relevance in consumer research is doubted. From a theoretical perspective, gender seems to possess its merits as it explains differences in consumer reactions and behaviors. From a practitioner's perspective, the findings of gender research are difficult to implement. Firstly, because gender itself is a fuzzy concept which is not only difficult to measure but where the measurement methods itself are subject to heavy debate. Secondly, a generic advertising strategy exists at least for the male segment – sticking to traditional portrayals – which should work independent of one's gender. Thus gender might be a more important variable for female target groups than for males. But in a lot of fields it still keeps battling with sex for which of the two possesses the greater explanatory power. Slow change in societies might enhance the importance of gender in general and render it important for consumer research on time. Thus research should not completely withdraw from gender research. Rather it should adopt a monitoring position and watch the change in gender importance.

During all this discussion it is important to realize that it – as it is essentially about sex equality – involves a large amount of prejudices, of wishful thinking, and of ideologically-based argumentation. There is no sense in constructing an explanatory power for gender simply because one does not want to accept *sex* differences as real. Per se there is nothing wrong with sex differences as different talents in individuals always provide chances instead of disadvantages. Sex equality is definitely an important goal for the time coming, but there can be equality even if men and women are different. There is definitely a certain amount of transition going on in society but not *everything* is changing. This is not a disadvantage per se.

7.3 Where Do We Go From Here?

Drawing from the limitations of the present study, future studies might investigate the following issues:

- The most obvious limitation of this study is the specificity of the sample. Other populations than students should be examined or even attempts made to obtain a representative sample for examining country-specific gender issues.
- Measurement problems of gender have been amply discussed so as a second limitation. Although I do not believe that the overall tendencies will change to a great extent, different scales should be used in further research to get results based on very general groundings which are not restricted to one or the other conceptualization of gender.
- Similarly, there are information processing measurements which have not been examined in the study at hand. Future studies could examine the flexibility of masculine and feminine individuals in choosing and switching their processing strategies or concentrate on the specific use of informational cues and the differences therein between masculine and feminine people. Also, the suggested gender effects on information processing should be tested on a large *female* sample.
- In measuring advertising effectiveness it was tried to incorporate the behavioral component by asking for purchase intent. However, intent is still intent only and no purchase so that the actual behavioral– and thus turnover and profit – effects could not have been assessed. As well the results of this research are restricted to the low involvement product category, and the effect might still be different for clearly feminine or masculine products.

More specific research could go into detail about the gender's information processing strategies and their impact on male and female decision making, building on the studies by Coughlin and O'Connor (1985) and Qualls (1987). This would bring insights into especially the case of joint buying decisions.

For more psychologically and sociologically oriented researchers it might be interesting to examine the influence of reference groups on male femininity, which has only been glanced at in the theory section of the present study. Reference groups might indeed have a powerful influence not so much on the individual personality characteristics but on the selection of those which are openly shown. As a large number of buying decisions are made in public, the gender of reference groups could be important given the discussion on the social desirability of feminine personality traits. Further research might also extend the findings to different product categories, investigate differences between low and high involvement goods and examine products which have a distinct gendered image. It is expected that the effects are different for masculine, feminine, or neutral products.

The androgynous information processing advantage suggested by the results of the present sample is definitely a promising area for future researchers. Not only needs this suggestion be substantiated by further empirical evidence but it is also necessary to develop a usable operationalization of androgyny for that purpose. For that, the construction of gender should be discussed in the light of current social changes and adequate measurement scales developed.

Summary

While sex has been an important factor in selecting target groups and designing appropriate advertising and promotional strategies, gender has entered the field of consumer research only in recent decades. Since then, the interest in gender has been fuelled by the rise of the feminist movement and changing social roles of women and – later – of men. In the social sciences gender is defined as the psychological status of masculinity and femininity, two dimensions which are – independent of each other – part of every individual's self-definition. That women's and men's roles are indeed changing is manifest in a number of demographic and psychographic variables. Because this can be the case more for one area than for another, the question to what degree human behavior is shaped by biological predisposition or by socialization forces is also addressed.

So far two areas of research have attracted a lot of attention: one of these is women's reactions to different advertising portrayals of their own sex. The use of stereotypes and how gender influences advertising response was investigated in a number of studies. In general, women tend to prefer portrayals showing them in a modern rather than in a traditional role. The second and still larger research area is sex differences. This book concentrated on the special field of sex differences in information processing. The results found that women generally employ a detailed information processing strategy, while men are heuristic processors who rely heavily on schematic information.

Building on these two fields of research, this book addresses two questions: First, knowledge on women's advertising response is extended to the second sex and men's reactions to modern and traditional role portrayals of their own sex are tested. Second, in an issue seldom addressed in the literature the question of whether gender could also have some power in explaining different information processing strategies is examined.

These two questions were tested in a laboratory experiment, conducted among 320 students at different universities in Vienna. Students were confronted with different advertisements, portraying a man either in a modern or a traditional role, and read two different product descriptions where in one experimental condition met their existing product schema and in the other experimental condition did not. Detailed information processors were thereby expected to process information when it was incongruent to their existing product schema. Advertising response was measured via attitudinal measures and purchase intent. To assess the degree of processing of the given information, participants were asked to recall and recognize elements from the product description. Respondents additionally completed three types of validated scales to measure their gender (their masculinity and femininity) as a multi-dimensional construct.

The analysis then assessed the influence of masculinity and femininity on the selected dependent variables as well as used the scales scores to categorize respondents into masculine, feminine, undifferentiated, and androgynous individuals – a procedure frequently employed in the literature but also subject to controversial discussions. Androgynous means that an individual is both masculine and feminine, whereas undifferentiated people do not score high on either of the two dimensions.

The results showed that for men high in masculinity it is especially critical that the male portrayal in the ad matches their own personality and attitudes. These respondents definitely preferred a traditional masculine role portrayal over a modern – feminine – one. In turn, individuals high in femininity did not show a specific preference for a certain type of portrayal but also did not reject the modern one, as did high masculinity males. Their personality thus influences their advertising response in a sense that they are more open to new role descriptions. Modern males did not, however, dislike the traditional portrayal, probably because traditional male roles are not – contrary to women's roles – dependent, but show a rather strong and independent character. Therefore, for practical application it is advisable to pay attention to the audience's gender not only when targeting women, but also when targeting men. Especially when advertising to an audience holding traditional role norm attitudes, advertisers should refrain from "new man" experiments.

Contrary to advertising response, information processing strategy is a mechanism which is heavily related to the existence of biological "hardware", i.e. the brain. Also, studies showed convincing processing differences between men and women and research on gender influence was almost non-existent. Information processing strategy was thus interpreted as based more on biological predisposition than on social circumstances and gender influence was not likely to play a role. The empirical results showed, however, that masculinity and femininity were related to the employment of a heuristic versus a detailed processing strategy though the connection was somehow diffused and ambiguous. The present data thus does not allow a conclusion in one direction or the other, yet. It still suggests that there is some influence – specifically that androgynous individuals might possess a certain advantage in processing information. This finding might be of interest to future research on the topic. For now, practitioners should still stick to observed males-females differences when designing their advertising messages.

References

Ahlstrom, Dick (1999, November 4). Students told not to confuse sex and gender. *The Irish Times*.

Aiken, Lewis R. Jr. (1963). The relationship of dress to selected measures of personality in undergraduate women. *Journal of Social Psychology*, 59, 119-128.

Allison, Neil K., Coogan, Donna, Golden, Linda L., Mullet, Gary, M. (1980). Sex-typed product images: the effects of sex, sex-role self-concept and measurement implications. *Advances in Consumer Research*, 7, 604-609.

Alreck, Pamela L., Settle, Robert B., Belch, Michael, A. (1982). Who responds to gendered ads and how? *Journal of Advertising Research*, 22 (2), 25-32.

Areni, Charles S., Kiecker, Pamela, Palan, Kay M. (1998). Is it better to give than to receive? Exploring gender differences in the meaning of memorable gifts. *Psychology and Marketing*, 15 (1), 81-109.

Aube, Jennifer, Koestner, Richard (1992). Gender characteristics and adjustment: A longitudinal study. *Journal of Personality and Social Psychology*, 63 (3), 485-493.

Bagozzi, R. P., Gopinath, M., Nyer, P. U. (1999). The role of emotions in advertising: *Journal of the Academy of Marketing Science*, 27, 184-206.

Bakan, D. (1966). *The Duality of Human Existence* Chicago: Rand McNally.

Ballard-Reisch, Deborah, Elton, Mary (1992). Gender orientation and the Bem Sex Role Inventory: a psychological construct revisited. *Sex Roles*, 27 (5-6), 291-306.

Barak, Benny, Stern, Barbara B. (1986). Sex-linked trait indexes among baby-boomers and pre-boomers: a research note. *Advances in Consumer Research*. 13, 204-209.

Bearden, William O., Etzel, Michael J. (1982). References group influence on product and brand purchase decisions. *Journal of Consumer Research*, 9 (September), 183-194.

Beckmann, Petra (2003). Die Beschäftigungsquote – (k)ein guter Indikator für die Erwerbstätigkeit von Frauen? IAB-Kurzbericht Nr. 11/2003, Institut für Arbeitsmarkt- und Berufsforschung. Retrieved October 16th, 2004 from the website of the Institut für Arbeitsmarkt- und Berufsforschung www.iab.de.

Beere, Carole A. (1990). *Gender Roles: A Handbook of Tests and Measures*. Westport: Greenwood Press.

Bellizzi, Joseph A., Milner, Laura (1991). Gender positioning of a traditionally male-dominant product. *Journal of Advertising Research*, (June/July), 72-80.

Bem, S. L., Lenney, E. (1976). Sex typing and the avoidance of cross-sex behavior. *Journal of Personality and Social Psychology*, 33, 48-54.

Bem, Sandra L. (1974). The measurement of psychological androgyny. *Journal of Consulting and Clinical Psychology*, 42 (2), 155-162.

Bem, Sandra L. (1977). On the utility of alternative procedures for assessing psychological androgyny. *Journal of Consulting and Clinical Psychology*, 45 (2), 196-205.

Bem, Sandra L. (1981). Gender schema theory: a cognitive account of sex typing. *Psychological Review*, 88 (4), 354-364.

Bem, Sandra L. (1982). Gender schema theory and self-schema theory compared: A comment on Markus, Crane, Bernstein, and Siladi's "Self-schemas and Gender". *Journal of Personality and Social Psychology*, 43, 1192-1194.

Bereska, Tami M. (2003). The changing boys' world in the 20th century: reality and fiction. *The Journal of Men's Studies*, 11 (2), 157-174.

Block, J. H. (1984). How gender differences affect children's orientations to the world. In Sex Role Identity and Ego Development, San Francisco: Jossey-Bass.

Bordo, S. (1993). *Unbearable Weight: Feminism, Western Culture, and the Body*. Berkeley, CA: University of California Press.

Brannon, Laura A., Brock, Timothy C. (1994). Test of schema correspondence theory of persuasion: Effects of matching an appeal to actual, ideal and product "selves". In Clark, Eddie M., Brock, Timothy C. (Eds.), Attention, Attitude, and Affect in Response to Advertising, Hillsdale, NJ: Lawrence Erlbaum.

Brassington, Frances, Pettitt, Stephen (2003). Principles of Marketing. 3rd, Essex: Pearson.

Bresnahan, Mary Jiang, Inoue, Yasuhiro, Liu, Wen Ying, Nishida, Tsukasa. Changing gender roles in prime-time commercials in Malaysia, Japan, Taiwan, and the US. *Sex Roles*, 45 (1-2), 117-131.

Brock, T. C., Brannon, L. A., Bridgwater, C. (1990). Message effectiveness can be increased by matching appeals to recipient's self-schemas: Laboratory demonstrations and a national field experiment. In Agres, S., Edell, J., Dubitsky, T. (Eds.), *Emotion in Advertising: Theoretical and Practical Explorations*, Westport, CT: Quorum Books, 285-315.

Burns, Alvin C. (1977). Wives' masculine-feminine orientations and their perceptions of husband-wife purchase decision making. In Greenberg, Barnett A., Bellenger, Danny N. (Eds.), *Contemporary Marketing Thought, AMA Educators' Proceedings Series #41*, Chicago: American Marketing Association, 521.

Carlson, Rae (1971): Sex differences in ego functioning: exploratory studies of agency and communion. *Journal of Consulting and Clinical Psychology*, 37 (2), 267-277.

Churchill, Gilbert A. Jr. (1999). *Marketing Research – Methodological Foundations*. 7th ed., The Dryden Press: Orlando.

Ciabattari, Teresa (2001): Changes in men´s conservative gender ideologies – cohort and period influences. *Gender and Society*, 15 (4), 574-591.

Clatterbaugh, K. (1996). *Contemporary Perspectives on Masculinity: Men, Women, and Politics in Modern Society*. New York: Westview Press.

Colarelli, Stephen M., Dettmann, Joseph R. (2003). Intuitive evolutionary perspectives in marketing practices. *Psychology and Marketing*, 20 (9), 837-865.

Coltrane, S. (1994). Theorizing masculinities in contemporary social science. In Brod, H., Kaufman, M. (Eds.), *Theorizing Masculinities*., Hillsdale, NJ: Sage Publications.

Constantinople, Anne (1973). Masculinity – femininity: an exception to a famous dictum? *Psychological Bulletin*, 80 (5), 389-407.

Conway, Michael (2000). On sex roles and representations of emotional awareness: masculinity, femininity, and emotional awareness. *Sex Roles*. 43 (9-10), 387-398.

Coughlin, Maureen, O'Connor, P. J. (1985). Gender role portrayals in advertising: an individual differences analysis. *Advances in Consumer Research*, 12, 238-241.

Crane, Marie, Hazel, Markus (1982). Gender identity : The benefits of a self-schema approach. *Journal of Personality and Social Psychology*, 43 (6), 1195-1197.

Darley, William K., Smith, Robert E. (1995). Gender differences in information processing: an empirical test of the selectivity model in advertising response. *Journal of Advertising Research*, 24 (1), 41-55.

Davis, F., Walsh, W. B. (1988). Antecedents and Consequents of Gender Role Conflict: An Empirical Test of Sex Role Strain Analysis. Paper presented at the 96th Annual Convention of the American Psychological Association, Atlanta, GA.

Deaux, Kay (1984). From Individual Differences to Social Categories: Analysis of a Decade's Research on Gender. *American Psychologist*, 39 (2), 105-116.

Deaux, Kay (1985). Sex and gender. *Annual Review of Psychology*, 36, 49-81.

Deaux, Kay, Lewis, L. L. (1983). Assessment of gender stereotypes: Methodology and components. *Psychological Documents*, 13, 25-34.

Deaux, Kay, Ullman, J. C. (1983). *Women of Steel.* New York: Praeger.

DePaulo, Bella M., Rosenthal, Robert (1979). Sex differences in accommodation in nonverbal communication. In Rosenthal, Robert (Ed.), *Skill in Nonverbal Communication,* Cambridge, MA: Oelgeschlager, Gunn&Hain.

Dolnicar, S., Heindler, M. (2004). If you don't need to know, don't ask! Does questionnaire length dilute the stability of brand images. In: *Processings of the 33rd EMAC Conference,* Murcia 2004.

Donaldson, M. (1993). What is hegemonic masculinity? *Theory and Society,* 22, 643-657.

Durkin, Kevin (1985). *Television and Sex Roles and Children: A Developmental Account Social Psychological Account.* Milton Keynes and Philadelphia: Open University Press.

Durkin, Kevin (1986). Sex roles and the mass media. In D.H. Hargreaves & A. M. Colley (Eds.), *The Psychology of Sex Roles,* London: Harper and Row.

Eagly, A. H. (1987). *Sex Differences in Social Behavior: A Social Role Interpretation.* Hillsdale, NJ: Erlbaum.

Eagly, A. H., Mladinic, A. (1989). Gender stereotypes and attitudes towards women and me. Personality and Social Psychology Bulletin, 15, 543-558.

Ebster, C., Reisinger, H. (2005). The role of physical attractiveness of the salesperson in personal selling. in: *Proceedings of the 33rd EMAC Conference,* Milano 2005.

Edwards, Valerie J., Spence, Janet T. (1987). Gender-related traits, stereotypes, and schemata. *Journal of Personality and Social Psychology,* 53 (1), 146-154.

Feather, N. T. (1978). Factor structure of the Bem Sex Role Inventory: implications for the study of masculinity, femininity, and sndrogyny. *Australian Journal of Psychology,* 30 (3), 241-254.

Fischer, Eileen, Arnold, Stephen J. (1990). More than a labor of love: gender roles and christmas gift shopping. *Journal of Consumer Research,* 17 (December), 333-345.

Fischer, Eileen, Arnold, Stephen J. (1994). Sex, gender identity, gender role attitudes, and consumer behavior. *Psychology and Marketing,* 11 (2), 163-182.

Frable, Deborrah E. S., Bem, Sandra L. (1985). If you are gender schematic, all members of the opposite sex look alike. *Journal of Personality and Social Psychology,* 49 (2), 459-468.

Fry, Joseph N. (1971). Personality variables and cigarette brand choice. *Journal of Marketing Research,* 8 (3), 298-303.

Furnham, A., Schofield, S. (1986). Sex-role stereotyping in British radio advertisements. *British Journal of Social Psychology,* 25, 165-171.

Furnham, A., Voli, V. (1989). Gender stereotyping in Italian television advertisements. *Journal of Broadcasting and Electric Media,* 33, 175-185.

Furnham, Adrian, Bitar, Nadine (1993). The stereotyped portrayal of men and women in British television advertisements. *Sex Roles,* 29 (3-4), 297-310.

Gainer, Brenda (1993). An empirical investigation of the role of involvement with a gendered product. *Psychology and Marketing,* 10 (4), 265-283.

Gardner, Meryl (1985). Does attitude towards one ad affect brand attitude under a brand evaluation set? *Journal of Marketing Research,* 22 (2), 192-198.

Gaudreau, P. (1977). Factor analyis of the Bem Sex-Role Inventory. *Journal of Consulting and Clinical Psychology.* 45 (2), 299-302.

Gentry, James W., Doering, Mildred (1977). Masculinity-femininity related to consumer choice. In Greenberg, Barnett A., Bellenger, Danny N. (Eds.), *Contemporary Marketing Thought, AMA Educators' Proceedings Series #41,* Chicago: American Marketing Association, 423-427.

Gentry, James W., Doering, Mildred (1979). Sex role orientation and leisure. *Journal of Leisure Research,* 11 (2), 102-111.

Gentry, James W., Doering, Mildred, O'Brien, Terrence V. (1978). Masculinity and femininity factors in product perception and self image. *Advances in Consumer Research,* 5, 326-332.

Gentry, James W., Haley, Debra A. (1984). Gender schema theory as a predictor of ad recall. *Advances in Consumer Research.* 11, 259-264.

Gill, Sandra, Stockard, Jean, Johnson, Miriam, Williams, Suzanne (1987). Measuring gender differences: the expressive dimension and critique of androgyny scales. *Sex Roles,* 17 (7-8), 375-400.

Golden, Linda L., Allison, Neil K., Clee, Mona, (1979). The role of sex-role self-concept in masculine and feminine product perceptions. *Advances in Consumer Research,* 6, 599-605.

Gough, H. (1952). Identifying psychological femininity. *Educational and Psychological Measurement,* 12, 427-439.

Gough, Harrison G. (1966). A cross-cultural analysis of the CPI femininity scale. Journal of Consulting Psychology, 30 (2), 136-141.

Gould, Stephen J., Stern, Barbara B. (1989). Gender schema and fashion consciousness. *Psychology and Marketing,* 6 (2), 129-145.

Gould, Stephen J., Weil, Claudia E. (1991). Gift-giving roles and gender self-concepts. *Sex Roles,.* 24 (9/10), 617-637.

Graham, Judy F., Standardi, Edward J. Jr., Myers, Joan K., Graham, Mark J. (2002). Gender differences in investment strategies: an information processing perspective. *The International Journal of Bank Marketing,* 20 (1), 17-26.

Grunert, K.G. (1990). Kognitive Strukturen in der Konsumentenforschung – Entwicklung und Erprobung eines Verfahrens zur offenen Erhebung assoziativer Netzwerke. Heidelberg.

Grunert, K.G. (1996). Automatic and Strategic Processes in Advertising Effects. *Journal of Marketing,* 60, 88-101.

Hacker, H. (1957). The new burdens of masculinity. *Marriage and Family Living,* 19.

Hall, J. A. (1978). Gender effects in decoding nonverbal cues. *Psychological Bulletin,* 85, 845-875.

Hantula, Donald A. (2003). Guest Editorial: Evolutionary psychology and consumption. *Psychology and Marketing,* 20 (9), 757-763.

Helmreich, R. L., Spence J. T., Gibson, R. H. (1982). Sex role attitudes: 1972-1980. University of Texas at Austin. *Personality and Social Psychology Bulletin,* 1982 (8), 656-663.

Helmreich, Robert L., Spence, Janet T., Holahan, Carole K. (1979). Psychological androgyny and sex role flexibility: a test of two hypotheses. *Journal of Personality and Social Psychology,* 37 (10), 1631-1644.

Hoffman, Rose Marie (2001). The measurement of masculinity and femininity: historical perspective and implications for counseling. *Journal of Counseling and Development,* 79 (4), 472-485.

Hogg, Margaret K., Garrow, Jade (2003). Gender, identity, and the consumption of advertising. *Qualitative Market Research,* 6 (3), 160-174.

Holt, Cheryl L., Ellis, Jon B. (1998). Assessing the current validity of the Bem Sex Role Inventory. *Sex Roles,* 39 (11-12), 929-941.

Horrocks, R. (1994). Masculinity in Crisis: Myths, Fantasies, and Realities. New York: St. Martin's Press.

Hupfer, Maureen (2002). Communication with the agentic woman and the communal man: are stereotypic advertising appeals still relevant? *Academy of Marketing Science Review Online,* 3. Retrieved October 10, 2003 from http://www.amsreview.org/amsrev/theory/hupfer03-2002.html.

Hurtz, Wilhelm, Durkin, Kevin (1997). Gender role stereotyping in Australian radio commercials. *Sex Roles,* 36 (1-2), 103-114.

Huston, A. C. (1983). Sex typing. In Mussen, P. H. (Ed.), Handbook of Child Psychology, New York: Wiley.

Hyde, Janet S. (1981). How large are cognitive gender differences? A meta-analysis using ω^2 and d. *American Psychologist,* 36 (8), 892-901.

Hyde, Janet S. (1990). Meta-analysis and the psychology of gender differences. *Signs,* 16 (1), 55-73.

Hyde, Janet S., Plant, Elizabeth A. (1995). Magnitude of psychological gender differences – another side to the story. *American Psychologist,* 50 (3), 159-161.

Jaffe, J. M., Lee, Y. E., Huang, L. N., Oshagan, H. (1995). Gender, Pseudonyms, and CMC: Masking Identities and Baring Souls. Paper presented at the International Communication Association Conference, Albuquerque, NM.

Jaffe, Lynn J. (1990). The effect of positioning on the purchase probability of financial services among women with varying sex-role identities. *Advances in Consumer Research,* 17, 874-879.

Jaffe, Lynn J. (1991). Impact of positioning and sex-role identity on women´s responses to advertising. *Journal of Advertising Research,* 31 (3), 57-64.

Jaffe, Lynn J. (1994). The unique predictive ability of sex-role identity in explaining women´s response to advertising. *Psychology and Marketing,* 11 (5), 467-482.

Jaffe, Lynn J., Berger, Paul D. (1988). Impact on purchase intent of sex-role identity and poduct positioning. *Psychology and Marketing.* 5 (3), 259-271.

Jaffe, Lynn J., Berger, Paul D. (1994). The effect of modern female sex-role portrayal on advertising effectiveness. *Journal of Advertising Research,* 34 (July), 32-42.

Jaffe, Lynn J., Berger, Paul D., Jamieson, Linda F. (1992). Comprehension, positioning, segmentation and purchase probability. *OMEGA – International Journal of Management Science,* 20 (1), 51-57 (Jaffe et al., 1992a).

Jaffe, Lynn J., Jamieson, Linda F., Berger, Paul D. (1992). Impact of comprehension, positioning, and segmentation on advertising response. Journal of Advertising Research, 32 (May/June), 24-33 (Jaffe et al., 1992b).

Jones, W. H., Chernovetz, M. E., Hansson, R. O. (1978). The enigma of androgyny: Differential implications for males and females? *Journal of Consulting and Clinical Psychology,* 46, 298-313.

Kacen, Jacqueline J. (2000). Girrl power and boyyy nature. The past, present, and paradisal future of consumer gender identity. *Marketing Intelligence and Planning,* 18 (6), 345-355.

Kahle, Lynn R., Homer, Pamela (1985). Androgyny and midday mastification: do real men eat quiche? *Advances in Consumer Research,* 12, 242-246.

Kamins, M. A. (1990). An investigation into the match-up hypothesis in celebrity advertising : When beauty may be only skin deep. Journal of Advertising, 16 (March), 4-13.

Kelly, Jeffrey A., Furman, Wyndol, Young, Veronica (1978). Problems associated with the measurement of sex roles and androgyny. *Journal of Consulting and Clinical Psychology,* 26 (6), 1574-1576.

Kempf, DeAnna S., Laczniak, Russell N., Palan, Kay M. (1997). Gender differences in information processing confidence in an advertising context. A preliminary study. *Advances in Consumer Research,* 24, 443-449.

Kessler, Suzanne (1990). The medical construction of gender: Case management of intersexed infants. *Signs. Journal of Women in Culture and Society,* Autumn, 3-26.

Kimmel, Michael S. (1988). Rethinking "masculinity": New directions in research. In: Kimmel, Michael S. (Ed.). *Changing Men: New Directions in Research on Men and Masculinity,* 3rd, Newbury Park, CA: Sage Publications, 9-24.

Koestner, Richard, Aube, Jennifer (1995). A multifactorial approach to the study of gender characteristics. *Journal of Personality,* 63 (3), 681-710.

Kolbe, Richard H., Albanese, Paul J. (1997). The functional integration of sole-male image into magazine advertisements. *Sex Roles,* 36 (11-12), 813-836.

Kolbe, Richard H., Langefeld, Carl D. (1993). Appraising gender role portrayals in TV commercials. *Sex Roles,* 28 (7-8), 393-417.

Kotler, Philip (2003). *Marketing Management, International Edition.* 11th, Upper Saddle River, NJ: Prenhall.

Krahe, Barbara (1989). Sex-role orientation and memory for gender-related terms: Another uncertain link. British Journal of Social Psychology, 28 (4), 327-340.

Kroeber-Riel, Werner, Weinberg, Peter (1999). *Konsumentenverhalten.* 7th ed., München: Vahlen.

Lang-Takac, Esther, Osterweil, Zahava (1992). Separateness and connectedness. Differences between the genders. *Sex Roles,* 27 (5-6), 277-289.

Laroche, Michel, Saad, Gad, Cleveland, Mark, Browne, Elizabeth (2000). Gender differences in information search strategies for a christmas gift. *Journal of Consumer Marketing,* 17 (6), 500-524.

Leigh, Thomas, Rethans, Arno J., Reichenbach Whitney, Tamatha (1987). Role portrayals of women in advertising: Cognitive responses and advertising effectiveness. *Journal of Advertising Research,* 27 (Oct/Nov), 54-63.

Levy, S. J. (1959). Symbols for sale. Harvard Business Review, 37, 117-124.

Lobel, Thalma E. (1994). Sex typing and the social perception of gender stereotypic and non-stereotypic behavior. The uniqueness of feminine males. *Journal of Personality and Social Psychology,* 66 (2), 379-385.

Lobel, Thalma E., Rothman, Gabriella, Abramovizt, Esther, Maayan, Ziva (1999). Self-perception and deceptive behavior. The uniqueness of feminine males. *Sex Roles,* 41 (7-8), 577-587.

Lubinski, David, Tellegen, Auke, Butcher, James N. (1983). Masculinity, femininity, and androgyny viewed and assessed as distinct concepts. *Journal of Personality and Social Psychology,* 44 (2), 428-239.

Lynn, Michael, Kampschroeder, Karl, Pereira, Arun (1999). Evolutionary perspectives on consumer behavior: An introduction. *Advances in Consumer Research,* 26, 226-230.

Maccoby, E.E., Jacklin, C. N. (1974): The Psychology of Sex Differences. Stanford, CA: Stanford University Press.

Maccoby, Eleanor E. (1988). *The Two Sexes: Growing up Apart, Coming Together.* Cambridge, MA: The Belknap Press of Harvard University Press.

Maldonado, Rachel, Tansuhaj, Patriya, Muehling, Darrel D. (2003). The impact of gender on ad processing. A social identity perspective. Academy of Marketing Science Review Online, 3. Retrieved October 10, 2003 from http://www.amsreview.org/articles/maldonado03-2003.pdf.

Malter, Alan (1996). An introduction to embodied cognition: Implications for consumer research. *Advances in Consumer Research,* 23, Corfman, Kim P., Lynch, John (eds.), Provo, UT: Association for Consumer Research, 272-276.

Mandler, G. (1982). The Structure of Value: Accounting for Taste. In: H. Margaret, S. Clarke and S.T. Fiske (eds), *Affect and Cognition: The 17th Annual Carnegie Symposium on Cognition,* Hillsdale, NJ: Lawrence Erlbaum.

Manstead, A. S. R., McCulloch, C. (1981). Sex-role stereotyping in British television advertisements. *British Journal of Social Psychology,* 20, 171-180.

Marchand, R. (1985). Advertising the American Dream. Berkeley, CA: University of California Press.

Markus, Hazel, Crane, Marie, Bernstein, Stan, Siladi, Michael (1982). Self-schemas and gender. *Journal of Personality and Social Psychology,* 42 (1), 38-50.

Markus, Hazel, Oyserman, Daphna (1989). Gender and thought: The role of the self-concept. In Crawford, Mary, Gentry, Margaret (Eds.): *Gender and Thought: Psychological Perspectives,* New York: Springer.

Martin, Brett A. S. (2003). The influence of gender on mood effects in advertising. *Psychology and Marketing,* 20 (3), 249-273.

Martin, John, Roberts, Mary L. (1983). Effect of sex of owner and personal circumstances on attitudes toward a service establishment. *Advances in Consumer Research,* 10, 339-344.

Martin, Warren S., Bellizzi, Joseph (1982). An analysis of congruence relationships between self-image and product-image. *Journal of the Academy of Marketing Science*, 10 (4), 473-489.

Mason, K. O., Czajka, J. L., Arber, S. (1976). Change in U.S. women's sex role attitudes 1964-1974. *American Sociological Review*, 41, 573-596.

Mazella, Carmela, Durkin, Kevin, Cerini, Emma, Buralli, Paul (1992). Sex role stereotyping in Australian television advertisements. *Sex Roles*, 26 (7-8), 243-259.

McArthur, L. Z., Resko, B. G. (1975). The portrayal of men and women in Americas television commercials. *Journal of Social Psychology*, 11, 109-127.

McCracken, E. (1993). *Decoding Women's Magazines: From Mademoiselle to Ms.* London: MacMillan.

McCreary, Donald R., Newcomb, Michael D., Sadava, Stanley W. (1998). Dimensions of the male gender role. A confirmatory analysis in men and women. *Sex Roles*, 39 (1-2), 81-95.

McGhee, P. E., Frueh, M. D. (1975). Traditional gender role development and amount of time spent watching television. *Development Psychology*, 11, 109.

McGivern, Robert F., Huston, Patrick J., Byrd, Desiree, King, Tina, Siegle, Greg J., Reilly, Judy (1997). Sex differences in visual recognition memory. Support for a sex-related difference in attention in adults and children. *Brain and Cognition*, 34, 323-336.

Mealey, Linda (2000): *Sex Differences*. San Diego, CA: Academic Press.

Meyers-Levy; Joan (1989). Gender differences in information processing. A Selectivity Interpretation. In: P. Cafferata & A.M. Tybout (eds.), *Cognitive and Affective Responses to Advertising*, Lexington and Toronto: Lexington Books.

Meyers-Levy, Joan (1988). The Influence of Sex Roles on Judgment. *Journal of Consumer Research*, 14 (4), 522-530.

Meyers-Levy, Joan (1994). Gender differences in cortical organization: Social and biochemical antecedents and advertising consequences. In Clark, Eddie M., Brock, Timothy C. (Eds.), Attention, Attitude, and Affect in Response to Advertising, Hillsdale, NJ: Lawrence Erlbaum.

Meyers-Levy, Joan, Maheswaran, Durairaj (1991). Exploring differences in males' and females' processing strategies. *Journal of Consumer Research*, 18 (1), 63-70

Meyers-Levy, Joan, Sternthal, Brian (1991). Gender differences in the use of message cues and judgments. *Journal of Marketing Research*, 28 (1), 84-96.

Meyers-Levy, Joan, Tybout, Alice M. (1989). Schema congruity as a basis for product evaluation. *Journal of Consumer Research*, 16 (1), 39-54.

Miller, R. S., Lefcourt H. M. (1982). The assessment of social intimacy. *Journal of Personality Assessment*, 46, 514-518.

Mitchell, Andrew A. (1986). The effect of verbal and visual components of advertisements on brand attitudes and attitude toward the ad. *Journal of Consumer Research*, 13 (2), 12-24.

Morris, George, P., Cundiff, Edward W. (1971). Acceptance by males of feminine products. *Journal of Marketing Research*, 8 (3), 372-374.

n.a. (1999): Männergesundheitsbericht Wien 1999. Retrieved June 14th, 2004 from the Homepage of the city of Vienna: www.wien.gv.at/who/manngb/99/.

n.a. (2003, june 7th): Wickel- statt Schreibtisch. Männer, die in Karenz gehen, sind in Österreich die Ausnahme. *Die Presse*.

Napoli, Julie, Murgolo-Poore, Marie, Boudville, Ian (2003). Female gender images in adolescent magazine advertising. Australasian Marketing Journal, 11 (1), 60-69.

Neto, Félix, Pinto, Isabel (1998). Gender stereotypes in Portuguese television advertisements. *Sex Roles,* 39 (1-2), 153-164.

Nyquist, Linda, Slivken, Karla, Spence, Janet T., Helmreich, Robert L. (1985). Household responsibilities in middle-class couples. The contribution of demographic and personality variables. *Sex Roles*, 12

(1-2), 15-34.

O'Neil (1990). Assessing men's gender role conflict. In Moore, D., Leafgren, F. (Eds.), *Problem Solving Strategies and Interventions for Men in Conflict*, Alexandria, VA: American Association for Counseling and Development, 23-38.

O'Neil, J. M., Helms, B. J., Gable, R. K., David, L., Wrightsman, L. S. (1986). Gender-role conflict scale: College men's fear of femininity. *Sex Roles*, 14, 335-350.

Odekerken-Schroeder, Gaby, De Wulf, Kristof, Hofstee, Natascha (2002). Is gender stereotyping in advertising more prevalent in masculine countries? A cross-national analysis. *International Marketing Review*, 19 (4), 408-419.

Oftung, Knut: *Fathers and Parental Leave in Norway*. Centre for Gender Equality (www.likestilling.no, accessed 13.10.2004).

Oliver, Mary B., Sargent, Stephanie L., Weaver, James B., III (1998). The impact of sex and gender role self-perception on affective reactions to different types of film. *Sex Roles*, 38 (1-2), 45-62.

Orlofsky, Jacob L. (1981). Relationship between sex role attitudes and personality traits and the Sex Role Behavior Scale-1. A new measure of masculine and feminine role behavior and interests. *Journal of Personality and Social Psychology,* 40 (5), 927-940.

Orth, Ulrich R., Holancova, Denisa (2004). Men's and women's responses to sex role portrayals in advertisements. *International Journal of Research in Marketing*, 21, 77-88.

Pajares, F., Valiante, G. (2001). Gender differences in writing motivation and achievement of middle school students: A function of gender orientation. *Contemporary Educational Psychology*, 26, 366-381.

Palan, Kay M. (2001). Gender identity in consumer behavior research. A literature review and research agenda. *Academy of Marketing Science Review Online*, 10. Retrieved October 10, 2003 from .http://www.amsreview.org/articles/palan10-2001.pdf.

Palan, Kay M., Areni, Charles S., Kiecker, Pamela (1999). Reexamining masculinity, femininity, and gender identity scales. *Marketing Letters*, 10 (4), 363-377.

Palan, Kay M., Areni, Charles S., Kiecker, Pamela (2001). Gender role incongruency and memorable gift exchange experiences. *Advances in Consumer Research*, 28, 51-57.

Parsons, T., Bales, R.F. (1955). *Family, Socialization, and Interaction Process*. Glencoe, IL: Free Press.

Payne, Thomas J., Connor, Jane M., Colletti, Gep (1987). Gender-based schematic processing. An empirical investigation and reevaluation. *Journal of Personality and Social Psychology*, 52 (5), 937-945.

Pedhazur, Elazar J., Tetenbaum, Toby J. (1979). Bem Sex Role Inventory: A theoretical and methodological critique. *Journal of Personality and Social Psychology*, 37 (6), 996-1016.

Peevers, B. H. (1979). Androgyny on the TV screen? An analysis of sex-role portrayals. *Sex Roles*, 5, 797-809.

Pleck, J. H., Sonenstein, F. L., Ku, L. C. (1993). Attitudes towards male roles among adolescent males: A discriminant validity analysis. *Sex Roles*, 30, 481-501.

Pollack, W. (1999). *Real Boys: Rescuing our Sons from the Myths of Boyhood*. New York: Henry Holt.

Prakash, Ved (1992). Sex roles and advertising preferences. *Journal of Advertising Research*, 32(May/June), 43-52.

Prakash, Ved, Flores, Caeli R. (1985). A study of psychological gender differences: applications for advertising format. *Advances in Consumer Research*, 12, 231-237.

Prenner, Peter, Scheibenhofer, Elisabeth (2001). Qualifikation und Erwerbsarbeit von Frauen in Österreich 1970 – 2000. *Sociological Series*, 49, Institute for Advanced Studies, Vienna.

Putrevu, Sandra (2001). Exploring the origins and information processing differences between men and women: Implications for advertisers. *Academy of Marketing Science Review Online* (10). Retrieved October 10, 2003, from http://www.amsreview.org/articles/putrevu10-2001.pdf.

Qualls, William J. (1987). Household decision behavior. The impact of husbands' and wives' sex role orientation. *Journal of Consumer Research*, 14 (September), 164-279.

Ramanaiah, N. V., Martin, H. J. (1984): Convergent and discriminant validity of selected masculinity and femininity scales. *Sex Roles*, 10, 493-504.

Renn, Jennifer A., Calvert, Sandra L. (1993). The relation between gender schemas and adults recall of stereotyped and counterstereotyped televised information. *Sex Roles*, 28 (7-8), 449-459.

Roberts, M. L. (1984). Gender differences and household decision making: Needed conceptual and methodological advances. In Kinnear, T. C. (Ed.), *Advances in Consumer Research*, 11, 276-278.

Rojahn, K., Pettigrew, T. F. (1992). Memory for schema-relevant information: A meta-analytic resolution. *British Journal of Social Psychology*, 31 (2), 81-109.

Rosenthal, R., Rubin, D. B. (1982). Further meta-analytic procedures for assessing cognitive gender differences. *Journal of Educational Psychology*, 74, 708-712.

Saad, Gad (2004). Applying evolutionary psychology on understanding the representation of women in advertisements. Psychology and Marketing, 21 (8), 593-612.

Saad, Gad, Gill, Tripat (2000). Applications of evolutionary psychology in marketing. *Psychology and Marketing*, 17 (12), 1005-1034.

Schmitt, Bernd H., Leclerc, France, Dubé-Rioux, Laurette (1988). Sex typing and consumer behavior. A test of gender schema theory. *Journal of Consumer Research*, 15 (1), 122-128.

Schneider-Dueker, M. (1978). Deutsche Neukonstruktion des Bem Sex-Role-Inventory. *Arbeiten der Fachrichtung Psychologie* Nr. 51, Universität des Saarlandes, Saarbrücken.

Schneider-Dueker, Marianne, Kohler, André (1988). Die Erfassung von Geschlechtsrollen – Ergebnisse zur deutschen Neukonstruktion des Bem Sex Role Inventory. *Diagnostica*, 34 (3), 256-270.

Schultze, S., Knussmann, R., Christiansen, K. (1991). Male sex role identification and body build. *Homo,* 42 (3), 203-215.

Sechrest, Lee (1976). Personality. In Rosenzweig, M. R., Porter, L. W., *Annual Review of Psychology*, 27, 1 – 22, Palo Alto: Annual Reviews Inc.

Seidler, V. J. (1997). *Man enough: Embodying Masculinities*. London: Sage Publications.

Sharpe, Mark J., Heppner, Paul P. (1991). Gender role, gender-role conflict, and psychological well-being in men. *Journal of Counseling Psychology*, 38 (3), 323-330.

Silverman, Julian (1970). Attentional styles and the study of sex differences. In Mostofsky, David I. (Ed.), *Attention: Contemporary Theory and Analysis*, New York: Appleton-Century-Crofts, 61-98.

Sirgy, Joseph M. (1982). Self-concept in consumer behaviour: A critical review. *Journal of Consumer Research*, 9, 287-300.

Skelly, G. U:, Lundstrom, W. J. (1981). Male sex role portrayals in magazine advertising: 1958-1983. *Sex Roles*, 18, 181-188.

Skitka, Linda J., Maslach, Christina (1990). Gender roles and the categorization of gender-relevant behavior. *Sex Roles*, 22 (3-4), 133-150.

Slinker, B. H. (1984, April). Would you buy a burger from this man? A car? Some stocks? *Madison Avenue*, 26, 52-53.

Smits, Jeroen, Mulder, Clara H., Hooimeijer, Pieter (2003). Changing gender roles, shifting power balance, and long-distance migration of couples. *Urban Studies*, 40 (3), 603-613.

Sneath, Julie Z., Kennett, Pamela A., Megehee, Carol M. (2002). The self-service versus full-service decision: gender-based assessment of risk. *Journal of Targeting, Measurement, and Analysis for Marketing*, 11 (1), 56-67.

Snow, R. P. (1983). *Creating Media Culture*. Beverly Hills, CA: Sage Publications.

Spence, J. T. (1984). Masculinity, femininity, and gender-related traits: A conceptual analysis and critique of current research. *Progress in Experimental Personality Research*, 13, 1-97.

Spence, J. T., Helmreich, R., Stapp, J. (1972). The Attitudes Towards Women Scale: An objective instrument to measure attitudes toward the rights and roles of women in contemporary society. *JSAS Catalogue of Selected Documents in Psychology*, 2, 66.

Spence, J. T., Helmreich, R., Stapp, J. (1973). A short version of the Attitude Towards Women scale (AWS). *Bulletin of the Psychonomic Society*, 2 (4), 219-220.

Spence, Janet T. (1993). Gender-related traits and gender ideology. Evidence for a multifactorial theory. *Journal of Personality and Social Psychology*, 64 (4), 624-635.

Spence, Janet T., Helmreich, R., Stapp, J. (1974). The Personal Attributes Questionnaire: A measure of sex role stereotypes and masculinity-femininity. *JSAS Catalog of Selected Documents in Psychology*, 4, 43. (Ms.No. 617).

Spence, Janet T., Helmreich, Robert L. (1981). Androgyny versus gender schema: A comment of Bem's Gender Schema Theory. *Psychological Review*, 88 (4), 365-368.

Spence, Janet T., Helmreich, Robert L., Stapp, Joy (1975). Ratings of self and peers on sex role attributes and their relation to self-esteem and conceptions of masculinity and femininity. Journal of Personality and Social Psychology, 32 (1), 29-39.

Stern, Barbara B. (1987). Gender research and the services consumer. New insights and new directions. *Advances in Consumer Research*, 14, 514-518.

Stern, Barbara B. (1988). Sex-role self-concept measures in marketing. A research note. *Psychology and Marketing*, 5, (1), 58-99.

Stern, Barbara B. (2003). Masculinism(s) and the male image. What does it mean to be a man? In Reichert, Tom, Lambiase, Jacqueline (Eds.), *Sex in Advertising – Perspectives on the Erotic Appeal,*. Mahwah NJ: Lawrence Erlbaum, 215-228.

Stern, Barbara B., Barak, Benny, Gould, Stephen J. (1987): Sexual identity scale: a new self-assessment measure. *Sex Roles*, 17 (9-10), 503-517.

Stern, Barbara B., Gould, Stephen J., Tewari, Sonia (1993). Sex-typed service images. An empirical investigation of self-service variables. *The Service Industries Journal*, 13 (3), 74-96.

Stillings, N., Feinstein, M., Garfield J., Rissland, E., Rosenbaum, D., Weisler, S., Baker-Ward, L. (1987). *Cognitive Science: An Introduction*. Cambridge, MA: MIT Press.

Stuteville, John R. (1971). Sexually polarized products and advertising strategy. *Journal of Retailing*, 45 (1), 13-20.

Symons, D. (1979). *The Evolution of Human Sexuality*. Oxford: Oxford University Press.

Terman, L., Miles, C. C. (1936). *Sex and Personality*. New York: McGraw-Hill.

The World Bank: *GenderStats, Database of Gender Statistics* (http://devdata.worldbank.org/genderstats, accessed 13.10.2004).

Thompson, Edward H. Jr., Pleck, Joseph H. (1988). *The Structure of Male Role Norms*. In: Kimmel, Michael S. (Ed.). Changing Men: New Directions in Research on Men and Masculinity, 3rd, Newbury Park, CA: Sage Publications, 25-36.

Tieger, T. (1980). On the biological basis of sex differences in aggression. *Child Development*, 51, 943-963.

Till, Brian D., Busler, Michael (2000). The match-up hypothesis: Physical attractiveness, expertise, and the role of fit on brand attitude, purchase intent and brand beliefs. *Journal Of Advertising*, 29 (3), 1-13.

Tolley, Stuart B., Bogart, Leo (1994). How readers process newspaper advertising. In Clark, Eddie M., Brock, Timothy C. (Eds.), *Attention, Attitude, and Affect in Response to Advertising*, Hillsdale, NJ: Lawrence Erlbaum.

Tseelon, E. (1995). *The Masque of Femininity*, Thousand Oaks, CA: Sage Publications.

Tucker, William T. (1976). A long day of discrepant behavior. In Bernhardt, Kenneth L. (Ed.), *Marketing 1776 – 1976 and Beyond, AMA Educators' Proceedings*, Chicago: American Marketing Association,

351-353.

Twenge, Jean M. (1997). Changes in masculine and feminine traits over time. A meta-analysis. *Sex Roles*, 36 (5-6), 305-325.

Vigorito, Anthony J., Curry, Timothy J. (1998). Marketing masculinity. Gender identity and popular magazines. *Sex Roles*, 39 (1-2), 135-152.

Vitz, Paul C., Johnston, Donald (1965). Masculinity of smokers and the masculinity of cigarette images. *Journal of Applied Psychology*, 49 (3), 155-159.

Wang, Cheng Lu, Bristol, Terry, Mowen, John C., Chakraborty, Goutam (2000). Alternative modes of self-construal: Dimensions of connectedness-separateness and advertising appeals to the cultural and gender-specific self. *Journal of Consumer Psychology*, 9 (2), 107-115.

Ward, Colleen, Sethi, Renuka R. (1986). Cross-cultural validation of the Bem Sex Role Inventory. *Journal of Cross-Cultural Psychology*, 17 (3), 300-314.

Website of Today's Parent, Canada (www.todaysparent.com, accessed 13.10.2004)

Weinzinger, Brigid, Wagner, Sigrid (2004): *Grüner Frauenbericht 2004*. Die Grünen Österreich.

Whetton, C., Swindells, T. (1977). A factor analysis of the Bem Sex-Role Inventory. *Journal of Clinical Psychology*, 33, 150-153.

Whitley, B. E. (1984). Sex-role orientation and psychological well-being: Two meta-analysis. *Sex Roles*, 12, 207-220.

Whittler, Tommy E. (1991). The Effects of Actors' Race in Commercial Advertising: Review and Extension. *Journal Of Advertising* 20 (1), 54-60.

Widgery, Robin, McGaugh, Jack (1993). Vehicle message appeals and the new generation woman. *Journal of Advertising Research*, 33 (September/October), 36-42.

Wilson, David, McMaster, John, Greenspan, Ruth, Mboyi, Lillian (1990). Cross-cultural validation of the Bem Sex Role Inventory in Zimbabwe. *Personality and Individual Differences*, 11 (7), 651-656.

Wolheter, M., Lammers, H.B. (1980). An analysis of male roles in print advertisements over a 20-year span: 1958-1978. *Advances in Consumer Research*, 7, 760-761.

Wong, Frank Y., McCreary, Donald R., Duffy, Karen G. (1990). A further replication of the Bem Sex Role Inventory. A multitrait-multimethod study. *Sex Roles*, 22 (3-4), 249-259.

Worth, Leila T., Smith, Jeanne, Mackie, Diane M. (1992). Gender schematicity and preference for gender-typed products. *Psychology and Marketing*, 9 (1), 17-30.

Zajonc, R. B. (1980). Feeling and thinking: Preferences need no inferences. *American Psychologist*, 35, 151-175.

Zuo, Jiping (1997). The effect of men's breadwinner status on their changing gender beliefs. *Sex Roles*, 37 (9-10), 799-816.

Zurawik, David (2003, August 13th). Make way for the metrosexual man: Unlike the old TV staples – the breadwinner, the cop, the doctor – he's getting in touch with his feminine side. *Ottawa Citizen*.

Appendix

The Male Role Norm Scale (Thompson & Pleck, 1988)

Construct	*Gender Role Attitudes*	
Original Scale	**Male Role Norm Scale (MRNS);** Thompson & Pleck (1988) (own translation for study in Austria, retranslated for control of accuracy)	Status Scale α = 0,81 Toughness Scale α = 0,74 Antifemininity Scale α = 0,76
Measure	7-point rating scale 1 – I do not agree at all 7 – I totally agree	

Items	

Status Norm

1. Success in his work has to be man's central goal in life.
2. The best way for a young man to get the respect of other people is to get a job, take it seriously, and do it well.
3. A man owes it to his family to work at the best-paying job he can get.
4. A man should generally work overtime to make more money whenever he has the chance.
5. A man always deserves the respect of his wife and children.
6. It is essential for a man to always have the respect and admiration of everyone who knows him.
7. A man should never back down in the face of trouble.
8. I always like a man who's totally sure of himself.
9. A man should always think everything out coolly and logically, and have rational reasons for everything he does.
10. A man should always try to project an air of confidence even if he doesn't feel confident inside.
11. A man must stand on his own feet and never depend on other people to help him do things.

Toughness Norm

12. When a man is feeling a little pain he should try not to let it show very much.
13. Nobody respects a man very much who frequently talks about his worries, fears, and problems.
14. A good motto for a man would be "When to going gets tough, the tough get going".
15. When a man is feeling a little pain he should try not to let it show very much.
16. Nobody respects a man very much who frequently talks about his worries, fears, and problems.
17. A good motto for a man would be "When to going gets tough, the tough get going".
18. I think a young man should try to become physically tough, even if he's not big.
19. Fists are sometimes the only way to get out of a bad situation.
20. A real man enjoys a bit of danger now and then.
21. In some kinds of situations a man should be ready to use his fists, even if his wife or his girlfriend would object.
22. A man should always refuse to get into a fight, even if there seems to be no way to avoid it.

Antifemininity Norm

1. It bothers me when a man does something that I consider "feminine".
2. A man whose hobbies are cooking, sewing, and going to the ballet probably wouldn't appeal to me.
3. It is a bit embarrassing for a man to have a job that is usually filled by a woman.
4. Unless he was really desperate, I would probably advise a man to keep looking rather than accept a job as a secretary.
If I heard about a man who was a hairdresser and a gourmet cook, I might wonder how masculine he was.

Construct	**Personality Traits**	
Original Scale	Bem Sex Role Inventory (BSRI); Bem (1974)	Masculinity: α = 0,86 Femininity: α = 0,80 – 0,82
Translated Scale	BSRI – German version Schneider-Dueker, Kohler (1988)	Masculinity: α = 0,85 Feminity: α = 0,74
Measure	7-point rating scale 1 – never or almost never applicable 7 – always or almost always applicable (Bem, 1974)	

Items

Masculinity

Acts as a leader, aggressive, ambitious, ana-lytical, assertive, athletic, competitive, defends own beliefs, dominant, forceful, has leadership abilities, independent, individualistic, makes decisions easily, masculine, self-reliant, self-sufficient, strong personality, willing to take a stand, willing to take risks

Femininity

Affectionate, cheerful, childlike, compassionate, does not use harsh language, eager to sooth hurt feelings, feminine, flatterable , gentle, gullible, loves children, loyal, sensitive to the needs of others, shy, soft spoken, sympathetic, tender, understanding, warm, yielding

Construct	**Global Gender**
Items	masculine – not masculine, feminine – not feminine
Measure	7-point semantic differential

Printed in the United States
207280BV00003B/3/A

9 783836 421621